Un-Making Law

Un-Making Law

The Conservative Campaign to
Roll Back the Common Law

Jay M. Feinman

Beacon Press, Boston

BEACON PRESS
25 Beacon Street
Boston, Massachusetts 02108-2892
www.beacon.org

Beacon Press books
are published under the auspices of
the Unitarian Universalist Association of Congregations.

07 06 05 04 8 7 6 5 4 3 2 1

Composition by Wilsted & Taylor Publishing Services

Library of Congress Cataloging-in-Publication Data

Feinman, Jay M.
    Unmaking law: The Conservative Campaign to Roll Back the Common Law / Jay M.
Feinman.
    p. cm.
  Includes bibliographical references and index.
  ISBN 0-8070-4426-1 (cloth : acid-free paper)
    1. Common law—United States. 2. Law reform—United States. 3. Justice and
politics. I. Title.

  KF394.F45 2004
  340'.3'0973—dc22

                                                        2004004903

Contents

Introduction oo

1. The Resurrection of Classical Common Law oo

2. Injuries, Victims, and the Attack on Tort Law oo

3. A Realistic View of Tort Law oo

4. Consumers, Workers, and the Tyranny
of Freedom of Contract oo

5. Freedom of Contract and Fair Contract oo

6. Property Rights and the Right's Property oo

7. Takings and Transcendental Nonsense oo

8. The Movement to Un-Make the Law oo

Conclusion oo

Updates oo

Notes oo

Acknowledgments oo

Index oo

Introduction

For the past twenty-five years, a movement has been underway to reduce the legal protections available to ordinary people and to increase the legal benefits given to automobile manufacturers, drug companies, gun makers, software publishers, land developers, HMOs, and other holders of wealth and power. Today, this movement is at its strongest, and it aims to diminish the ability of government to act on behalf of consumers, workers, small business people, homeowners, and the environment, and therefore to limit the ability of government to redress inequalities of wealth, power, and status.

The campaign has had dramatic effects. It has increased the burden on victims of accidental injuries and reduced the responsibility of corporations for the injuries they cause. It has made it easier for large companies to extend their economic power by imposing contract terms on people who have less sophistication and less bargaining power. It has limited government's ability to protect our natural environment. And more changes are on the way.

Professor Stephen Sugarman of the University of California, Berkeley law school first noted how the California Supreme Court began to "un-make" personal injury law (known to lawyers as "tort law") after three liberal justices were voted off the bench in 1986 and replaced by conservatives.[1] That was only the tip of the iceberg. Today this right-wing movement aims to un-make the entire common law, the law of property, contracts, and torts. Although constitutional law and criminal law get more headlines, these are the areas of law that affect most of the everyday activities of ordinary people. Sometimes "the common law" also denotes law made by judges, as distinguished from statutes, but this attack on property, contract, and tort law has been waged in the courts and the legislatures.

Consider a few examples discussed in this book:

Steven Olsen is different from other children in San Diego. Instead of learning to walk as a toddler, Steven did not learn to walk until he was five years old. Steven also is blind, and he has had to undergo continual medical treatment and physical, speech, and occupational therapy. The cause? When Steven was two, a doctor negligently failed to discover and treat an abscess in his brain. A jury awarded Steven $1.9 million to compensate him for his medical bills and lost future wages, and $7 million to compensate him for not being able to see, play, and enjoy life as other children do because of the doctor's negligence. But under a 1975 California statute promoted by doctors and insurance companies and used as a model by conservatives ever since, Steven's recovery for noneconomic loss was cut to $250,000, an amount that was not even large enough to cover his attorney's fees.[2]

Carl Malmstrom was fifty-six years old when he was recruited by Kaiser Aluminum and Chemical Company. Concerned about job security at his age, he asked for and received assurances that the job was permanent and that he should have no fears of being laid off; his boss told him, for example, that Kaiser "never laid off anyone unless there was due cause obviously of some nature." Four years later, he was transferred from California to Florida, receiving renewed assurances that he could work until he retired at age sixty-five. Eight months later, Kaiser fired him because of corporate cutbacks and, allegedly, age discrimination. The court hearing the case, departing from twenty years of precedents, refused even to consider Kaiser's promises to Carl, because of boilerplate language in a standard form employment contract that Carl had signed.[3]

Loveladies Harbor, Inc., a land developer, acquired 250 acres on Long Beach Island, New Jersey, a barrier island at the New Jersey shore known for its quiet summer homes and limited commercial development. After dredging and filling in 199 acres of wetlands and building 375 houses, the corporation sought to develop the rest of the tract, all of which consisted of wetlands or shorefront tidelands. To protect the environmentally sensitive property, the Army Corps of Engineers denied Loveladies Harbor permission to build. The developer sued under the Fifth Amendment to the Constitution, asserting that by limiting it from developing the rest of its land, the government had "taken" its property without just compensation. The court agreed, holding that the government had deprived the developer of all economically beneficial use of its land, even though it already had developed four-fifths of the tract.[4]

Of course, individuals and groups always try to shape the law to serve their interests. Times change and attitudes change. As a result, the law always has been a mixture of elements that support business interests and elements that control business, and recent decades represent a conservative response to liberal developments in the 1960s and 1970s. From that perspective, the changes in the law might be seen as unfortunate but unremarkable. But the Right's current attack on the common law *is* remarkable, for three reasons.

First, the law has dramatically changed to the detriment of ordinary people, and more changes are in sight. To the extent that conservatives transform the common law, injury victims will find it harder to get into court to sue the wrongdoers who hurt them, harder to win when they get there, and harder to be adequately compensated for their injuries if they do win their suits. Consumers, employees, insurance policyholders, and HMO patients will be increasingly subject to terms dictated by the big businesses with whom they deal, even when they have not agreed to those terms, may not even have known about the terms, and cannot challenge the terms in court. The government will be less able to prevent environmental harm, suburban sprawl, and the destruction of forests, beaches, and wetlands, and even will find it difficult to carry on normal governmental activities such as establishing health and safety protections for workers and preventing the spread of disease. The changes are sweeping and pervasive, but only small portions of this transformation are well known, among either legal professionals or the general public.

Second, the individual developments in property, contract, and tort law are not isolated or accidental. Instead, they are elements of a comprehensive and coordinated campaign to reshape the common law. Product manufacturers, insurance companies, land developers, the software industry, HMOs, and others have banded together to seek gains at the expense of ordinary people. Politicians, academics, and ideologues have joined the cause to advance their own interests and to promote a conservative agenda. A network of trade groups, think tanks, right-wing foundations, membership organizations, lobbyists, and litigation centers link the elements of the campaign in a coordinated effort of funding, lobbying, networking, and advocacy to advance the new approach to law.

Third, and most strikingly, this campaign to transform the law is not really conservative at all—it is radical. In mounting the campaign, conservatives reject the main currents of American law that have developed over the past hundred years. At the beginning of the twentieth century, conservative judges advanced a concept of law based in the natural rights of property, abstract freedom of contract, and limited liability for tortious harm; the practical effect of this concept was to enable big businesses to exercise their economic power with minimal interference by the government. The story of American law through the twentieth century is a critique of this idea and the development of alternative bodies of law that consider other interests as well, including the protection of unsophisticated consumers in contract law, the promotion of safety and the compensation of injury victims in tort law, and the assertion of the public interest in the use of property.

The radical conservative movement aims to turn back the clock and revive the long-discredited idea that the market should be left to work, and the law should step out of the way. The ultimate goal is to restore the equally discredited belief that abstract principles of justice can be mechanically applied by courts to solve every legal problem. The campaign does more than try to transform legal rules. It also espouses an ideology that claims that inequalities of wealth and power are natural and good, that government should not intervene to correct those inequalities, and that a legal system that enables or even enhances those inequalities is nonpolitical and just.

In this way, the attack on the common law is part of the broader conservative agenda to reduce the ability of government to promote the common good. Starving government through tax cuts, rewriting environmental laws, privatizing government programs, appointing business-friendly regulators, packing the courts with right-wing judges, and transforming the common law all have the same objective: let business do its business and get government out of the way.

This book provides the first comprehensive account of the conservative attempt to un-make the common law. It describes the changes in the law, adopted and proposed, and shows the harm they portend for individuals in their daily lives. It explains how businesses and conservatives have organized their economic and political power to manipulate public opinion, lobby, and litigate to promote these changes. And it explains why the conservatives' changes are wrong—not just questionable or debatable, but wrong.

The opening chapter summarizes the conservative approaches to the common law, old and new. The current conservative movement presents a Reaganesque ideal of a society of free individuals satisfying their needs through market transactions, unimpeded by a paternalistic, overbearing government. That narrative resurrects the classical approach to the common law that reigned at the turn of the twentieth century, when law served the newly powerful corporate oligarchs. Generations of scholars and judges thoroughly debunked the classical theory and constructed a more balanced common law that focused on real-world conditions of inequality and injury and on principles of fairness and social welfare. By rejecting that history, the conservative vision is both radical and false.

The next two chapters describe the tort reform movement. This part of the conservative effort tries to make it harder for injured victims to get to court, to win if they get there, and to collect damages for their injuries when they do win their suits. Insurance companies, doctors, manufacturers, and conservative activists have successfully promoted legislation and litigation campaigns to reduce victims' rights, and they are now seeking changes at the national level that would fundamentally alter the tort system. These efforts are at odds with the well-established position of the law. Since the early twentieth century, courts and legislatures have recognized that tort law needs to expand its scope to provide remedies in more situations, not fewer, in order to promote safety and fairness. Chapter 3 also demonstrates that the conservative portrayal of a tort system dominated by sue-happy plaintiffs and greedy lawyers is a myth; the tort system works reasonably in protecting the public and compensating victims.

Chapters 4 and 5 address contract law. Big businesses increasingly have sought changes in contract law that would allow them to totally control the terms of their relationships with employees and customers, using seldom-read and poorly understood form contracts to impose terms, denying responsibility for many of the promises they make, and preventing employees and customers from going to court to challenge the contracts. This effort, viewed in the context of the history of contract law, is at odds with reasonable business practices and accepted contract law principles.

The property rights movement, described in Chapter 6, resurrects long-dead ideas about the right to own property free of government regulation and then attempts to enshrine these ideas in constitutional law. The effect of this transformation would be to reduce the ability of government to regulate land developers, polluters, or other businesses without paying them for doing so. As the next chapter explains, nearly a hundred years of property scholarship and Supreme Court decisions have shown these ideas to be nonsense, with no sound basis in legal theory or constitutional interpretation.

The attempts to transform tort, contract, and property law are parts of a whole. The last chapter exposes the movement behind the attempts. This movement is a concerted effort by an array of business groups and conservative ideologues to transform the common law. That effort is part of a much broader campaign by conservatives to reduce the ability of government to do good. The shift of politics to the right, the rise of market fervor, and the transformation of the common law are all part of the conservative campaign to reshape American society.

The fundamental flaw—or the fundamental lie—of the conservative ideology is the illusion of simplicity. The conclusion suggests that our common law needs to embrace the complexity of the world to make progress and protect the people's rights.

1

The Resurrection of Classical Common Law

The central story in American politics in recent decades has been the ascendancy of conservatism.[1] Classical liberals, libertarians, the religious right, social conservatives, fiscal conservatives, business conservatives, compassionate conservatives, and neocons have shifted political discourse to the right. Particularly since the election of 2000, the divergent elements of the conservative movement have set aside differences in a coordinated effort to exert control over all institutions of government—including the common law.

The Individual, the Market, and the Common Law

The master narrative of the conservative movement is Reaganesque: Once upon a time there was a golden age when a man (always a man) could stand on his own two feet, his rights inviolate. Individual liberty, personal responsibility, and economic opportunity were the foundations of American life. Society was organized and controlled by two institutions: the market and the state. The market was primary; through it, people could maximize their potential, realize their dreams, and rise or fall on their own merits. The state was subordinate; beyond its minimal functions of guaranteeing physical security, providing public goods, and protecting individual rights, government offered only the possibility of unwise and pernicious interference in the social order created by the market.[2] In general, people should look out for themselves, and government should get out of their way.

The narrative is hardly new or unique. Richard Posner, federal judge and leader of the law and economics movement, traces the ideology's roots to the classical liberalism of John Stuart Mill:

The government's role is to provide an unobtrusive framework for private activities. Government provides certain goods, such as national defense and (in some versions) education, that private markets will not provide in sufficient quantities. But beyond that it merely protects a handful of entitlements (property rights and some personal liberties) that are necessary to prevent markets from not working at all or from running off the rails.[3]

But the breadth of the market fervor in the modern conservative era is striking. "More than anything else," said Reagan—presumably more than peace, justice, community, or social welfare—"I want to see the United States remain a country where someone can get rich."[4] And so the market provides the solution for every social ill: It is superior to welfare programs for eradicating poverty, according to Manhattan Institute scholar Charles Murray.[5] Racial discrimination can be eliminated by market competition, so there is no need for civil rights laws, writes University of Chicago law professor Richard Epstein.[6] The ills of urban public school systems can be cured by the market solution of parent choice with government-funded vouchers.

In the conservative narrative, the ideal state of affairs was corrupted by liberal politicians who expanded the role of government beyond protecting individual rights and preserving market competition, and thereby disrupted the natural and just order of things. To reverse this corruption, the country needs to be reclaimed from big government.

The mainstream discourse of conservatism seldom makes explicit the place of the common law in this picture, but a vision of the common law is central to the conservative ideology, and the conservative ideology is central to contemporary changes in the common law. The Right's ideal of individual freedom and limited government and its conception of property, contract, and tort law are mutually reinforcing. The protection of absolute private property is "the foundation from which America's prosperity has been launched."[7] Under attack since at least the New Deal by eager environmentalists and overzealous bureaucrats, property rights have "become the line drawn in the sand between tyranny and liberty," according to Nancie Marzulla of the right-wing litigation center Defenders of Property Rights.[8] The "sanctity of contract" also is a condition of freedom, writes federal judge Alex Kozinski, who led an attack on modern interpretations of contract law by California courts. The role of courts, therefore, is simply to enforce the contracts the parties appear to have made, not to assess their reasonableness or fairness: "Like other aspects of personal autonomy, [freedom of contract] is too easily smothered by government officials eager to tell us what's best for us."[9] Tort law supplements property and contract law in the relatively few cases of wrongful acts that cause injury. The Reagan administration's Tort Policy Working Group, which laid the groundwork for the modern tort reform effort, called fault "the only vehicle in tort law capable of distinguishing wrongful (or undesirable) from beneficial (or desirable) conduct,"[10] but the fault principle has been corrupted, according to former congressman Dick Armey's Citizens for a Sound Economy: "An elite group of greedy trial lawyers is exploiting our legal system and turning it into 'jackpot justice.' "[11]

It should be obvious how an ideology of individualism and the free market favors the conservative, business-oriented agenda in property, contract, and tort law. What is also crucial but may be less obvious is that this ideology promotes an understanding of the common law as nonpolitical. The common law is portrayed exclusively as a realm of corrective justice, righting wrongs between individuals according to objective principles of law, as contrasted with the political choices made in electoral politics and in legislation. In this understanding, the choice of common law rules that favor the conservative conception of private property, freedom of contract, and limited tort law is not a political choice; indeed, it is hardly a choice at all. Instead, the substance of the common law and the process of judicial decision making reside as a neutral background against which "real" political conflicts are played out. The common law, like the interstate highway system, is simply part of the natural, nonpolitical infrastructure of society. In this way, conservatives attempt to withdraw from the realm of politics the allocation of economic, political, and social values by the common law.

But like the interstate highway system, the conservative vision of the common law is neither natural nor nonpolitical. (The interstate highway system, the "cathedral of the car culture," was the product of a political victory by a coalition, including truckers, auto manufacturers, big city politicians, and road contractors, that ended up shaping urban planning and starving the railroads.[12]) Instead, it furthers economic interests and promotes an ideology in support of those interests. Businesses and interest groups argue, litigate, and lobby for the conservative vision of the common law and the particular changes in the law that follow from it.

What is most remarkable about this movement is that the challenges to the common law that conservatives are promoting really are radical—radical because they reject the mainstream of American law that developed over the past hundred years. The radical conservative vision embodies ideas that are extreme in their rejection of most of American law, outmoded in their adoption of ideas that were discarded almost a century ago, and simply wrong in their attempt to resurrect discredited legal principles.

Classical Legal Thought

At the end of the nineteenth century, conservative judges and scholars created an idealized vision of law and society known as "classical legal thought."[13] A fantastic mix of natural law, Social Darwinism, and laissez faire economics, this classical vision bore little resemblance to the real world of the Standard Oil trust, the Granger movement, and the Wobblies, but that did not matter. This was law for the age of science, when Christopher Columbus Langdell, first dean of the Harvard Law School, designed a curriculum based on the idea that there were only a few fundamental principles of law, and that lawyers and judges "could have such a mastery of these as to be able to apply them with constant facility and certainty to the ever-tangled skein of human affairs."[14] Classical legal thought also was law for the Gilded Age, the age when (like today) "conservatives—or better, pro-corporate apologists—hijacked the vocabulary of Jeffersonian liberalism and turned words like 'progress,' 'opportunity,' and 'individualism' into tools for making the plunder of America sound like divine right," as Bill Moyers described it.[15] More importantly, this was (like today) the age of wealth ensconced as government power. At the turn of the twentieth century, when the average family's income was under $500 a year, John D. Rockefeller amassed a billion-dollar fortune from his oil monopoly; Andrew Carnegie, $400 million from steel; Frederick Weyerhauser, $200 million from lumber; and brothers Andrew and Richard Mellon, $100 million each, also from oil. These titans of business, and their counterparts in railroads, sugar, finance, and other newly dominant industries, exerted effective control over many legislatures and courts, federal and state, a "bold and aggressive plutocracy [that] has usurped the government," according to James B. Weaver, 1892 Populist candidate for president.[16]

Classical legal thought imagined a world of independent individuals, each of whom acts within a broad sphere of legal autonomy to pursue his own self-interest. The market was the model of social organization, and the acquisitive capitalist the paragon of personal behavior. The role of government, on the other hand, was precisely defined and narrowly circumscribed. The legislature had limited authority to regulate narrowly and traditionally defined harmful activities, such as crimes. The courts, applying a complete, coherent, and formal body of law, policed the boundaries of legislative authority and defined the ground rules for interaction among private individuals, namely the rules of property, tort, and contract.

Where once property had largely been associated with land, the generalization of the market in classical law led to an understanding of property as "everything which has exchangeable value," as Justice Swayne wrote in dissent in the *Slaughterhouse Cases*.[17] An individual's right to own property included the creation, exchange, and accumulation of wealth of all kinds, from dynastic trusts to corporate wealth. The state could control property rights only in limited ways; classical property law "sanctioned capitalist accumulation, the starkest form of property-as-wealth . . . and it created a large private domain of unregulated and unregulatable market activity."[18]

Classical contract law described a broad realm in which individuals could realize the value of their property and otherwise exercise their autonomy by consenting to agreements with other autonomous individuals. "Freedom of contract" was both a political slogan and an operative legal principle from which the entire body of contract doctrine flowed.

While contract law defined a broad scope of individual autonomy, tort law encompassed a much narrower realm in which the law recognized liability for harm wrongfully committed.[19] Tort law was corrective justice through which the law provided recompense when one person caused injury by invading the preexisting right to bodily security of another person. Corrective justice required that, for liability to be imposed, the defendant must have been at fault and must have caused the injury, and in classical tort law, each of these elements had a narrow, fixed meaning.

In deciding common law cases, courts were seen as nonpolitical institutions, not exercising discretion or making political judgments. A court engaged in legal reasoning began with the few basic propositions that lay at the heart of the common law subjects, such as "an exercise of consent creates a contract." Then, it used inexorable deductive logic to generate narrower doctrinal rules ("all the terms of a contract must be definite") and decisions in individual cases ("an offer to sell salt in carload lots is not enforceable because it failed to specify how many carloads were being offered"), all of which were merely specific instances of the basic propositions.

There always was a potential contradiction in the classical image. Common law rights were absolute, but government was not entirely powerless. The state could, for example, limit the use of property in the exercise of the "police power" to protect the public health, safety, and morals. What if the exercise of the police power invaded the otherwise-sacrosanct rights of property? The rigidity of the classical mind refused to entertain the conflict. The sphere of individual liberty (defined by the common law) and the sphere of government authority (defined by the police power) simply did not overlap, like a disjunctive Venn diagram. A landowner's common law property rights naturally included the right to farm but not the right to operate a slaughterhouse, so the state could restrict the latter but not the former.

When brought to bear on actual cases, classical legal thought had one frequent, practical result: the courts protected the ability of big business to exert economic power with minimal government interference. As legal historian Lawrence Friedman commented, the U.S. Supreme Court's late-nineteenth-century decisions were noteworthy for their combination of conservative economics and radical judicial power. The state courts followed suit; between 1885 and 1899, for example, the Minnesota Supreme Court struck down seventy regulatory statutes as unconstitutional, with most coming in the last few years of the century.[20]

The applications of this approach have become infamous. In one of its most notorious manifestations, *Lochner v. New York*, the U.S. Supreme Court invalidated a New York statute that limited bakery workers to a sixty-hour work week as an impermissible invasion of their freedom of contract. Under an ideal market—disregard the inequalities of the real world—"there is no reasonable ground for interfering with the liberty of person or the right of free contract, by determining the hours of labor, in the occupation of a baker."[21]

The Critique of Classical Law and the Rise of the Modern Common Law

Classical legal thought was absurd even at the moment of its creation, and, prior to the current attempt by conservatives to resurrect it, the main story of the common law over the past hundred years has been the attack on classical legal thought and the development of an alternative vision of law.[22] Successive movements in jurisprudence and generations of judges pointed out the unreality and injustice of the individualist, market-oriented vision and reconstructed the law in response to its demise.[23] Greed is not the highest of human virtues, and the market is not the measure of all things. Instead, people live and work in networks of social relations, and the public has an interest in correcting the excesses of the market in support of just social relations. Abstract, general principles cannot be mechanically applied to decide particular cases. Courts necessarily make law as well as apply it, drawing on their own sense of justice and public policy. The rules of contract, property, and tort law are as much expressions of public policy as is any legislative act.

A cornerstone of the detailed critique of classical law was first articulated by an obscure specialist in jurisprudence and then quickly applied by other scholars. In a series of brilliant articles published between 1913 and 1917, Wesley Newcomb Hohfeld, a professor at Stanford and later Yale law schools, merged analytical jurisprudence and Progressive politics to expose the fallacies of the classical concepts. Although dry and technical (Hohfeld's Yale students, finding his scholarship impenetrable and his teaching unbearable, petitioned Yale's president to fire him), this scholarship acted as the note of proper pitch that shattered the glass edifice of classical legal thought.[24]

The core of Hohfeld's analysis was an exquisite description of the "fundamental legal conceptions as applied in judicial reasoning." Hohfeld precisely defined and distinguished the kinds of legal interests, or "entitlements," a person can have. Each entitlement has an opposite. With respect to any legal issue, a person must have either one of the primary interests or its opposite, but not both, such as the "privilege" to use the land in a certain way without interference or the "duty" (enforceable by others) not to do so. Each interest also has a correlative interest that defines a relationship between two people with respect to a certain issue; if the landowner has the "privilege" to use the land, his neighbor has a "no-right," or the legal inability to do anything about the owner's privileged use.

Hohfeld's pedantic construction of legal interests appears to be the height of nominalism, but its implications were devastating. General concepts such as "property" are composed of discrete elements (the entitlements) that tell us who holds particular legal interests but do not tell us who *should* hold them. Instead, judges and legislatures determine who has which rights, and there are always winners and losers in the process.

In Hohfeld's analysis, the classical vision of rights is absurd. Rights are social, defining relationships among people, and they are constructed, allocated by the legal system. But allocated on what basis? Not on the basis of "natural rights," because there are no such things. "The real question in each new case," explained Hohfeld's Yale colleague Arthur Corbin, "always is as to the limits to be placed upon each of the parties in the 'free struggle of life.' Where the situation is a novel one, this is, of course, purely a problem of economic and social policy, conceal it how we will."[25]

Progressive economists in the tradition of John R. Commons and Richard T. Ely translated Hohfeld's insights into the economic and political realms. The most influential was Robert L. Hale, who began as a corporate lawyer, turned to graduate study in economics, then to teaching in Columbia's economics department and its law school. Instead of considering a market based on property and contract rights as an area of freedom, Hale focused on the law's coercive power.[26] Applying and contextualizing Hohfeld's analysis, Hale dissected concepts such as "liberty," "property," "freedom," and "coercion" to show that they represented the exercise of legal power, not the absence of it, and so lacked the axiomatic content ascribed to them by classical law. Property, for example, consisted of a set of Hohfeldian interests that enabled an owner to summon the power of the state in withholding access to his property from others.[27] Similarly, bargains are not exercises of freedom of contract but are mutually coerced against a background of market inequality, which is established by legal entitlements; where the state does not protect workers who join unions, their freedom of contract to bargain with employers is limited. By the time the critique had crested in 1930, legal theorist Felix Cohen would summarize much of the classical method as "transcendental nonsense," or the use of such empty concepts to reach circular results.[28]

The critics demonstrated that courts were engaged in the allocation of rights, not the application of rights, and in that respect they were making policy judgments very much as legislatures did. Therefore, the common law's individualist, market-oriented principles were incomplete at best. The critics offered to supplement or replace those principles from two directions.

The first direction, grounded in their scientific and functionalist bent, was empirical. Law ought to attend to the realities of the world, complex as they might be. The principles of individualism and the market were found wanting when tested against the circumstances of lack of personal choice in an imperfect world, concentrations of economic power, and networks of social relations. In applying the principles of freedom of contract, for example, a court had to take account of the inequality of workers who were not legally protected if they joined a union.

The second direction, grounded as much in their Progressive politics as in their academic approach, focused on a concern for social welfare as an antidote to excessive individualism. Here, too, instrumental policymaking to achieve Progressive social objectives required a departure from the classical ideal; the abstraction of freedom of contract had to yield to the social need for maximum-hours legislation. In every legal subject, the critics demonstrated that the classical method and substance needed to be discarded in favor of a more complex, functional analysis.

The critique of classical legal thought percolated through the courts and the legal academy from the 1920s through the 1970s. The revised common law that was created by that critique embodied three principles.

First, people are not just self-interested individuals, and market values are not the sole measuring stick of social good. Instead, people are social beings, and the public as a whole has an interest in nonmarket values such as fairness, equality, and protection of the disadvantaged. In contract law, for example, a court should not simply enforce the words of a standard form employment contract as the sole expression of the parties' agreement. Instead, it should look at what the employer and employee said and did and the context in which they said and did it, trying to arrive at the understanding that a reasonable person in that context, acting in good faith, would achieve. When some element of the document expresses a term that was probably not read or understood by the employee and imposes an unfair burden, such as a clause by which she gives up the right to sue the employer for race or sex discrimination, the court may refuse to enforce the surprising, onerous term.

Second, abstract, general principles cannot be mechanically applied to decide particular cases. Courts necessarily make law as well as apply it, drawing on their own sense of social needs and public policy. To do this, courts have to immerse themselves in the world they regulate. For example, there are no objective principles of fault and causation that determine who ought to bear the burden of an accidental injury. Deciding whether cigarette manufacturers should be responsible for the disease and death of smokers requires a complex judgment about the personal responsibility of individuals, the responsibility of a manufacturer to the users of its product, tort liability as an incentive for making a safer product, the relative effectiveness of warnings and commercial advertising, and whether the costs of catastrophic injuries should be distributed among all product users or left to fall on individual victims.

Third, the rules of the common law are not neutral or nonpolitical. Property, contract, and tort rules are as much expressions of public policy as are minimum wage laws or environmental protection statutes. Courts as much as legislatures necessarily and appropriately engage in policymaking when they formulate and apply doctrine. Deciding whether the owner of environmentally fragile tidelands can fill them in to construct a housing development entails the allocation of economic and social values, not the recognition of preexisting natural rights of property.

The spread of the critique of classical legal thought and its incorporation into the law from the 1930s through the 1970s produced a striking if unsurprising fit between the common law and other vehicles of public policy. Just as Social Security, Medicare, and the civil rights acts addressed issues of poverty, health, and inequality, the law of property, contracts, and torts used flexible tools to regulate harmful uses of land, remedy unfairness in business and consumer transactions, and promote safety and reduce the burden of accidental injury. Property law expanded to further the interests of people who were economically disadvantaged, from urban tenants to rural farm workers, and of the public at large, by upholding historic preservation legislation, for example. Contract law saw a wave of consumer-oriented legislation and judicial decisions, requiring greater disclosure of contract terms, regulating the content of consumer transactions, and allowing courts to pay more attention to the situation of less-sophisticated and less-powerful parties. Tort law imposed liability on manufacturers of dangerous products to give them a greater incentive to make safe products and to spread the costs of injury.

The Resurrection of Classical Law

After the remarkable legal developments that began in the 1920s and crested in the 1960s and 1970s, it would be normal to have a period of consolidation and even reaction, a more conservative approach drawing back from a more liberal one. But the conservative campaign to roll back the common law is more than a reaction to perceived excesses of the past. Instead, its vision rejects the century-long history of the common law just described and aims to un-make modern law.

In the conservative vision, the market is the primary economic, social, and political institution, and its primacy obviates the balancing of individualist principles and nonmarket values, such as fairness, that has characterized the law. The state has a limited and subordinate role in advancing social welfare; its principal function is to enforce a legal regime that facilitates operation of the market, including especially a well-defined law of property and contract. Courts fulfill this function by applying a formal body of doctrine that enables market actors to know the law and channel their conduct accordingly; rigid rules also prevent courts from intervening too extensively into the realm of private conduct, since they are less-trustworthy judges of social welfare than are market participants.

The conservative campaign attempts to implement this vision across the law of torts, contracts, and property. During the past twenty years, the campaign has enjoyed notable successes through legislation and judicial decisions, as conservatives and business interests have gained influence throughout the government. The campaign is ongoing, with important battles under way in each of the areas of law. If this vision comes to pass, the kind of government that has developed throughout the twentieth century would be eviscerated. Severe limits, perhaps near-total limits, would be placed on the collective power of the people to protect the environment and to regulate business practices that harm people economically or even physically. Nor could government easily intervene to protect those people for whom the market did not provide its benefits, from the elderly poor to the unsophisticated consumer. As the idea of government as an agent of the common good declined, self-interest would be the order of the day in politics as in business, and he who paid the piper would call the tune. The large corporations, the rich, and the powerful would dominate the government, the economy, the universities, and the other institutions that set the agenda for society.

2

Injuries, Victims, and the Attack on Tort Law

The longest-running front in the Right's campaign to reshape the common law has played out in personal injury law, what lawyers call "tort law." For more than a quarter century, a coalition of insurance companies, doctors, automobile manufacturers, tobacco companies, gun manufacturers, other large corporations, their big-firm lawyers, conservative foundations, think tanks, and politicians has attempted to reduce the legal protections available to injured patients, workers, and consumers. This "tort reform" movement—Ralph Nader calls it "tort deform"[1]—has enjoyed many successes because of its political influence, power lobbying, aggressive litigation, and production of an elaborate public campaign of misinformation that convinces people that reducing their rights is actually in their own interest.

In a series of important victories in nearly every state legislature, in the state courts, in Congress, and in the U.S. Supreme Court, the movement has eroded longstanding rights of injury victims. At the same time, some courts have taken a narrower approach to tort cases generally, reflecting a drawing back from some of the more progressive decisions of the 1960s and 1970s and a generally more conservative posture on liability. The election of George W. Bush in 2000 and the shift to Republican control of the Congress in 2002 fueled by tort reformers' campaign contributions, reenergized the movement and produced even more dramatic proposals.

A key example is the attempt to reduce the ability of victims of medical negligence to recover damages, an issue important enough to command mention in President Bush's 2003 and 2004 State of the Union addresses. Three-fifths of the states have adopted some tort reform proposals, and an effort has been under way to adopt federal statutes such as the cleverly named Patients First Act and the Help Efficient, Accessible, Low-Cost, Timely Healthcare Act of 2003 (the HEALTH Act).[2] These bills would transform suits against doctors, hospitals, and HMOs for medical malpractice; product liability actions against drug companies and the makers of medical devices such as artificial heart valves and silicone breast implants; and Medicaid fraud cases against health-care systems, among many others.[3] Aimed at the latest in a recurring series of alleged crises in liability insurance in general and medical malpractice insurance in particular, they would shorten the time period during which victims can sue, limit the damages available to compensate victims, abrogate the rule of joint and several liability (under which a victim can recover against one defendant if another defendant cannot pay), limit attorney fees, restrict punitive damages, and cut off some benefits to a victim's family if the victim dies.

These changes are sweeping as general propositions, and their effect in particular cases would be dramatic. Steven Olsen, the twelve-year-old boy from San Diego mentioned in the Introduction, was caught in the provisions of a California statute that provided a model for the federal proposals. Steven is blind, mentally handicapped, and subject to seizures. In a good year, his parents report, he will not have to be admitted to the hospital, but he still will endure more than seventy doctor visits, one hundred sixty physical and speech therapy appointments, and several trips to the emergency room. When Steven was two and walking with his parents, he fell and his face hit a twig, which lodged between his upper lip and gums. A week after initial treatment, he began suffering from fevers and headaches. A hospital pediatrician diagnosed an abscess in the central nervous system, but other doctors refused to perform a CT scan—it would have cost $800—to verify the abscess. Instead, they misdiagnosed Steven as suffering from viral meningitis, prescribed treatment, and discharged him. The next day his brain herniated from the abscess, causing his permanent injuries.

Steven's parents sued on his behalf. Their doctors' medical group settled, but the hospital (the employer of a negligent doctor) refused to settle and went to trial. The jury found for Steven and took the only action the law allows to compensate him, awarding damages of $1.9 million for lost future earnings, medical bills, and the other expenses of providing care for Steven for the rest of his life. The jury also awarded $7.1 million for his pain and suffering and for not being able to see, play, and enjoy life like other children.[4]

But Steven never received full compensation for his injuries. Under a 1975 California statute promoted by doctors and insurance companies, Steven's $7 million recovery for noneconomic loss was slashed to $250,000.

The federal bills would mandate the same effect in every state, and, after inflation, $250,000 in 1975 dollars is worth about $72,000 today. Worse yet, medical malpractice litigation is notoriously expensive, requiring extensive discovery, the testimony of medical experts, professionally produced exhibits, and the like. Steven's costs and legal fees amounted to $914,000; because the jury's award for noneconomic losses was reduced by the statute, those costs had to come out of his recovery for the expenses of his care and lost income.

Steven's case was one of simple, if tragic, negligence by a physician. The federal bills also would limit or eliminate altogether the liability of manufacturers of dangerous drugs and medical devices. A. H. Robins, manufacturer of the notorious Dalkon Shield IUD contraceptive, was driven into bankruptcy after litigation revealed that Robins had lied to the FDA, physicians, and patients to conceal the health risks of the device, including pelvic inflammatory disease, spontaneous septic abortion, sterilization, and even death. At the time Robins entered bankruptcy, it had paid judgments or settlements in nine thousand cases, with five thousand more pending and new cases being filed at the rate of ten a day.[5] In another setting, Carol Lynn Wooderson, a newlywed in Lawrence, Kansas, suffered kidney failure and a gangrenous colon after taking Ortho-Novum I-80, an oral contraceptive; she recovered $2 million for her mammoth medical expenses, lost income, and pain and suffering, and received $2,750,000 in punitive damages because Ortho, the manufacturer, had ignored medical and scientific evidence of the dangers of its high-estrogen pill and downplayed the risks when communicating with patients and their doctors. Under the tort reformers' proposals, Robins might still be in business, and Ortho would owe no punitive damages.[6]

And more: Many victims of medical negligence or dangerous drugs would be unable to sue altogether because no lawyer would take their cases. By limiting attorney's fees, compensatory damages for noneconomic loss, and punitive damages, the bill makes it economically infeasible for lawyers to invest in a whole class of cases. Because they take cases on a contingent fee basis and advance the costs of litigation, victims' lawyers will only take cases where the probable recovery is much greater than the expense of investigating and pursuing the case. When the victim is an elderly person, a housewife, or a low-income wage earner, the economic loss will be small, because of their short life expectancy or low earning capacity. Tort reformers would make it difficult or impossible for these victims to sue doctors or drug companies that injured them, a loss that would fall disproportionately on women and minorities.

And finally, the most extraordinary thing about the federal bills is that they would nationalize malpractice law. Tort law has traditionally and consistently been the province of the states, allowing each state to set its own rules, strict or flexible, as its courts and legislatures thought best. If enacted, these statutes would supplant centuries of state law at a stroke, and they are only one example of a recent array of statutes and proposals in Congress that would take over entire areas of tort law. Despite their usual claim of fealty to states' rights and federalism, conservatives and business interests increasingly have turned to Congress to immunize gun manufacturers, chemical companies, and others from liability, or to remake wholesale the law concerning injuries caused by doctors, product manufacturers, airlines, and other industries.

The federal proposals provide a particularly egregious example of tort reformers' broad-scale attack on the ability of victims to seek redress from wrongdoers. The scope of the attack ranges from the beginning to the end of the legal process, with three clear goals: to make it harder for injured people to get into court, to make it harder for them to win if they do get there, and to reduce the damages they can recover if they manage to win.

The Conservative Vision of Tort Law

"Tort" comes from a Latin root meaning "twisted" or "turned aside." Behavior that causes a tort is behavior that is turned aside from normal conduct in that it is wrongful, unreasonable, or dangerous. When such conduct causes injury, the law gives people a remedy. Recovery in the tort lawsuit compensates the victim for the injuries suffered, through damages to pay for medical bills, lost income, and noneconomic loss (often called pain and suffering). Because potential injurers know that they will be liable for the injuries they cause, they have an incentive to act carefully and avoid wrongful behavior that injures others. Because the compensation comes to the victim from the person whose act caused the injury, the system has a symmetrical fairness, too.

The problem with tort law today, according to tort reformers, is that the system itself has become twisted, more twisted than the underlying, injury-causing behavior. There has been a "litigation explosion" that has bred a "litigation habit" among the American people.[7] "An elite group of greedy trial lawyers is exploiting our legal system and turning it into 'jackpot justice.'"[8] Judges are alternately and contradictorily activist crusaders for more liability and too weak to keep the system in check: "Some members of the judiciary have become quite willing to adopt exotic legal theories and less willing to temper the abuses of plaintiffs' lawyers."[9] The results of litigation are unpredictable, a "lawsuit lottery, where a few win and the rest of us lose,"[10] or, as Solicitor General Theodore Olson describes it, "demented, with freakish punitive damage bonanzas for persons who pour coffee on themselves or ricochet golf balls into their own foreheads."[11] At the same time, the system is grossly inefficient, with too much of the money burned up in expensive and time-consuming litigation and too little going to deserving victims. This has caused a "liability crisis" or an "insurance crisis" that drives obstetricians out of practice, causes drug manufacturers to abandon promising research, and puts manufacturers of small planes out of business. It also imposes a "tort tax" on all of us, raising the prices of goods and services, causing the loss of jobs, and threatening American competitiveness, all because of the costs and fears of lawsuits. More profoundly, "Robin Hood Jurisprudence"[12] (an odd pejorative, since Robin Hood was the hero of the common folk of Sherwood Forest) or "the All-American Blame Game" has corrupted our moral fiber, so that "we've now become a society of victims in search of a scapegoat to sue whenever anything goes wrong."[13]

The tort reformers' view of the ills of the system is captured and promoted in a wealth of anecdotes, usually exaggerated, misstated, or simply false, about loony lawsuits and outrageous verdicts. Ronald Reagan's favorite story was the man in a telephone booth who was struck by a drunk driver; instead of suing the driver, the man sued the telephone company and won. Actually, Charles Bigbee, the victim, sued and settled with the driver, who may or may not have been drunk, and also sued the telephone company. The booth was adjacent to a busy highway and near a driveway, and another booth in the same location had been demolished in an accident less that two years earlier. As Bigbee saw the car coming toward him and tried to escape, the door of the booth jammed, leaving him helpless.[14]

Tort reform publicist Peter Huber recounts the tale of a "prankster" who fell through a painted skylight while committing a burglary and then successfully sued the building owner for his injuries. The victim actually was a recent high-school graduate who had climbed on the roof of his school to retrieve a floodlight for a nearby basketball court; the skylight was covered with tar and indistinguishable from the rest of the roof, school officials knew that students and workers walked on the roof, and there had been a similar accident a few months before.[15]

George W. Bush's presidential campaign wailed about the Washington man who sued the dairy industry and Safeway supermarkets because drinking whole milk increased his risk of stroke. In fact, the court tossed out the suit, but Bush wanted his lawyer punished for daring to represent his client by bringing the claim.

Corporate lawyer and limited-liability advocate Philip K. Howard decries the removal of swings, slides, and monkey bars from playgrounds by towns and schools afraid that injured children will sue. His lament ignores the facts that the movement for safer playground equipment is worldwide, including in not notably litigious places such as the European Union, Argentina, and Singapore, and many new playgrounds are being built and equipped in the United States, including wild skate parks with gravity-defying half-pipes and handrails.[16]

Everyone's favorite horror stories of frivolous lawsuits involve McDonald's. An irresponsible woman spilled coffee on herself and then collected millions. Actually, Stella Liebeck, the seventy-nine-year-old victim in the case, suffered third-degree burns that required skin grafts and a week of hospitalization, because McDonald's served its coffee 30 degrees hotter than its competitors, too hot to drink but hot enough to burn. Prior to Liebeck's case, McDonald's had received more than seven hundred complaints about the temperature. Even then, the jury reduced Liebeck's compensatory damages by 20 percent because she was partly at fault, and the judge cut the jury's punitive damage award from $2.7 million (the jury's estimate of how much McDonald's made from two days' coffee sales) to $480,000.[17] And, most recently, the opportunistic New Yorkers who sued McDonald's because eating Big Macs and fries made them obese had their suit thrown out of court —even from the tort reformers' perspective, the system worked. Nevertheless, McDonald's, Kraft, and other food companies, fearing more suits, began cutting fat from their products and disclosing more nutrition information—the system worked again.[18]

The tort reformers' solution to this alleged crisis is a purported return to basic principles, an attempt to reestablish an outdated understanding of torts to address contemporary social issues. This conception is part of the broader conservative scheme to recast the common law, and it resembles the individualist, formulaic approaches to contracts and property.

The conservative conception assumes that there are clear rules that should determine liability. A court deciding a tort case can apply these rules to tell when a defendant is at fault, and when the defendant's fault caused the plaintiff's harm. Fault and causation can be objectively determined, like scientific facts, and both are narrow to boot. In the conservative vision, these objective principles best serve the ends of tort law and economic and social welfare generally. The objective principles provide reasonable incentives to potential wrongdoers for balancing productive behavior and safety and reasonable standards for compensating victims. The result is adequate safety, fair compensation for plaintiffs, a liability system that does not burden market entrepreneurs too much, and, therefore, a higher level of productivity and social welfare. At the same time, this focus promotes personal responsibility in society, where an excessive reliance on compensation through tort liability saps individual will and responsibility.

This vision of tort law and tort reform crystallized during the Reagan administration in the *Report of the Tort Policy Working Group*.[19] The Working Group was chaired by Richard K. Willard, assistant attorney general in charge of the Civil Division, and more recently general counsel of The Gillette Co. and advisor to conservative think tanks and litigation centers. The Working Group's report came during one of the periodic "insurance crises" that spurred tort reform. Concise and unencumbered by a detailed consideration of evidence and issues, it came as conservatives and business interests inside and outside the administration were gearing up for a major push toward tort reform. Although its broad ambitions were never realized, parts of its recommendations were quickly adopted in most of the states, and it set the pattern for future proposals.[20]

The report begins by identifying a "rapidly expanding crisis in liability insurance availability and affordability," and dismisses in four pages any explanation for the crisis—economic conditions, a fall in interest rates, or insurance company mismanagement—other than defects in tort law. It then focuses on four tort "problem areas" as the cause of the crisis. Three of the areas identified relate to the core elements of the conservative vision: the decline of fault as a basis of liability, the undermining of causation, and the "explosive growth" in damage awards caused by disregard of the established principles of fault and causation. The fourth problem area is the allegedly high transaction costs of the system, which are only of benefit to lawyers and presumably are caused by litigating exaggerated or spurious claims. In short,

> Too many defendants are found liable (or forced into settlements) where there should be no liability, either because they engaged in no wrongful activity or because they did not cause the underlying injury.
>
> Damages have become excessive, particularly in the area of noneconomic damages such as pain and suffering, mental anguish, and punitive damages.

As a result of these problems, the burden of the tort system on the economy is too large, with insurance against the risk of liability either unavailable or unaffordable.[21]

The report then presents a list of reforms "which if implemented should return tort law to a credible fault-based compensation system that provides a fair and reasonable level of compensation to deserving plaintiffs through a more predictable and affordable liability allocating mechanism." The first two reforms reestablish the core principles: "retain fault as the basis for liability" and "base causation findings on credible scientific and medical evidence and opinions." Other reforms aim to reduce victims' damages, by eliminating joint and several liability and limiting noneconomic damages (including limiting or abolishing punitive damages), for example. The two final recommendations go to process: reduce contingency fees and establish alternative dispute resolution mechanisms with strong disincentives to litigation. Along the way, the report suggests other means of reducing liability, such as preventing courts from finding a drug or other product unsafe if government regulators such as the Food and Drug Administration have passed on it.[22]

Professor Stephen Sugarman opined that the report reflects an attempt "to turn the tort law clock back to the 1950s," to a time when businesses were less often liable for the injuries they caused—and his assessment may be generous by fifty years.[23] The report's vision depends entirely on a perception that the system has gone overboard. Only by limiting the power of courts and juries and creating financial disincentives for lawyers to pursue victims' claims can the system be restored to its appropriate posture in which only the truly deserving would be compensated, and then only to the extent of their actual injury.

It is even more striking how the report has set the agenda for the tort reform movement to the present. The federal bills discussed at the beginning of this chapter, for example, do little more than repackage the report's proposals. And the range of tort reform proposals and enactments in other forums likewise mirror the report. From the Working Group's report to the present, tort reformers argue, as stated earlier, that three steps are needed to shift from the present unfair, expensive, out-of-control system to the ideal. First, make it harder for injury victims to get to court. Second, make it more difficult for plaintiffs to win if they get to court. Third, restrict damage recoveries for plaintiffs who do win. The result: unworthy and unscrupulous plaintiffs will be screened out, and defendants will only be liable to the deserving for reasonable damages.

Keeping Victims out of Court

One way to keep a victim out of court is to make it harder for the victim to find a lawyer by making it less profitable for a lawyer to take a case and, if she does take it, to create financial incentives not to pursue it aggressively. In practically every personal injury case, the plaintiff's attorney is compensated on a contingent fee basis, receiving an agreed-on portion of the plaintiff's recovery if he or she wins and nothing if the plaintiff loses. Contingent fee contracts provide an important benefit to injured people. A person of moderate means who could not afford to pay a lawyer out of pocket can "afford" the best lawyer, because the lawyer will be paid out of the eventual recovery. A lawyer must invest time and expenses in the case, so lawyers under contingent fee contracts also play a part by screening cases for their merit. Despite tort reformers' complaints about the burden of frivolous cases, it makes no economic sense for a lawyer to take a case that is a likely loser or in which there is little hope of substantial damages.

More than twenty states already regulate contingent fee agreements, either in all cases or, as a result of tort reform efforts, in medical malpractice and other health-care liability cases, but proposals for stricter limitations are pending in other states and in Congress. Some of the restrictions are generally regarded as reasonable: Utah, for example, limits plaintiffs' attorneys in suits against doctors and other health-care providers to one-third of the recovery.[24] Other proposals are draconian. The organization Common Good, promoted by Hudson Institute fellow Michael Horowitz and corporate lawyer and tort reform advocate Philip K. Howard, has introduced a proposal in thirteen states so far that would cap the fees of the victim's lawyer at 10 percent of the first $100,000 and 5 percent of anything more (The arithmetic yields a fee of $10,000 on a $100,000 recovery, $55,000 on $1 million, and $95,000 on $2 million).[25] Because *The Collapse of the Common Good* (as Howard's latest pro-defendant book is entitled) is threatened by the frivolous complaints of victims and their lawyers but presumably not by the dilatory, scorched-earth defense tactics of injurers and their lawyers, this proposal, like all the others, contains no restriction on the fees of defendants' attorneys.

Even these restricted fees may seem reasonable. But their effect is to penalize victims or their lawyers and to screen out an increasing number of worthy claims. The numbers are not what they seem, because they do not account for the costs of litigation. Expert witness fees, court reporters, exhibits, and other expenses can easily add up to tens of thousands of dollars, even hundreds of thousands, in complex cases. In the Woburn, Massachusetts environmental pollution case that was the subject of *A Civil Action*, the book by Jonathan Harr and the film starring John Travolta, the plaintiffs' costs—not the lawyers' fees, just the costs—were $2.5 million. In a more typical case alleging a defect in a car, costs of $300,000 would not be unusual.[26] The plaintiff's lawyer has to pay these expenses up front out of her own pocket, with the risk that they will never be repaid if the plaintiff loses. If these costs are taken into account before computing the lawyer's fee, the fee is reduced accordingly; if they are not, they reduce the plaintiff's recovery.

More fundamentally, reducing fees makes lawyers less likely to take particular kinds of cases: those in which liability is less than certain, those in which the probable damage award is small, and those in which the time and expense of litigation seriously cut into the expected recovery. For example,

Mary Jane Connors underwent a laparoscopy and a hysteroscopy in order to help her become pregnant.[27] A few days after the surgery, she felt severe pain in her leg and hip; the pain persisted, and she permanently lost the use of her leg. The dispute at trial centered around whether Dr. Brumsted, the surgeon, had negligently used a retractor and damaged Connors's nerve, causing the injury; Brumsted claimed he had been careful and that the injury was the result of an unusual anatomical feature of Connors' leg. After one trial that ended in favor of Brumsted and his colleagues, the judge ordered a new trial because he had made a mistake in charging the jury. At the second trial, the jury found for Connors and awarded damages of $800,000. The defendants appealed, and the case was affirmed by the court of appeals, seven years after the initial surgery.

Think of this case from the time Mary Jane Connors first walks into a lawyer's office. There is a disputed factual issue about Brumsted's negligence that will require the use of expensive medical experts, and there is the resulting uncertainty of how the jury will decide. There are other legal issues in the case, requiring research and introducing more uncertainty. The process is certain to be protracted; as it turned out, the trial, appeal, new trial, and new appeal took seven years from the date of the surgery. Assume that the costs, which must be advanced by the plaintiff's lawyer and then reimbursed out of the recovery, were a relatively modest $50,000, reducing the award to $750,000. Under the Utah rule, the attorney receives $250,000. Under Common Good's proposal, $42,500. At what point does Mary Jane Connors not get a lawyer and Dr. Brumsted's negligence go unsanctioned?

Another means of reducing access to the courts is through "early offer" mechanisms, proposed by the Bush presidential campaign, the business group Committee for Economic Development, and Republican senator Mitch McConnell. Under these schemes, defendants in tort cases could offer to pay a plaintiff's economic losses, often before the plaintiff's lawyer had an opportunity to fully investigate the case. If the plaintiff accepted the offer, she would be barred from seeking recovery for noneconomic losses (pain and suffering), and her attorney would be limited to an hourly fee that could not be greater than 10 percent of the first $100,000 received and 5 percent of the remainder. If the plaintiff rejects the offer and goes to trial, she could recover her economic loss less the amount of insurance or other benefits received, but could recover damages for noneconomic loss only if she proved by "clear and convincing evidence" that the loss was caused by "intentional or wanton misconduct." Both of these are much higher than normal standards; in a typical tort case, the plaintiff only has to prove that it is more likely than not that the defendant was negligent. And the plaintiff's lawyer's fees would be limited to the 10 percent and 5 percent rules, measured against the difference between what the defendant initially offered and what the jury eventually awarded the plaintiff.[28]

In practice, early offers give defendants a tremendous incentive to make lowball offers before the plaintiff has all the facts and put tremendous pressure on plaintiffs and their lawyers to take them. If Mary Jane Connors were a homemaker and had medical insurance, the doctor who injured her could make a low offer to cover her economic losses minus insurance coverage, which would be minimal. The offer could come before her attorney had an opportunity to engage in discovery of the facts in the complex case, such as deposing the operating room personnel, leaving her with the choice of taking a small amount or facing a difficult and uncertain recovery; that is, that would be her choice if she could find an attorney at all, given the drastic limitation on the normal contingency fee.

A limitation of access to lawyers on a grander scale is the object of legislation making it more difficult for states to hire private attorneys to assist in major litigation. The landmark litigation of this kind involved suits brought by all states against the tobacco companies. For decades, suits by smokers and their heirs against cigarette manufacturers had met an impenetrable wall of corporate secrecy and adverse judicial decisions. In 1994, however, Attorney General Michael Moore of Mississippi sued the tobacco industry to recover the money the state had spent on health care resulting from smoking-related illnesses. Eventually other states joined in, and in 1998 the tobacco companies and the states entered into a settlement agreement under which the companies would pay $242.8 billion for the injury they caused.[29]

The state attorneys general had neither the resources nor the expertise to pursue such a massive products liability litigation, so they turned to those who did: a multistate team of plaintiffs' personal injury lawyers. The effort was immense, the risks were great—these were thought to be the unwinnable cases—and the expenses were enormous. As they would in any other personal injury case, the private lawyers hired by the states agreed to a contingent fee. As it turned out, the rewards of success justified the risk; the attorneys received $12 billion in fees (an amount that was probably less than defense lawyers received over the decades of defense of tobacco—in one year, the industry spent $600 million defending lawsuits).[30]

Since the states' tobacco litigation was so successful, states and cities have used the same technique to attempt to remedy other public harms. More than thirty cities, including Atlanta, Chicago, Detroit, Los Angeles, and New Orleans, have sued gun manufacturers, arguing that they make more handguns than can legally be sold and used, knowing that a network of illegal dealers funnels them into the hands of criminals. The state of Rhode Island hired a major plaintiffs' firm to sue paint manufacturers for making lead paint that causes mental retardation and other injuries to children.[31] The probability of success in these suits is always in doubt, and the ability to bring them and others against public hazards such as handguns and lead paint depends on the ability of governments to enter into contingent fee contracts with private lawyers.

Accordingly, tort reformers have proposed severe limitations on the ability of states and cities to engage private counsel and to sue. Some proposals, for example, establish a special, politically freighted approval process for contingent fee contracts and limit the amount of the fee without regard to the complexity or the riskiness of the litigation; one of the first such statutes was signed by Texas governor George W. Bush in 1999.[32]

A final means of keeping victims out of court is to limit their ability to join together in a class action. Often used in consumer and civil rights cases as well as tort claims, class actions enable plaintiffs who would not be able to find a lawyer to take their case individually to bring many similar cases in one suit. Aggregating small claims also benefits the legal system, by allowing issues of law or fact common to many individual claims to be litigated all at once. For example, fourteen thousand schools around the country joined in a class action against asbestos manufacturers for costs incurred in asbestos removal, and the class of plaintiffs in the Agent Orange litigation eventually ballooned to include 2.5 million veterans and family members claiming injury due to exposure to that herbicide during the Vietnam War.

A series of tort reform proposals aims to move most class actions out of state courts into federal courts, which are traditionally less plaintiff-friendly, to give defendants greater powers to challenge whether a class action is appropriate, to delay the proceedings, to limit plaintiffs' attorneys' fees, and to punish attorneys who bring defective class actions. When the Class Action Fairness Act came up for a vote in the House of Representatives on June 12, 2003, corporate interests were fully mobilized. Its passage was assisted by 475 lobbyists—more than one for every member of the House—including 45 from the U.S. Chamber of Commerce and 11 from Ford Motor Co., which at the time happened to be faced with a $2.7 billion class action settlement for making cars with faulty ignitions.[33]

Changing Liability Rules

Injury victims who manage to get their cases to court find a changed landscape of liability rules, with tort reformers promoting further changes. The number one recommendation of the Tort Policy Working Group was to "retain fault as the basis for liability."[34] The changes in liability rules reveal the true twin purposes of the conservative approach to tort law: to retain fault as the basis of liability in some cases and to abandon it in other cases, the choice being determined by the desire to limit liability, rather than to maintain principled rules.

For most tort cases, the basic fault principle is negligence, or causing injury to someone by failing to act with reasonable care. The negligence principle first took center stage at the end of the nineteenth century, to replace an agglomeration of inconsistent rules. Over the next hundred years, the negligence principle became generalized, applying to more and more types of cases, removing exceptions and qualifications to negligence-based liability.

The conservative shift in tort law has halted and in some respects reversed the spread of negligence. The ostensible basis for this abandonment of tort's core fault principle is that judges and juries, influenced by liberal activism, antipathy toward corporations, or sympathy for injured victims, cannot be trusted to apply the principle correctly. Therefore, higher courts and legislatures have to make liability-limiting rules that appear to depart from the fault principle but actually enforce it.

The most dramatic departure from the negligence principle is the insulation of whole groups of wrongdoers from liability for negligence. A principal step in the generalization of negligence was the abolition of traditional immunities, such as the rules that protected governments and charities from being sued and the rule that one family member could not sue another. In a retreat from that step, one special-interest group after another has gone to Congress or state legislatures to obtain immunity from suit for negligence.[35]

The National Rifle Association and the Shooting Sports Foundation (the gun industry trade group with a $100 million war chest) have promoted the most egregious example. The Protection of Lawful Commerce in Arms Act, which actually protects both lawful and unlawful commerce in Saturday night specials and other handguns, would prohibit all suits against gun manufacturers for injuries suffered by the unlawful misuse of a gun. If the act were adopted, the families of persons killed by the Washington, D.C., sniper in 2002 could not sue the Tacoma, Washington, gun store that sold the sniper the rifle used, allegedly without keeping the required records. David Lemongello and Kenneth McGuire, police officers in Orange, New Jersey, could not sue either. They were shot and disabled by a 9 mm pistol while trying to prevent a service station robbery. The gun was one of a dozen selected by James Gray but purchased by Tammy Lee Songer at a West Virginia gun shop; Songer made the purchase, with the store clerk's acquiescence, because the required Brady Law background check would have revealed that Gray was an illegal gun dealer with a criminal record. Officers Lemongello and McGuire sued the gun dealer and manufacturer, alleging that their negligence in allowing guns to get into the hands of criminals contributed to their disabling injuries. Thirty states already have enacted legislation protecting gun manufacturers from suits to recover the costs of health care and policing caused by their reckless distribution of handguns. Some of these lawsuits have been successful, and others have not, but the legislation prevents courts even from considering the issue.[36]

The Biomaterials Access Assurance Act of 1998 also provided product manufacturers immunity from their negligence.[37] The Act immunizes suppliers of raw materials and component parts used in medical implants, as long as the materials sold meet the specifications of the sale. The Act was precipitated by cases in which DuPont was sued for selling Teflon to the manufacturer of implants designed to cure temporomandibular joint (TMJ) disorders. The TMJ implants fractured in the jaw, causing immune reactions and often breaking the surrounding bone. The injured victims sued Vitek, the implant manufacturer, and, because the suits led to Vitek's bankruptcy, sued DuPont as well. Because DuPont had not manufactured the implants and Teflon was not a dangerous product in its other uses, from spacecraft to nonstick frying pans, it defeated the claims. But complaining about the chilling effect of litigation, DuPont and other manufacturers successfully petitioned Congress to pass the Act, which allows a supplier to invoke special procedural devices to defeat a products liability claim that otherwise might be available under state law.[38]

Even the massive energy bill in 2003 contained a controversial immunity provision. The bill that passed the House of Representatives included unprecedented immunity from products liability suits for manufacturers of MTBE, a gasoline additive that has polluted water supplies around the country. Over twenty suits were pending against the manufacturers, including one by the state of New Hampshire, and many suits had already been settled for more than $100 million. The legislation, backed by powerful congressmen Tom DeLay, Joe Barton, and Billy Tauzin from the MTBE-producing states of Texas and Louisiana, would preempt pending and future suits. Controversy over this immunity was one reason that the energy bill stalled.[39]

While negligence cases are most numerous in tort law, the most significant area of development in the past fifty years has been the law of products liability. Courts increasingly recognized that injuries caused by dangerous products were a social problem of great magnitude that could not be addressed either by trusting the market to work things out or by the law of negligence. In a California case in 1944, for example, Gladys Escola, a waitress, was injured when a Coke bottle she was putting in the refrigerator exploded in her hand. The majority of the California Supreme Court adopted a tortured reading of the law of negligence to let Escola recover, but Justice Roger Traynor, one of the principal architects of the legal transformation of the late twentieth century, in a landmark concurrence laid the path for a more direct approach: "It should now be recognized that a manufacturer incurs an absolute liability when an article that he has placed on the market... proves to have a defect that causes injury to human beings.... Public policy demands that responsibility be fixed wherever it will most effectively reduce the hazards to life and health inherent in defective products that reach the market."[40] As a result of the widespread adoption of Traynor's thinking, compensation to victims of dangerous products expanded dramatically, and consumer products became much safer because of manufacturers' fear of expanded liability.

Over time, the scope of strict products liability expanded, encompassing cases in which the product was defectively made (such as a Coke bottle that exploded) and defectively designed (a truck transmission that shifted out of Park unexpectedly); products liability also addressed cases in which a product was unsafe due to inadequate warnings or safety instructions (household products that are highly flammable, for example), although those cases more closely resembled ordinary negligence. The doctrine permitted actions by injured bystanders as well as the actual users of products, actions against retailers, franchisors, and predecessor and successor corporations, and actions involving leased goods, used goods, and even "products" such as rental apartments.[41]

The conservative shift in the courts and the tort reform movement have eroded products liability to the point where a leading torts textbook captions its discussion "Development, Rationales, and Decline of Strict Products Liability." Professor Sugarman characterizes the approach of the current California Supreme Court, once the pathbreaking source of *Escola* and other cases, as "slowly, but steadily, pushing California products liability law away from any remaining pretense of strict liability."[42]

The ultimate prize for tort reform advocates is congressional action to nationalize products liability law, which traditionally has been the province of the states. So far the attack on products liability has been met with only modest success in the Congress. Particular industries have obtained special-interest legislation, such as medical implant suppliers protected by the Biomaterials Access Assurance Act, but broader measures have been blocked. In 1996, both the House and the Senate passed the Common Sense Product Liability Legal Reform Act, which would have capped punitive damages in products liability cases, but President Clinton vetoed the bill and challenged Senator Bob Dole to confront the issue in that fall's presidential campaign.[43] Tort reformers persist, however. American Tort Reform Association (ATRA) counsel Victor Schwartz, in his "Menu for the New Millennium" outlining the tort reform lobby's agenda for the second Bush administration—"an Administration that seeks to have *fair* rules," according to Schwartz—calls for "national uniform product liability laws"; ATRA's proposals for fair rules would remove strict liability and revert to negligence.[44]

The campaign has met with greater success in the increasingly business-friendly state legislatures and state courts. Forty-five state legislatures have passed some tort reform statutes, and more than half of those have addressed products liability specifically. Many state courts have shifted from aggressively creating new liability rules to cautiously preserving the status quo or even more aggressively cutting back on the gains of the past few decades.

A basic principle of products liability has been that an injured victim can sue any company in the chain of distribution. In *Vandermark v. Ford Motor Co.*, for example, a leading California case, Ford and its dealer, Maywood Bell Ford, tried to point the finger at each other for a brake defect that caused Chester Vandermark's car to pull off the road and smash into a pole. Justice Traynor's opinion rejected that maneuver, holding that both would be bound, and that "they can adjust the costs of such protection between them in the course of their continuing business relationship."[45] A third of the states have reversed that posture through tort reform statutes that immunize retailers and other product sellers from liability. While half of these statutes allow the victim to sue the retailer if the manufacturer is insolvent or beyond the jurisdiction of state courts, the other half leave the victim without a remedy against the retailer even if the victim is unable to sue the manufacturer.[46]

Not every injury caused by a product gives rise to a claim; if a toaster ignites bread and causes a fire, it is defective, but if a user drops the toaster on her foot, the manufacturer is not liable. The core issue in products liability law, therefore, is whether a product is defective. Two tests have been widely adopted to determine whether a product is designed defectively: whether the product's dangers would not reasonably be expected by a user (the "consumer expectations test"), and whether the risks of the product outweigh its benefits (the "risk/utility test"). Both tests have recently been narrowed in many jurisdictions.

The consumer expectations test embodies the principle that products should not be more dangerous than people ordinarily expect them to be. Chocolate pecan candies should not contain pieces of shell large enough to break a tooth, and automobiles should not explode while idling at stoplights.[47] Courts increasingly have limited the application of the consumer expectations test. A California court held that Jack Clark, a patron at the Mexicali Rose restaurant, should have expected the 1-inch chicken bone in his enchilada, which lodged in his throat and caused serious injury.[48] Here the court prevents the jury from determining the reasonable expectations of a consumer of enchiladas, usurping that role for itself as a matter of law.

The risk/utility test balances the benefits provided by a product against its costs. In its classic formulation by Vanderbilt University professor John Wade, the test directs a court to consider the usefulness of the product to the user and to the public, the likelihood that it will cause injury, the availability of substitutes, the manufacturer's and the user's ability to control the risk, the user's awareness of the danger, and the feasibility of the manufacturer's spreading the loss by setting the price of the product higher or carrying liability insurance.[49] The first and last factors particularly distinguish the test from a negligence standard; the focus is broader than the reasonableness of the manufacturer's conduct, considering also the social utility of the product and the loss-spreading capacity of the manufacturer.

Recent statutes and judicial decisions in a number of jurisdictions have moved the risk/utility test to a negligence standard and so have introduced a fault requirement into what was previously strict products liability. The Louisiana Products Liability Act illustrates this.[50] To establish that a product is defective, a victim must prove that at the time of manufacture, there existed an alternative design for the product that would have prevented the injury, and that the likelihood and severity of the injury outweighed the costs of adopting the alternative design—that is, that the manufacturer was negligent. Unlike Wade's formulation, the court is not to consider whether the product lacks social benefit and whether the manufacturer can spread the loss by increasing the price. And under this formulation, the risk/utility test trumps the consumer expectation test; even if the product is more dangerous than a user would expect, it is not necessarily defective.

The narrowing of the risk/utility test gives defendants a tremendous advantage, because often a victim will be able to prove that a product malfunctioned but not necessarily be able to show exactly why or how an alternative design could have prevented the injury. Robert Kallio was driving his Ford F-150 pickup truck home from work when he shifted the automatic transmission into "Park" and left the cab to cover some tools in the truck bed that were exposed to the rain. As he jumped on the bumper, the truck suddenly shifted into reverse and Kallio leaped to the ground, where the truck ran over both his legs and one of his hands. At trial, Kallio proved that the transmission was improperly designed because it shifted out of "Park" on its own, but not how it could have been made differently. The Minnesota Supreme Court held that his proof was sufficient, but under the conservatives' narrow view of risk/utility, Kallio would have received no compensation for his injuries.[51]

The requirement of a reasonable alternative design and the exclusion of liability for "inherently dangerous" products present a particular barrier to recovery in cases in which there is no alternative product but the harm caused is greater than the social benefits. This principle has been most controversially raised in the area known as generic liability, what Professor Carl Bogus calls "the third revolution in products liability." (The first revolution was strict liability for defectively manufactured products, such as the exploding Coke bottle. The second revolution was products whose design made them unreasonably dangerous, such as Kallio's truck.)[52] Generic liability refers to those products for which there is no substitute design or product, but for which the costs of the product may exceed its benefits. The two leading examples: orally gratifying nicotine delivery systems (cigarettes) and inexpensive, easily concealed, lethal weapons (cheap handguns). Legislatures and courts, adopting the conservative position, responded to the threat of these cases by declaring that the risk/utility test could not be applied to impose liability on particular products or categories of products in this way. The New Jersey statute, for example, immunizes products if there is no "practical and technologically feasible alternative design that would have prevented the harm without substantially impairing the reasonably anticipated or intended function of the product."[53]

In some other cases, tort reformers propose taking the question of the dangerousness of the product away from the jury altogether or submitting the question with a strong presumption of reasonableness. When a drug manufacturer receives Food and Drug Administration (FDA) approval for a product, an auto maker complies with federal safety standards, or a corporation otherwise complies with governmental requirements, the product would be presumed to be safe under this rule. (Perversely, however, the reverse presumption does not operate; the manufacturer's failure to comply with an applicable government standard does not require that the product be considered defective.)[54] The problem is that regulatory agencies, even at their best, are incapable of adequately considering and testing every possible product risk and establishing clear regulations to deal with them. At their worst, as Professor Bogus describes it, agencies can be "captured, exhausted, besieged, ossified, cycled, demoralized, . . . co-opted [and] starved," subject to political influence and control by those they are meant to regulate, and underfunded.[55]

The result of these changes would be to prevent recovery by victims such as Lee Ann Gryc, a four-year-old whose pajamas ignited when she reached across an electric stove, causing second- and third-degree burns and permanent scarring on 20 percent of her body. The flannel fabric in the pajamas complied with the test in the federal Flammable Fabrics Act, but Riegel Textile Corporation, the manufacturer, knew that it was unsafe because it was not treated with flame retardant. The court described the statute as "unreliable" and "adopted as a result of industry influence and, therefore, served to protect the textile industry rather than the public."[56] The jury awarded Lee Ann $750,000 in compensatory damages and $1 million in punitive damages; under the tort reformers' rules, she would not have recovered anything.

The struggle over the content of products liability law and the conservative trend is exemplified in the drafting of the Restatement of products liability by The American Law Institute (ALI). The ALI was founded in 1923 by an august group of lawyers, judges, and law professors "to promote the clarification and simplification of the law and its better adaptation to social needs." A self-appointed and self-perpetuating organization, the ALI's principal enterprise is to prepare "Restatements of the Law." With a mix of rules, comments, citations, and illustrations, the Restatements skirt the border between what the ALI authors think the law is and what they think the law should be. The concept of restating the law has always been controversial; torts critic Leon Green described the original Restatement of Torts as "a sort of dehydrated something" with "stiffness and pompousness of expression "smothering important ideas . . . in a welter of insignificant ones."[57]

When the time came for the third round of Restatements in the 1990s, the first torts topic addressed was products liability. Traditionally the drafting of Restatements has been characterized by the preparation of drafts by law professors and the painstaking parsing of the drafts by the ALI membership. The products restatement, however, became the focus of enormous political controversy. Added to the usual processes were consultations with the Association of Trial Lawyers of America (composed of plaintiffs' personal injury lawyers), the Defense Research Institute (corporate defense lawyers), and the Product Liability Advisory Council (representing business interests). The consultations were necessary since the subject had become expressly political, concerning the clash of interests of consumers, workers, and manufacturers.[58] The result was a document that was widely attacked and defended. Scholars and courts argued whether it accurately stated what the courts were doing; a week after the ALI adopted the Restatement, the Connecticut Supreme Court stated that the court's "independent review of the prevailing common law reveals that the majority of jurisdictions" disagreed with the Restatement, and Professor John Vargo later published a mammoth 462-page law review article with 2,403 footnotes that demonstrated that the Restatement was a misstatement of the law.[59] Critics also argued that it represented a capitulation to tort reformers; Professor Frank Vandall characterized it as "a wish list for manufacturing America."[60]

Whether the products restatement was the product of dispassionate scholarship or quasi-legislative interest group politics, it symbolizes the shift to a much more business-friendly body of tort law. It removes consumer expectations as a basis of liability; under the Restatement, a manufacturer is not liable for making a product that is more dangerous than its users would expect. At the same time, it moves the risk/utility test to a constricted form of negligence: The victim must show that there was a "reasonable alternative design" of the product at the time of manufacture, and the list of factors to be weighed in the risk/utility balance is narrower than commonly used by courts. The Restatement bars liability for inherently dangerous products, such as tobacco and handguns, and prescription drugs and medical devices are excluded from the already narrow Restatement rules and are instead treated under a "super negligence" standard, that, according to Professor Teresa Moran Schwartz, "is decidedly favorable to defendants and is likely to reduce rather considerably the role of the common law in assuring the safety of prescription products."[61]

Limiting Damages

Victims who manage to find lawyers, get to court, and win their cases face a final conservative challenge: receiving compensation for their injuries. Tort reformers have targeted traditional damage rules as a way of reducing defendants' costs and discouraging plaintiffs. These rules include joint and several liability, under which a victim who cannot recover from one defendant (because that defendant is bankrupt, for example) can recover from another defendant; the collateral source rule, under which insurance payments a victim received are not used to reduce the amount a defendant must pay; and the single judgment rule, under which the victim receives a single payment for the amount of damages, rather than having to wait for payments over time. The two principal areas of controversy, however, concern the attempt to cap compensatory damages, especially noneconomic damages, and to make it harder to recover punitive damages.

When a victim wins a typical torts case, the victim receives "compensatory damages," under which the wrongdoer has to compensate the victim for the harm caused. Compensatory damages include economic loss, such as the cost of medical expenses, property damage, and lost income, and noneconomic loss, commonly called damages for pain and suffering. Damages for pain and suffering include the physical pain caused by an injury and the emotional harm caused by the restriction on one's life activities. They are not as easily fixed in a dollar amount as a medical bill or a lost paycheck, but they are just as real. Steven Olsen, the handicapped twelve-year-old discussed at the beginning of the chapter, cannot do the things that other children do, and his inability to do them is a real cost created by his doctor's negligence. Money cannot entirely make up for Steven's loss, but the award of noneconomic damages affirms the significance of his injury, requires that the negligent doctor bear the cost of his wrongdoing to the extent that Steven's losses can be measured in money, provides a fund for activities that may in some small way make up for Steven's loss, and provides a means of funding Steven's attorney's fees, allowing the award of economic damages to remain intact.

Traditionally, the amount of damages has been within the discretion of the jury, subject to review for reasonableness by the trial judge and appellate courts. Tort reformers have been successful in removing this discretion in some or all cases in about half the states, with federalization threatened.[62] The main focus has been on medical malpractice cases. California was a leader; in 1975, its Medical Injury Compensation Reform Act set a limit of $250,000 on noneconomic damages in medical malpractice cases, a limit that has not been raised since, and the one that reduced Steven's damages from $7.1 million to less than 4 percent of that amount.[63] Other states include limits on the total damages that can be awarded, including economic damages, without regard for the nature of the injury or the amount of resulting harm. The Virginia law is particularly harsh, limiting all damages to an amount set at $1.5 million in 1999 and gradually increasing to $2 million in 2008. A Fredericksburg jury awarded Craig Allen $6.5 million for an inflammation of the spine that his doctor misdiagnosed as a side effect of medication, but the judge was required by the statute to cut the award to $1.55 million. That amount was less than the $1 million in lost income and $2.5 million in medical expenses that even the defendant conceded Allen was entitled to. New Mexico similarly limits total damages for the victim and family to $600,000, with additional provision for the cost of medical care. In several states with caps, the negligent doctors or hospitals (or their insurance companies) do not have to pay even the limited amounts themselves; state-run victim compensation funds pay a substantial portion.[64]

The final target of the tort reform attack is punitive damages. In awarding punitive damages, as a New Jersey court stated in *Coryell v. Corbaugh* in 1791, one of the earliest American cases on the topic, the jury's task is "not to estimate the damages by any particular proof of suffering or actual loss; but to give damages for example's sake, to prevent such offences in [the] future.... Such a sum...would mark [the jury's] disapprobation, and be an example to others."[65] Awarded only in the most egregious cases of intentional wrongdoing, punitive damages punish the defendant, deter that defendant and other potential wrongdoers from engaging in reprehensible conduct, and encourage the plaintiff to bring litigation that serves the public interest.[66]

Punitive damages are in some respects an odd target for tort reformers. Huge awards are highlighted in the media and decried by tort reformers: $4.8 billion against GM for redesigning the Chevrolet Malibu's gas tank in a more dangerous manner once it learned that federal regulators were using less-rigorous crash tests,[67] $5 billion against Exxon for the *Exxon Valdez* oil spill (still on appeal, a decade and a half later),[68] and $145 billion in a class action by smokers against the tobacco companies, subsequently reversed on appeal (as are many large awards).[69] Actually, though, punitive damage awards are rare, very large awards are rarer still, and most of the awards that are made

arise from business disputes between companies, not from tort suits by injured individuals. A Justice Department study of 762,000 cases in the seventy-five largest counties in the United States, for example, found only 190
tort cases and 174 other cases in which punitive damages were awarded, with
recoveries of more than a million dollars in only 12 percent of those cases.[70]

Nevertheless, the attempt to limit or abolish punitive damages has been
a mainstay of tort reform campaigns. As Bush administration solicitor general Theodore Olson, then representing the industry group Civil Justice Reform Group, put it, when bemoaning the *Exxon Valdez* judgment: "Punitive
damages have replaced baseball as our national sport. The system is a per-
verse combination of lottery and bullfighting, selecting beneficiaries and
targets almost at random and inflicting brutal punishment on the latter if
they wander into the arena."[71]

The Tort Policy Working Group made an early and extreme proposal:
only allow punitive damages in cases bordering on criminal conduct and
limit the amount to $100,000, which would include pain and suffering dam-
ages as well; if those limitations cannot be enacted, then abolish punitive
damages altogether.[72] Since then, tort reformers have proposed statutes that
limit the occasions when punitive damages can be granted and even then
limit the amounts; forty states have adopted legislation in response. Meanwhile, a group of corporate and foundation litigators, with heavy support
from the business community, have successfully litigated a series of cases establishing constitutional limitations on punitive damages.

The legislative campaign to limit punitive damages has several elements.
One aims to create a new rule for when punitive damages can be awarded.
Courts have used a number of vague standards for determining when punitive damages could be awarded (including malice, ill-will, wanton misconduct, flagrant indifference to the safety of others, or abuse of power), all of
which go to the ultimate question of "whether the defendant's conduct merits punishment as just dessert or shows the need for deterrence," as a leading treatise sums it up.[73] Tort reformers aim for a narrower standard. The
HEALTH Act, for example, requires "malicious intent to injure" or "delib-
erately fail[ing] to avoid unnecessary injury that [the defendant] knew the
claimant was substantially certain to suffer."[74] The state that currently comes
closest to that standard is Wisconsin, which allows punitive damages only if
"the defendant acted maliciously toward the plaintiff or in an intentional

disregard of the rights of the plaintiff." In a case in which three workers were killed by the collapse of a crane during the construction of the Milwaukee Brewers' baseball stadium, the court ruled that the statute meant what it said, so punitive damages could be awarded only if the companies operating the crane intended to injure the workers or knew that injury was substantially certain; as plaintiffs' attorney Robert Habush described it, this required them to prove "that the Mitsubishi superintendent who made the decision to do the lift in windy conditions intended to kill these three guys."[75]

Five states bar punitive damages when a defendant has complied with government safety standards, even if its conduct is otherwise blameworthy.[76] This rule would prevent cases such as *O'Gilvie v. International Playtex, Inc.*, in which the U.S. Court of Appeals upheld a $10 million punitive damage award against Playtex in the death of Betty O'Gilvie. Although Playtex complied with all FDA requirements in the labeling of tampons, it knew that its super-absorbent tampons posed a risk of toxic shock syndrome and failed to adequately warn Betty and thousands of other users of the danger.[77]

Another aim is to limit how much wrongdoers have to pay as punitive damages. Almost a third of the states have a cap on punitive damages, typically at a flat dollar amount or as a multiple of compensatory damages. In Colorado, for example, the punitive damages may not exceed the amount of compensatory damages, and in Connecticut, two times compensatory damages. Some states have alternatives: in Indiana, three times actual damages or $50,000, and in North Dakota, two times actual damages or $250,000, whichever is greater. A number of states also require that some of the punitive damage award not go to the plaintiff but to a fund established for that purpose.[78]

Most of the tort reform project has to be carried on state by state, or occasionally in the Congress, because of tort law's status as a common law subject. But punitive damages are unique, in that clever tort reform lawyers representing business interests have successfully constitutionalized the area, bringing the weight of the U.S. Supreme Court to bear on the subject. Participants in the Court's leading punitive damages case in 2003, for example, included the Product Liability Advisory Council (which has filed over six hundred amicus briefs), tort reform author and corporate lawyer Philip K. Howard on behalf of his organization Common Good, the U.S. Chamber of

Commerce, law and economics professors A. Mitchell Polinsky and Steven Shavell with the right-wing group Citizens for a Sound Economy, the American Tort Reform Association, the Washington Legal Foundation, Abbott Labs, Wyeth, Exxon Mobil, Halliburton, and Ford. The effect has been to preempt much of the prevailing state and federal law and set tough new standards limiting when punitive damages can be awarded and in what amount.

The litigation campaign against punitive damages enjoyed its first success in 1996 in the Court's decision in *BMW of North America v. Gore*.[79] After Ira Gore, Jr., had purchased a BMW sports sedan for $40,750 from a Birmingham, Alabama, dealer, he discovered that the top, hood, trunk, and quarter panels had been repainted to conceal damage from acid rain. Gore sued because a repainted car was worth less than a new car, and he asked for punitive damages because of BMW's previously concealed practice of repainting damaged cars and selling them as new. The jury awarded compensatory damages of $4,000 (the diminished value of Gore's repainted car) and additional damages of $4 million to punish BMW, an amount equal to the decreased value of all the repainted cars BMW had sold in the past few years. (The Alabama Supreme Court subsequently reduced the punitive damage award to $2 million.)

The U.S. Supreme Court struck down the punitive damages as unconstitutionally excessive. In part of its ruling, the Court defined three "guideposts" that became standards for evaluating whether an award is excessive: the reprehensibility of the conduct, the relationship between the actual harm suffered by the victim and the punitive damage award, and the relationship between the size of the award and penalties authorized or imposed by law in comparable cases. In this case, BMW's wrongdoing was purely economic, the $2 million award was five hundred times Gore's actual damages, and the highest fine in Alabama for such conduct was only $2,000, so the jury's verdict could not stand.

In later cases, the Court defined further ways to reduce punitive damage awards. In *Cooper Industries, Inc. v. Leatherman Tool Group, Inc.*, an unfair competition case involving copying of the popular Leatherman multifunction tool, the jury awarded $50,000 in actual damages and $4.5 million in punitive damages, finding that Cooper had maliciously copied Leatherman's product and advertisements. The trial judge found the award not to be excessive, and the court of appeals affirmed this. The Supreme Court reversed the decision, stating that the trial judge was too deferential to the jury and the court of appeals was too deferential to the trial judge. From now on, reviews of jury awards would be "de novo"; whatever juries found, judges would decide for themselves if the *BMW* factors had been met, and if trial judges were too lenient, appellate judges would rein them in.[80]

Then, in *State Farm Mutual Automobile Insurance Co. v. Campbell*, in 2003, the Court went even further.[81] Curtis Campbell was at fault in causing an auto accident. The victims offered to settle for $50,000, the limit on Campbell's State Farm insurance policy, but State Farm refused and took the case to trial. The verdict was for $185,849, and for several years State Farm refused to pay the amount above the policy limits. Eventually, State Farm did pay that amount, but Campbell sued for the emotional harm he had suffered due to State Farm's bad faith refusal to settle the claim against him. The trial demonstrated that State Farm had for twenty years employed a national scheme of limiting its payouts through fraud, lies, document destruction, and "mad-dog defense tactics," and that the victims of the scheme seldom sued. In addition to an award of $2.6 million for emotional distress (which the judge reduced to $1 million), the jury awarded $145 million in punitive damages to punish State Farm for its wrongdoing and to deter future misdeeds.

The Supreme Court reversed. Although, as Justice Kennedy delicately put it, State Farm's conduct "merits no praise," in deciding how much State Farm needed to be punished and deterred from future misconduct, the jury and court could only consider the wrong done to Campbell, not the broader pattern of long-term, national wrongdoing of which it was a part. And while ostensibly declining to impose a bright-line test for the ratio of punitive to compensatory damages, Kennedy stated that "few awards exceeding a single-digit ratio" will be constitutional. Indeed, where there are large compensatory damages, as in this case, perhaps only a one-to-one ratio of punitive to compensatory damages is constitutional. As a result, where a wrongdoer imposes greater harm on an individual, the proportion of punitive damages available is smaller. And where the wrongdoer imposes harm on many individuals nationwide, the court has to disregard that bigger problem and focus only on the individual case.

Less Compensation, More Victims

Tort law is pervasive and important in American society. For victims, it provides an important source of compensation for their harm. Most people, fortunately, will never suffer a catastrophic injury, but they benefit from tort law, too. Its compensation function stands in the background, like private insurance, seldom called on but essential when needed. As a statement by the legal system, and therefore by the society as a whole, that the victim has been wronged and the defendant has done wrong, it vindicates our collective sense of fairness. Most importantly, it makes all kinds of activities safer, from the manufacture of prescription drugs to the provision of medical care, by warning those whose activities produce injuries that they ultimately must bear the cost of those injuries. Everyone benefits from the tort system, and those who are not injured may benefit even more than those who are injured, because they are the beneficiaries of increased safety.

If the campaign to undermine tort law is successful, these benefits will be lost. People who are injured by dangerous products or negligent doctors will find it harder to get to court and recover damages. Some wrongdoers, including large chemical companies and reckless gun manufacturers, will be immune from suit altogether. Other defendants will face lax liability rules, allowing negligent drug companies to hide behind FDA approval and presenting victims injured by complex products with an insurmountable burden of proof. If they do win, they will recover smaller damages, often smaller than their medical expenses and lost wages, and, under restrictions on punitive damages, the worst offenders will have the greatest protection from plaintiffs' claims. Because of the new, restrictive rules, many victims will never be able to find a lawyer to take their case at all, and low-income workers, the elderly, and women will be hardest hit of all.

The most important effect of these changes, however, will be to produce more victims. Businesses aim to make profits, and under the tort reformers' proposals, producing injury will become more profitable and producing safety will cost them profits. For a large corporation, the cost of paying tort damages and the cost of making safe products to reduce damages are balanced against each other. If the law requires them to pay less damages, they will produce more injuries.

The Right's attempt to un-make the common law argues that this result is necessary and good. Tort law should limit liability, especially in the current situation of a crisis of too many claims. As the next chapter explains, those claims are false. Over the past hundred years, tort law has become more fair and has made life safer as it has expanded liability. The system that the tort reform movement attacks is based on a realistic assessment of the needs of society, and, if anything, more tort litigation is needed, not less.

3

A Realistic View
of Tort Law

Each of the individual tort reform proposals is driven by self-interest. Eli Lilly, Smith & Wesson, and Ford each want to be sued less often for injuring or killing people, to win more often when they are sued, and to pay less damages if they happen to lose. But here, as in the rest of the conservative assault on the common law, interest and ideology go hand in hand. The individual proposals are connected by a common vision of tort law that acts as propaganda to legislators, judges, potential jurors, and the public at large. The successes of the tort reform movement have come through the propagation of this ideology as much as through campaign contributions and lobbying.

The tort reform ideology contains two myths. The first myth looks back longingly to a golden age of tort law, in which a principle of true fault reined, only real wrongdoers were held liable, and unfortunate victims were fairly compensated; the golden age was corrupted by the expansion of liability beyond all reason and fairness. By enacting the range of tort reform proposals described in Chapter 2, the golden age will be restored. In fact, the golden age never existed, and, as the story of the critique of classical law in the early decades of the twentieth century and the development of modern law in the half-century following demonstrate, it cannot exist. The second myth looks at the present state of tort law and finds the system broken, with liberal judges and emotional juries responding to the pleas of greedy plaintiffs and avaricious trial lawyers and imposing liability willy-nilly on guiltless defendants. A realistic look at the tort system exposes that myth; tort law works well, and if anything, we need more lawsuits, not fewer.

The Origins of Classical Tort Law

Tort law has ancient origins; Roman law's Institutes of Justinian explicated the difference between obligations arising *ex contractu* (out of promises) and *ex delicto* (out of wrongs), and the latter terminology has survived to this day in the civil law, where torts are known as "delicts."[1] For all practical purposes, however, tort law is a modern phenomenon. No lawyer or scholar in England or America attempted a systematic exposition of this area of law before 1850, and cases were few and far between, because serious accidents were much less common in a preindustrial age. Personal injury law is largely a product of industrialization. Harnessing the power of engines and machines created the ability to inflict massive injuries on other people on a regular basis, often on large numbers of people at a time. The railroad and the factory in the nineteenth century, and automobiles, mass-manufactured products, and chemicals and drugs since, created a demand for a new body of law to address the routine power to maim and kill.[2]

As tort law developed in the nineteenth century, it was an agglomeration, drawing on ancient precedents, emerging social science, and judgments of social policy. After 1870, tort law began to resemble its modern form, with a tripartite division of the subject into intentional torts, negligence, and strict liability. Most important was the identification of negligence as the central principle of tort law.

Negligence meant unreasonableness, and negligence began to be considered as a general rule of liability. But negligence posed a problem for classical legal thinkers. Negligence was the duty "of all to all," as Oliver Wendell Holmes, Jr., wrote in his landmark article "The Theory of Torts."[3] But what was the content of that duty; what obligations did a person—or a corporation—owe to others to avoid injuring them? If the state could define the content of the duty, it could impose heavy burdens on individuals and industry, effectively redistributing wealth and power.

This problem was more than academic. The English House of Lords in 1868 held that a landowner was liable even though he was not at fault for flooding a neighbor's land, when the construction of a reservoir caused water to escape through an undiscovered, abandoned coal mine.[4] Treatise writer Francis Wharton warned of the "practical communism" that would result from the failure to narrow legal responsibility: "The capitalist, therefore, becomes liable for all disasters of which he is in any sense the condition.... Making the capitalist liable for everything, therefore, would end in making the capitalist, as well as the noncapitalist, liable for nothing, for there would be soon no capitalist to be found to be sued."[5]

The response to this challenge was to view tort law solely as a realm of

Aristotelian corrective justice, correcting a rip in the social order that had been caused by wrongful behavior, rather than imposing liability to serve social ends. Classical legal scholars systematized tort law around the negligence principle as defined by objective causation and fault, with a particular enthusiasm for limitations of liability.[6] Wharton was a principal expositor of objective causation. Any accident could be traced to a single effective cause by a truly responsible party, so the court need not, and should not, choose among a range of potential defendants. For others, of whom Holmes was the most prominent, custom provided an objective basis of fault that enabled a court to limit liability by taking cases away from the jury.[7] Judges could take the advice of the jury on the question of customary standards of behavior, but they could also declare rules on their own. The effect in classical tort law, as under the proposals of contemporary tort reformers, was to limit the liability of businesses and leave many victims uncompensated.

The Rise of Modern Tort Law

By the early twentieth century, the classical vision of tort law was under forceful attack. The first step was to undermine the concept of objective causation. Henry Edgerton, a George Washington University law professor and later a prominent New Deal judge, and Leon Green, a Texas trial lawyer and populist who became dean of Northwestern University's law school and professor at the University of Texas, were the principals in the attack. Causation, they demonstrated, was never a basis of liability, objectively or otherwise. Causation was a physical fact, and any accident had a multiplicity of causes.

In the famous *Palsgraf* case, for example, Helen Palsgraf was taking the Long Island Railroad to the beach one summer day and was injured as a result of an improbable chain of events.[8] A train conductor, helping a passenger onto a departing train, dislodged the passenger's package, which fell to the ground; the package contained fireworks, which exploded on impact, and the explosion dislodged scales at the opposite end of the platform, which fell on and injured Palsgraf. What "caused" the injury to Palsgraf? Classicists would try to determine whether the negligence of the conductor (attributable to the railroad) was the "proximate cause" of the injury. Critics like Green rejected that approach; causation was a simple factual issue, and on these facts, the conductor's act caused the injury, as did the passenger's carrying a package that did not indicate the danger of its contents, and, for that matter, Palsgraf's decision to go to the beach. As Judge Andrews said in his dissenting opinion in the case, "A boy throws a stone into a pond. The ripples spread. The water level rises. The history of that pond is altered to all eternity."[9]

If causation could not be the basis of assigning liability, then how to determine if the railroad was liable, or the passenger, or no one at all? The critics also rejected an abstract notion of fault. Neither natural rights nor a vague concept of custom could tell the court whether the railroad should pay for Palsgraf's injury.

Instead, in Green's terms, the question was one of interest balancing. The task of the jury or the court, in determining when a duty was owed and when conduct was negligent, was to immerse itself in the facts of the case, to weigh the consequences of deciding one way or the other, and then to determine a just result. Green took the concept so far as to reorganize the entire subject, structuring his casebook not on the traditional doctrinal categories such as negligence but in factually organized chapters such as "Occupancy, Ownership, and Development of Land," "Traffic and Transportation," and "Family Relations." This approach to interest balancing undermined the idea of a Holmesian universal duty of "all to all." Instead, negligence became narrow and relational—whether the railroad owed a duty to Palsgraf not to dislodge another passenger's package.

The *Palsgraf* case became the most famous case in all of tort law for its discussion of how to make the calculation of duty, with a majority opinion by the legendary Benjamin Nathan Cardozo and a dissent by William Andrews. Although the opinions differed in approach, both agreed that the negligence inquiry could not be decided abstractly. For Cardozo, "Negligence, like risk, is thus a term of relation. Negligence in the abstract . . . is surely not a tort, if indeed it is understandable at all." For Andrews, "because of convenience, of public policy, of a rough sense of justice, the law arbitrarily declines to trace a series of events beyond a certain point. . . . It is all a question of expediency. There are no fixed rules to govern our judgment."[10]

Thus tort law became a question of public policy; in Green's famous phrase, tort law is "public law in disguise."[11] If judgments about tort liability entailed the balancing of social interests, however, that balancing should be done openly, rather than being concealed by abstract principles of fault or obscure legal doctrines. And most tort cases did not involve freakish accidents like the one that befell Palsgraf, but involved repeated injuries of the same type: workplace injuries, automobile accidents, adulterated food, and so on. The obvious next step was to consider whether approaches other than ordinary negligence litigation would better balance the interests in each of those areas.

The first area in which this analysis was implemented was workplace injuries. Beginning around the turn of the century, states supplanted the tort system altogether in this area, substituting workers' compensation systems. These systems are usually described as a social bargain, in which workers give up their right to sue employers for workplace injuries in return for a guarantee that they will receive medical expenses and scheduled disability payments without the need to establish fault. Even Holmes, who in *The Common Law* had opposed having the state act as "a mutual insurance company against accidents," came to recognize that the bulk of litigation had become "injuries to persons or property by railroads, factories, and the like. The liability for them is estimated, and sooner or later goes into the price paid by the public. The public really pays the damages, and the question of liability . . . is really the question how far it is desirable the public should insure the safety of those whose work it uses."[12]

The Expansion of Liability in Modern Tort Law

From at least the 1920s through the 1970s, the balancing of interests has led to the general expansion of liability. This expansion, in turn, reflects two basic insights about interest balancing. First, where classical scholars and judges saw tort law as the realm of *corrective* justice, providing a remedy for wrongs between individuals, modern tort law is a realm of *collective* justice. Each case is not singular but representative of a larger class of cases, and the resolution of each case ought to take account of the larger class of cases as a social problem; when a court decides a medical malpractice case, it should consider the effects its decision will have on doctors and patients generally. Tort law, in other words, is functional, serving the social goals of safety and compensation. This does not mean that tort law is unconcerned with fairness; to the contrary, fairness is essential, but fairness entails considering the ramifications of an individual decision and treating all cases of the same kind as part of a broad solution to a social problem.

Second, in considering resolutions to the social problem of injury, modern law has recognized a principle of "enterprise liability." Where classical law focused on individual responsibility for an individual wrongful act, modern tort law focuses on the responsibility of an enterprise for a class of injurious behavior. The principle asserts that enterprises, activities, and businesses—a railroad, a hospital, a product manufacturer—ought to bear their true costs, including the costs of injuries they produce, and that ordinarily those costs actually can be borne by all of its users through an increase in price. Enterprise liability promotes all three goals of safety, compensation, and fairness. When an enterprise is liable for the injuries it produces, it has an incentive to reduce injuries to the lowest reasonable level. By shifting the costs of an injury to all who benefit from an activity, enterprise liability effectively compensates by providing insurance against catastrophic losses otherwise suffered by individuals. Enterprise liability is fair because it imposes the costs of an activity, including the costs of injuries it produces, on those who profit from it.

Conservative advocates of tort reform propose limited rather than expanded liability, and they do so by ignoring these well-established insights. Their focus is the perceived injustice of imposing liability in the individual case, not the broad social problem of injury caused by defective products, negligent doctors, or toxic chemicals. And their baseline principle is that businesses should not be liable for the damage they cause, and individual victims should generally bear their own losses, uncompensated. These positions are a rejection of at least a half-century of the development of tort law.

One of the leading cases highlighting the principles of interest balancing and enterprise liability was *Escola v. Coca Cola Bottling Co. of Fresno*, a 1944 decision of the California Supreme Court noted in the previous chapter.[13] Gladys Escola, a waitress in Tiny's Waffle Shop in Merced, California, was injured when a glass bottle of Coca-Cola broke in her hand. The driver for the local Coca-Cola bottler had delivered several cases of Coke to the restaurant, placing them on the floor, one on top of the other, where they remained for at least thirty-six hours. Immediately before the accident, Escola picked up the top case and set it on a cabinet in front of the refrigerator. She then proceeded to take the bottles from the case with her right hand, one at a time, and put them into the refrigerator. After she had placed three bottles in the refrigerator and had moved the fourth bottle about 18 inches from the case, it exploded in her hand. The bottle broke into two jagged pieces and inflicted a deep 5-inch cut on Escola, severing blood vessels, nerves, and muscles of the thumb and palm of her hand.

Under a strict, traditional rule of negligence, Escola had to prove that the bottling company failed to exercise reasonable care to prevent the explosion of the bottle that injured her. That was difficult; the evidence at trial established that new bottles were fully tested, that used bottles were inspected four different times for cracks or other defects, and that the kind of break this bottle suffered was probably caused by external force, not excessive pressure in the bottle.

The majority of the court, in a convoluted opinion, helped Escola make an end run around her proof problems by inferring negligence. In his concurrence, Justice Roger Traynor, one of the architects of the modern law, shifted the analysis to directly confront the principles in one remarkable paragraph:

> I concur in the judgment, but I believe the manufacturer's negligence should no longer be singled out as the basis of a plaintiff's right to recover in cases like the present one.... Even if there is no negligence, however, public policy demands that responsibility be fixed wherever it will most effectively reduce the hazards to life and health inherent in defective products that reach the market. It is evident that the manufacturer can anticipate some hazards and guard against the recurrence of others, as the public cannot. Those who suffer injury from defective products are unprepared to meet its consequences. The cost of an injury and the loss of time or health may be an overwhelming misfortune to the person injured, and a needless one, for the risk of injury can be insured by the manufacturer and distributed among the public as a cost of doing business. It is to the public interest to discourage the marketing of products having defects that are a menace to the public. If such products nevertheless find their way into the market it is to the public interest to place the responsibility for whatever injury they may cause upon the manufacturer, who, even if he is not negligent in the manufacture of the prod-

uct, is responsible for its reaching the market. However intermittently such injuries may occur and however haphazardly they may strike, the risk of their occurrence is a constant risk and a general one. Against such a risk there should be general and constant protection and the manufacturer is best situated to afford such protection.[14]

Here the problem and solution are clearly framed. The case is not about Gladys Escola, or even exploding Coke bottles, but about dangerous manufactured products in general. The central issue is not the bottler's negligence, but public policy and the public interest. Public policy is best determined and the public interest best served by weighing the manufacturer's ability to control the risk, the "overwhelming misfortune" to the injured victim who is "unprepared" to bear a catastrophic loss, and the incentives to reduce a "menace to the public."

Traynor's opinion makes explicit what is implicit in every tort case. The court must make a public policy decision as to where the loss will fall. If the court requires Escola to prove the bottler's negligence and she is unable to do so, the court has decided that the public interest is best served by letting the loss lie where it falls. If it adopts Traynor's argument and imposes liability even without clear proof of negligence, the court has decided that the public interest is best served by shifting the loss. Either way, it is engaging in an allocation of rights and responsibilities with social consequences.

As interest balancing and enterprise liability spread in tort law through the mid-twentieth century, the two major developments in tort rules were the generalization of negligence and the rise of strict products liability. Where previously there had been pockets of no liability or limited liability, or special rules for particular defendants and circumstances, courts and legislatures began to recognize that the law of negligence ought to be uniform in principle if diverse in application.

One step in the generalization of negligence, which tort reformers aim to roll back, was making everyone responsible for failing to act with reasonable care by removing a set of archaic immunities and limited-duty rules. For example, there was an old maxim that "The King can do no wrong," adhered to even in newly democratic America, which held that governments were not liable for their torts. In 1946, Congress enacted the Federal Tort

Claims Act, which generally makes the United States liable for its torts as a private actor would be, subject to exceptions appropriate to its unique governmental functions, and most states have followed suit.[15]

Charities, too, were immune from suit, but that immunity also was abolished in most states. In *Bing v. Thunig,* for example, Isabel Bing was severely burned when an electric cautery device being used by a surgeon during her operation ignited a flammable antiseptic liquid that nurses negligently had allowed to accumulate on sheets under her. Under a tortured body of law dating to a 1914 decision, St. John's Episcopal Hospital, the principal defendant, would not be liable for the negligence of its employees, the nurses. But the New York Court of Appeals pointed out that "Liability is the rule, immunity the exception. It is not too much to expect that those who serve and minister to members of the public should do so, as do all others, subject to that principle and within the obligation not to injure through carelessness." Therefore, the court concluded, in adopting an enterprise liability approach, "Hospitals should, in short, shoulder the responsibilities borne by everyone else. The rule of nonliability is out of tune with the life about us, at variance with modern-day needs and with concepts of justice and fair dealing."[16]

In many other cases, the general negligence principle has supplanted rules of more limited duties. Traditionally, for example, a person owed no duty to control the conduct of another person or to warn third persons of dangers that person might present. In the much discussed case of *Tarasoff v. Regents of the University of California,* Dr. Lawrence Moore, a psychologist employed by the university, was treating Prosenjit Poddar.[17] Poddar killed Tatiana Tarasoff, and her parents sued, alleging that two months earlier, Poddar had expressed his intention to kill Tatiana, but that Dr. Moore had failed to warn her of the danger. Under the traditional rule, neither Moore nor the university would be liable. The court, however, applied the "fundamental principle" that liability should be imposed whenever there is negligence. The principle is not absolute, but courts depart from it only after a process of interest balancing, considering factors outlined in a line of California cases, including "the foreseeability of harm, . . . the policy of preventing future harm, . . . the extent of the burden to the defendant and consequences to the community of imposing a duty, . . . and the availability, cost and prevalence of insurance for the risk involved."[18] A psychotherapist bears a special relationship to his patient that supports a duty of reasonable care, so the therapist, like anyone else, must act reasonably with respect to the potential risk.

The generalization of negligence affected rules that evaluated the conduct of victims as well as injurers. Until the 1960s, nearly all states operated under a principle of "contributory negligence." If a plaintiff acts unreasonably—say, a pedestrian fails to look when entering a crosswalk—the plaintiff's contributory negligence absolves the defendant of liability, even if the defendant's negligence was much greater—the defendant was speeding, driving drunk, and talking on a cell phone. Although a variety of explanations have been offered for the rule, as the dean of torts scholars, William Lloyd Prosser noted, its origins lie in classical law:

> Probably the true explanation lies merely in the highly individualistic attitude of the common law of the early nineteenth century. The period of development of contributory negligence was that of the industrial revolution, and there is reason to think that the courts found in this defense, along with the concepts of duty and proximate cause, a convenient instrument of control over the jury, by which the liabilities of rapidly growing industry were curbed and kept within bounds.[19]

And contributory negligence received latter-day support by conservatives such as Lewis F. Powell, a tort reform advocate prior to his ascension to the Supreme Court; Powell argued that the rule should be kept as a counterweight to the jury's bias toward plaintiffs.[20]

Beginning in the 1960s, most legislatures and courts rejected contributory negligence in favor of comparative negligence. There are different versions of comparative negligence, but all share a basic principle: A plaintiff's negligence should not completely exonerate a defendant, but it should reduce the amount the plaintiff recovers. If the jury decides that the pedestrian was 20 percent responsible for the accident by failing to look before crossing, the negligent driver only has to pay 80 percent of the pedestrian's damages.

The second important movement in the law has been the rise of strict products liability. Many of the high-visibility controversies in tort law have concerned products cases, including asbestos, silicone breast implants, drugs such as fen-phen and Bendectin, Ford Broncos and their Firestone tires, and the humble McDonald's cup of coffee. Until the recent conservative reaction, the story of products liability was one of gradually expanding liability of product manufacturers and sellers in favor of injured consumers. The crucial point of the story, however, is not the expansion of liability but the way in which it was achieved: through the application of interest balancing and enterprise liability that have characterized modern tort law.

Products liability law has mixed origins in tort and contract law. Its contract origins were once a barrier to liability; a mail coach driver could not recover against the maker of a defective coach because the postmaster, not the driver, had contracted for the purchase of the coach.[21] Throughout much of the twentieth century, however, contract law was a source of expanded liability. Courts increasingly held that sellers impliedly warranted their goods to be safe, creating liability for a loaf of bread with a pin in it[22] or a Plymouth with defective steering.[23] Although products liability cases today are usually treated as tort cases, not contract cases, the contract and warranty strain is still important because it shows the representational basis of products liability: consumers expect goods to be safe for their ordinary uses, and liability should attach when their expectation of safety is disappointed.

Courts found tort law more congenial than contract law because it more directly expressed the public policy basis of the law. Justice Traynor's concurring opinion in *Escola v. Coca Cola Bottling Co* was an important landmark. In the early 1960s, the movement took root with the overt recognition of strict liability by the California Supreme Court in *Greenman v. Yuba Power Products, Inc.,* and the drafting by the American Law Institute of section 402A of the Restatement (Second) of Torts, subsequently adopted by most courts as the embodiment of strict liability.

William Greenman received a Shopsmith home power tool from his wife for Christmas. While using it as a lathe, he was struck in the head and seriously injured by a piece of wood that flew out of the machine. Inadequate screws had been used to control vibration, and alternate designs could have prevented the injury. Writing for a unanimous court, Justice Traynor vindicated his earlier opinion in *Escola* by clearly moving away from negligence. "A manufacturer is strictly liable in tort when an article he places on the market, knowing that it is to be used without inspection for defects, proves to have a defect that causes injury to a human being." The principle was by now so obvious, at least to Traynor, that he did not need to review the reasons for its adoption, but could simply summarize: "The purpose of such liability is to insure that the costs of injuries resulting from defective products are borne by the manufacturers that put such products on the market rather than by the injured persons who are powerless to protect themselves."[24]

Restatement section 402A stated the rule that a product seller is liable for injuries caused by a product that is "in a defective condition unreasonably dangerous"; moving away from negligence, liability attached even if "the seller has exercised all possible care in the preparation and sale of his product."[25] Subsequently, the section was cited by courts more than three thousand times and, in one way or another, shaped the law in every state.[26] The Restatement language was somewhat obscure; did it mean that a product was "in a defective condition" *because* it was "unreasonably dangerous, or did it contain independent requirements of a defective condition and unreasonable dangerousness? But many courts, in adopting the standard, clearly indicated their choice to favor strict liability by reading "defective" independently of the "unreasonably dangerous" language, because the latter phrase "burdened the injured plaintiff with proof of an element which rings of negligence," which was to be avoided now that negligence was irrelevant.[27]

The adoption of strict products liability presented a new set of issues for the courts, and many courts responded by expanding liability. For example, who is liable to whom? Early cases went beyond the case of a buyer suing a manufacturer; Gladys Escola's employer had purchased the cases of Coke, and William Greenman's wife had purchased the Shopsmith, but Escola and Greenman were foreseeable users of the products. Eventually, bystanders and other nonusers of products were allowed to recover. On the defendants' side, everyone in the chain of distribution was a potential defendant, including manufacturer, distributor, and retailer.

The definition of a defective product was relatively clear as to goods that were manufactured improperly, but a different problem is presented by products that are manufactured in accordance with a design that is itself unreasonably dangerous. Many courts use alternative tests for design defects, allowing recovery if the product violated the expectations of the ordinary consumer or if the risks of the product outweighed its utility. Consistent with enterprise liability, both place the costs of violation on the product seller rather than the victim.

And some defects concern dangers inherent in the product or those that can be avoided by proper use but that require warning or instruction. Here, products liability comes closer to negligence, but the standard employed in triggering the warning is less onerous to the plaintiff than in negligence cases, and courts expansively require warnings and assess their adequacy.

Liability expanded from the early 1960s through the mid-1980s, as courts recognized that social needs and enterprise liability favored expanded liability. But the expansion was not uniform, and a key difference between the period of expansion and the conservative reaction was process, not results. During this period, courts recognized that abstract principles of fault and formal legal reasoning could not decide the cases, whatever the eventual results.

One of the most prominent issues that illustrates this approach to tort law involves the drug diethylstilbestrol, or DES. DES was invented by British researchers in 1937 but never patented, so the formula was available to any drug company that wished to produce it. In 1941, twelve American companies applied to the FDA to produce DES for the treatment of excessive menstrual bleeding and other ailments. In 1947, the FDA also approved DES for the prevention of miscarriage during pregnancy, and in 1951 it concluded that the drug was "generally recognized as safe" (a term of art) when used for this purpose, enabling manufacturers to market it without further approval. By 1971, however, evidence had accumulated that DES caused the previously rare adenosis (precancerous vaginal or cervical growths) and vaginal adenocarcinoma (a form of cancer) in the daughters of women who had taken DES during pregnancy. These rapidly progressing and deadly diseases needed monitoring by biopsy and colonoscopy and frequently required massive surgery. Joyce Bichler's case was typical. When she was seventeen years old, she was stricken with cervical and vaginal cancer, requiring surgery to remove her reproductive organs and more than half her vagina, destroying her ability to bear children or enjoy normal sexual relations.[28]

The DES cases presented challenges on many levels. First, what standard of liability should apply? The plaintiffs argued that the drug companies were liable even under a negligence standard, because they had failed to adequately test DES before marketing it. If they had tested the drug on pregnant mice, they would have discovered the effect on DES daughters and not marketed the drug for use during pregnancy. But note that the drug was approved for use during pregnancy by the FDA. Tort reformers currently assert that the FDA can assess dangerousness better than juries can and that it is reasonable for manufacturers to rely on the FDA approval process (a process that in turn relies on information from the manufacturers); under this approach, DES manufacturers would have been immunized even if they could have prevented the harm.

Second, some victims faced a statute of limitations problem. The statute of limitations dictates the time in which a lawsuit may be brought. Usually in tort cases, the limitations period begins to run from the date of the injury, a rule that poses no problems in the case of a sudden, catastrophic event such as an auto accident. Exposure to toxic harms presents a more difficult problem, however. Many states apply a discovery rule, with the period beginning to run when the victim knows or reasonably should have known of the harm. In New York, on the other hand, exposure to the harm triggered the limitations period, so by the time DES daughters contracted cancer the statute already had run. The legislature, recognizing the social problem posed by DES cases, responded by changing to a discovery rule and reviving claims that had already expired.

The third issue, and the one that provoked the most litigation, concerned causation. A plaintiff has to prove that the defendant caused her injury, which presents little difficulty in a typical case; Gladys Escola knew that the exploding bottle came from the Fresno Coca Cola Bottling Company. But the distribution of DES was different. DES produced by all manufacturers (more than three hundred made it) was chemically identical. Pharmacists usually filled prescriptions from whatever brand they had on hand. Since the effects did not manifest themselves for decades, memories had faded and the records of physicians and pharmacists had been lost. Therefore, individual victims like Joyce Bichler could not prove that her mother had taken a drug made by Eli Lilly or Abbott or any other particular company.

A few courts threw up their hands at this point. The Missouri Supreme Court, for example, was troubled because imposing liability would be inconsistent with traditional fault principles, because the defendant in a particular case might not have manufactured the drug that caused the plaintiff's injury.[29] Other courts, applying modern tort thinking, were more creative, the California Supreme Court being the first. The court began with a basic insight:

> In our contemporary complex industrialized society, advances in science and technology create fungible goods which may harm consumers and which cannot be traced to any specific producer. The response of the courts can be either to adhere rigidly to prior doctrine, denying recovery to those injured by such products, or to fashion remedies to meet these changing needs.

It then focused specifically on balancing the public interests involved, with an emphasis on the principle of enterprise liability.

> As between an innocent plaintiff and negligent defendants, the latter should bear the cost of the injury. From a broader policy standpoint, defendants are better able to bear the cost of injury resulting from the manufacture of a defective product (citing Justice Traynor's *Escola* opinion).... The manufacturer is in the best position to discover and guard against defects in its products and to warn of harmful effects; thus, holding it liable for defects and failure to warn of harmful effects will provide an incentive to product safety.[30]

As a result of this process, the California court and others formulated rules of "market-share liability." Injured victims could recover from manufacturers a proportion of their damages equal to the proportion of the DES market held by each company. An individual plaintiff would not recover all of her damages from the company that had actually harmed her, but victims would be compensated by having all the companies pay in accordance with how much they had profited from the sale of the drug and how much harm they had done.

More Tort Law, Not Less

The conservatives' claim that we have strayed from a golden age of tort law is refuted by a hundred years of history. Their second claim, that the tort system is out of control, is equally false. Republican senator Mitch McConnell sums up this claim: (McConnell, who has introduced a series of tort reform bills, thought the issue so important that on the day British prime minister Tony Blair addressed a joint meeting of Congress on war in Iraq, McConnell introduced the Common Sense Consumption Act to protect McDonald's, Sara Lee, and other food purveyors from lawsuits.)

> Hardly a day goes by that we do not hear or read of the dramatic increase in the number of lawsuits filed, of the latest multimillion dollar verdict, or of another small business, child care center, or municipal corporation that has had its insurance cancelled out from under it.... Everyone is suing everyone, and most are getting big money.[31]

There are too many lawsuits filed, their number is increasing, plaintiffs win when they shouldn't, and they get large awards from sympathetic juries. The results are a "tort tax" raising the price of goods and services to pay for the liability costs and an "insurance crisis" raising liability insurance premiums to such heights that companies are deterred from developing new products, and doctors are driven out of practice.

In fact, while the tort system as developed by courts and legislatures through the 1970s is far from perfect, it functions reasonably well in deterring unsafe conduct and compensating victims, particularly when compared to the alternative of little liability and diminished government regulation preferred by tort reformers; if there is a major flaw in the system, it is the imposition of too little liability on too few defendants, resulting in compensation to too few victims.

The conservative claim that the tort system is broken rests largely on spurious anecdotes like the McDonald's coffee case, with occasional factual claims that are exaggerated or simply made up. Scholars have accumulated a body of evidence about the workings of the system, and the evidence mostly runs counter to the conservative claims.

The claim that there are too many tort cases presents an obvious question that conservative critics seldom address: Too many compared to what? The place to start is not with litigated cases but with injuries that could give rise to litigation. There is much data on injuries: over two hundred babies died in playpens between 1988 and 2001,[32] all-terrain vehicles caused 111,700 injuries and 547 deaths in 2000,[33] and the number of traffic fatalities declined from 42,130 in 1988 to 37,795 in 2001.[34] Connecting injury data with potential tort actions is difficult, however; some ATV accidents are caused by vehicle defects, some by driver negligence, and some by pure chance.

Over time, a number of studies have been conducted of the relationship between injuries and claims. Professor Michael Saks, in his exhaustive analysis of empirical studies on tort litigation, summarizes them by remarking not on the large number of claims, as tort reformers would have it, but on the dearth of claims:

> One of the most remarkable features of the tort system is how few plaintiffs there are. A great many potential plaintiffs are never heard from by the injurers or their insurers.
>
> . . .
>
> Perhaps the most precise conclusion is that filings [of tort cases] represent few false positive errors (defendants who are wrongly sued) and many false negative errors (meritorious claims that are never filed).[35]

A study by the Rand Corporation's Institute for Civil Justice reported that eighty-one of every one hundred people who suffered a disabling injury did nothing to seek redress. Of the remaining nineteen who even considered a claim, only seven consulted a lawyer, and only two of them sued.[36] Breaking down the claims, auto accidents—seldom grist for the tort reform mill—made up almost two-thirds of the claims.[37]

More studies have been done of medical malpractice claims, an area that has been a focus of tort reform efforts. An early study by the California Medical Association and California Hospital Association had experts compare patient records with insurance company files, and found that only 10 percent of negligently injured patients sought compensation. Even among patients who suffered "major, permanent injuries," only one in six sued.[38] The largest study of medical errors, conducted by Harvard researchers through a review of 31,000 patient records at hospitals in New York state, had similar findings. About one of every one hundred hospital patients suffered an injury that could have been the basis of a tort claim; this number is probably understated, because the review was based only on hospital records that might have been incomplete and did not include information that would have been turned up on discovery. Ten percent of the injuries resulted in long-term hospitalization, and 14 percent resulted in death. Yet only about one out of eight negligently injured patients filed a claim. The Harvard researchers concluded that while tort litigation "does in fact operate erratically, it hardly operates excessively."[39]

Despite allegations of sue-happy plaintiffs and greedy lawyers, these statistics are easy to understand. Sociologists call this part of the process "blaming and claiming." An injured person has to identify someone else as the cause of her injury and then pursue a claim against the injurer. In a medical injury case, she has to recognize that the harm may have been caused by a physician's negligence, a defective medical device, or a dangerous drug, rather than being an unfortunate but random outcome of medical treatment. In an auto accident, an injured driver has to recognize that a mechanical defect or improper design in the car may have contributed to the injury. Even when blame can be attached, most people prefer to take their lumps rather than litigate. Litigation is time-consuming, emotionally draining, unpredictable, and, for many people, culturally undesirable, so they will avoid it. And if they do want to litigate, they need to find a lawyer willing to take the case. Since tort cases are brought on a contingent fee basis, the lawyer has to decide that the probability of success and the size of the potential recovery justify the up-front investment of the lawyer's time and money. In malpractice cases, for example, lawyers reject as many as nine out of every ten potential cases; even victims who eventually recover damages, and therefore have demonstrably meritorious claims, often have difficulty finding a lawyer to take the case.[40]

This process weeds out some groups of victims more than others. A 1993 report by the General Accounting Office, the nonpartisan research arm of Congress, concluded that Medicare and Medicaid recipients—the elderly and the poor—were less likely than other victims of medical malpractice to file claims. The Harvard study confirmed this result; poor patients and uninsured patients—those most in need of compensation—were least likely to sue.[41]

If the incidence of tort litigation is not demonstrably too large, perhaps the problem is the rate of increase; people have become more litigious, and tort claims are increasing at too fast a rate. All claims about litigation rates should be approached with caution. The composition of cases differs over time, and tort cases have increased as new dangers have been presented and the law has expanded. But looking at all litigation (not just tort litigation), Americans were, if anything, more litigious in the eighteenth and nineteenth centuries than they are today. In Accomack County, Virginia, in 1639, there was one case for every four people, a rate several times higher than anywhere in America today. One of the longest studies of litigation, for the St. Louis Circuit Court, shows that the litigation rate in recent decades was about half what it was in the 1840s.[42]

More specifically, researchers from the Rand Institute point out that tort litigation is composed of three "worlds": routine personal injury suits, especially auto accidents; high-stakes cases involving catastrophic injuries and well-insured defendants, such as products liability and medical malpractice; and mass injury cases, such as asbestos litigation.[43] The first world is relatively stable. The National Center for State Courts, for example, reports that tort filings in state courts actually fell by 10 percent during the 1990s.[44] The second and third worlds move up and down as the law changes and latent injuries become newly manifest. Tort filings have increased dramatically in the federal courts, but much of that is made up of mass torts. Twenty thousand breast implant cases suddenly appeared in the federal courts in the early 1990s, and asbestos cases made up a fourth of all the products liability litigation in the federal courts.[45] Much more striking is the seldom complained of litigation explosion in businesses suing each other, which has increased twice as fast as tort cases and constitutes ten times more of the courts' caseload.[46] The rate of medical malpractice claims, by contrast, has remained relatively stable; from 1986 through 2002, the rate was about fifteen malpractice claims for every one hundred physicians.[47]

Tort reformers also complain that the tort system is distorted by jury verdicts that are too favorable to plaintiffs and damage awards that are too large. Of course, only a small proportion of cases actually go to trial—5 percent is a high estimate of cases as a whole—but those cases provide a basis for comparison when insurance companies and lawyers decide which cases to settle and for how much. The conclusions to be drawn from the research on verdicts and claims are that victims win about as often as they should, and verdicts are about as large as they should be, measured by statistical probability and the opinions of experts both inside and outside the legal system.

Cases that go to trial are the product of a winnowing process that begins with the victim's decision to recognize an injury as someone else's fault and extends through finding a lawyer, filing a suit, and engaging in settlement negotiations. The cases that are left at the end of the process are the most contested and most ambiguous cases, in which liability, the amount of damages, or both are most unclear. Given the uncertainty in these cases, we would expect plaintiffs and defendants each to win about half of the cases. (The question is actually more complicated, because plaintiffs and defendants might have different incentives; a doctor may be more concerned with preserving his reputation and so will be a more aggressive litigator than a patient. But over the run of tort cases, individual factors ought to balance out.) And that is what happens. Looking at all tort cases, plaintiffs win about half. That number is composed of wider variations in types of cases: victims win 70 percent of toxic torts, 60 percent of automobile negligence cases, 40 percent of products liability cases, and 30 percent of medical malpractice cases.[48]

Another way of looking at verdicts and awards is by comparing what the juries do to some external standard. There is, of course, no objective truth against which we can measure the verdict, but it is possible to compare jury decisions to decisions made by experts. A series of studies from the 1950s through the 1990s all reached the same conclusion: measured by any standard, juries get it right in a large majority of cases. The oldest and most famous study of jury behavior, the University of Chicago Jury Project of the 1950s, asked judges how they would have decided the cases in which they presided over jury trials. In about 80 percent of the cases, the judge agreed with the jury; showing that juries do not necessarily favor victims, the disagreements in the remaining cases favored plaintiffs and defendants about evenly.[49] Later studies provided similar results. A survey of judges in thirty-three states, a detailed analysis of 153 trials in Arizona, a study by the National Center for State Courts in California, and a study of twenty years of federal civil cases all concluded that judges substantially agree with juries on outcomes.[50]

A number of studies have used outside experts to evaluate jury decisions. Most of these involve medical malpractice cases, using physicians to evaluate case records and comparing their decisions to those of the juries that actually decided the cases. The consistent pattern is that the experts and the jurors agree. A research group directed by physicians examined over eight thousand malpractice cases in New Jersey, for example, and found that the jury verdicts in cases that went to trial tracked the opinion of the reviewing physicians. Review of the amounts of awards also demonstrates agreement; jury awards increase as the seriousness of the injury increases, except that injuries resulting in death receive somewhat less than serious injuries that the victim survives. The same is true of awards for noneconomic loss, or pain and suffering, where the award increases as the severity of the injury increases.[51]

This is not to say the every jury reaches a correct decision. Of course they do not, and in individual cases judges are able and quite willing to reduce the amount of damages awarded or reverse the verdict altogether. But tort reforms are directed at the system as a whole, and the evidence shows that as a whole, the charges of the tort reformers are without foundation.

One area that receives particular attention is punitive damages. Conservatives argue that punitive damages are like lightning; while they do not occur very often, when they do, the consequences are devastating. And even more than the fear of lightning, the fear of punitive damages affects everyday behavior; corporations avoid making new products or entire product lines and settle unmeritorious litigation because the threat of bankruptcy caused by punitive damages is too great.

But this perception does not accord with reality, either. There have been a number of studies of punitive damages conducted by independent scholars, the American Bar Association, the General Accounting Office, and the Rand Institute for Civil Justice. While they vary in detail, there is substantial agreement on certain basic findings.[52] Punitive damages are very rare, awarded in 1 or 2 to at most 6 percent of the cases that plaintiffs win. Awards are even less frequent in products liability and medical malpractice cases, the target of most tort reform measures. Intentional torts (such as libel) and business cases make up the bulk of punitive damage awards; a Justice Department study of cases in the seventy-five largest counties found that punitive damages were three times more likely to be awarded in contract cases than in tort cases.[53] Many of the cases involving individuals are insurance bad faith cases, where an insurance company wrongfully denies coverage under a policy, as in *State Farm Mutual Automobile Insurance Co. v. Campbell*, the Supreme Court's 2003 pronouncement on the issue, and the

John Grisham novel *The Rainmaker*. Although a few huge awards are high-lighted by newspapers and tort reform advocates, most awards are relatively modest and reasonably related to the compensatory damages. In medical malpractice and products liability cases, for example, Professors Rustad and Koenig report that the median punitive damage award is about 1.2 times the compensatory damage award.[54] And of the awards that are made, plaintiffs often see little or nothing; even before the Supreme Court's recent develop-ment of new standards for the review of punitive damages, it was not un-usual for plaintiffs who were awarded punitive damages by juries to receive fifty cents on the dollar, or nothing at all, either because the awards were re-duced by judges or because the defendants were unable to pay.

Whatever the actual extent of litigation, tort reformers say, the conse-quences of tort litigation are to impose an intolerable burden on society. Usually, the argument is made in two forms: First, there is a "tort tax" or "li-ability tax" imposed on every product and activity that increases costs un-reasonably for everyone and makes American business less competitive, and second, excessive liability has created an "insurance crisis" that forces busi-nesses to close and, most prominently, drives doctors who are unable to pay exorbitant malpractice insurance premiums out of practice.

A variety of numbers are offered for the extent of the tort tax, most of which are pure fiction or the product of dubious assumptions. As far back as 1988, tort reform publicist Peter Huber asserted that the annual tort tax equaled an astonishing $300 billion.[55] The figure was quickly picked up and spread by business advocates, including *Forbes* magazine, the President's Council on Competitiveness, Vice President Dan Quayle, and the 1992 Re-publican campaign platform.[56] Unfortunately, Huber's assertion was fan-tasy. The fantasy began with an off-the-cuff estimate of $80 billion by Robert Malott, CEO of chemical giant FMC, Republican fundraiser, and tort re-form advocate, which was reported in *Chief Executive*, a glossy magazine for top executives.[57] This was an estimate of direct costs of, variously, products liability cases, tort law, or the legal system as a whole. Neither Malott nor Huber reported a source for that $80 billion figure. But that was not enough. Extrapolating from a limited study on medical malpractice, Huber adopted a multiplier of 3.5 to add the "indirect costs" of the system, although neither direct nor indirect costs is a firm concept. With crude rounding, (the sum should be 3.5 x $80 billion = $280 billion indirect costs, plus $80 billion direct costs, for a total of $360 billion—but what's $60 billion here or there?), Huber arrived at the $300 billion figure.

Other estimates of the costs of the system have been offered, some with a gloss of respectability. Tillinghast-Towers Perrin, a consulting firm to the insurance industry, helpfully provides periodic estimates of tort costs at a level congenial to its customers; its first study was presented to the American Insurance Association, an industry trade group, in 1985.[58] Its cost figure—it is not even labeled an estimate—for 2002 was $233 billion, or $809 per American, "equivalent to a 5 percent tax on wages." This figure is arrived at by adding insurance payments for tort claims, the costs of handling those claims, insurance company costs and profits, and self-insurance. Some of the figures are dubious; the study attributes insurance company overhead, including television advertising and CEO salaries, to the tort system. But there are more fundamental problems.

First, the study is based on an odd notion of costs. A principal component is the amounts paid to tort victims. This may be a cost to insurance companies, but it is not a cost of the system. It is, rather, an amount to compensate the victim for a loss, a loss that occurs whether or not the insurance company pays or the tort system exists. If a victim incurs medical expenses and lost wages through an accident caused by a poor, uninsured defendant, in Tillinghast's view no cost has been incurred; only if a defendant or its insurance company pays is there a social cost.

Second, not until the last paragraph of its analysis of the costs of the system does the report suggest that tort law provides "indirect benefits that are not measured in this study." Included in those benefits: "The tort system may also act as a deterrent to unsafe practices and products." (Revealingly lacking the alleged certainty of the rest of the report, "may" not "does.") So if A. H. Robins or its insurer pays out millions of dollars in compensation because it knowingly manufactured an IUD that maimed and killed, that is a cost of the system, but if the device is driven off the market and the company into bankruptcy, and if other manufacturers are deterred from similarly dangerous conduct, those "indirect benefits" are not counted in an analysis that purports to be "objective and unbiased." The analysis also ignores the costs of alternatives. The tort reformers' proposed liability rule for defective products requires that the plaintiff prove that there was a reasonable alternative design to a defective product, and perhaps the same standard should be applied here. What would be the cost of an alternative system that would compensate victims and provide the deterrent effect of tort law?[59]

The insurance crisis or, more accurately, the periodic insurance crises, are somewhat more grounded in reality than the cost figures. In the mid-1970s, liability insurance suddenly became very expensive and, in some areas, unavailable; tort reforms followed. In the mid-1980s, the phenomenon recurred; more tort reforms in more places. In the past few years, still more premium increases and policy cancellations, with the predictable cries for more tort reforms. *Time Magazine* exemplified the hubbub, running essentially parallel cover stories on the crisis a decade and a half apart.[60] Products liability and medical malpractice have been the areas most prominently featured, with medical malpractice, especially high-risk specialties, the focus of the most recent crisis. When many obstetricians in Las Vegas reportedly stopped taking patients because of insurance increases, one pregnant radio host asked her listeners to help her find a doctor.[61] Joliet, Illinois, may lose its only remaining neurosurgeon because his insurance increased in a single year from $180,000 to $468,000.[62]

The horror stories can be multiplied, but they only tell part of the story. Conservatives have used the stories as a basis for proposing every conceivable tort reform in every jurisdiction at every time. The stories are real but they obscure the underlying issues. First, are they representative of a real crisis and, if so, where and under what conditions? The AMA identified nineteen states as "crisis states," in which "skyrocketing medical liability premiums" are "threatening access to care for patients."[63] In many of those states, though, the evidence of a liability crisis is uncertain at best. In Connecticut, for example, the number of medical malpractice suits filed in the state increased from 272 in 1992 to 368 in 2002, a modest 35 percent increase in a decade, and the number of ob-gyns and neurosurgeons licensed to practice in Connecticut actually increased at the height of the crisis.[64] In New Jersey, malpractice lawsuits decreased by 16 percent from 1997 to 2001, and the total amount paid by doctors in malpractice premiums and awarded by juries to successful malpractice plaintiffs was virtually constant in the decade from 1992 to 2001.[65] In Pennsylvania, the number of medical malpractice awards of $1 million or more fell in 2000 and again in 2001; in Philadelphia, the most litigious area in the state, the number of large awards was about the same in 1999 and 2000 and dropped by a third in 2001.[66]

Second, if there is a crisis, is it a liability crisis or an insurance crisis? That is, to what extent is the increasing cost and decreasing availability of liability insurance a product of a runaway tort system, or to what extent is it caused by other factors? For tort reformers, there is a simple, arithmetic relationship. Damage verdicts increase, so insurance payouts increase, so liability insurance premiums increase, so calamity follows: soaring prices, manufacturers shutting down, doctors driven out of practice. The solution: tort reform measures—especially, in the medical malpractice area, damage caps—which will reduce payouts and therefore reduce premiums.

The facts are more complicated. The General Accounting Office found that medical malpractice insurance payments increased significantly from 1998 to 2002, but premium increases varied greatly from state to state, from area to area within states, and across medical specialties; for example, from 1999 to 2002, base premium rates for general surgeons increased 130 percent in the Harrisburg, Pennsylvania, area but only 2 percent in Minnesota.[67] Even some prominent tort reformers deny the whole effect. In response to a study that refuted the link between tort claims and insurance premiums, Sherman Joyce, president of the American Tort Reform Association, argued that the only argument for tort reform is fairness, and "we wouldn't tell you or anyone that the reason to pass tort reform would be to reduce insurance rates." Roger Kenney of the Alliance of American Insurers similarly admitted that "Premiums can be affected by many things that have nothing to do with tort reform."[68] Those "many things" include, over long periods of time, a larger and more sophisticated plaintiffs' bar that is accessible to injured victims and better able to prove injuries, advances in science that have revealed the harm imposed by products from asbestos to drugs, and rises in average income and, dramatically, in the cost of medical care, which are the major components of compensatory damages.[69]

The business cycle and insurance company marketing practices contribute to the crisis, too, particularly because cycles in the malpractice insurance market are more volatile than the business cycle in the economy as a whole. J. Robert Hunter, director of insurance of the Consumer Federation of America and former federal insurance administrator and Texas insurance commissioner, conducted a study for Americans for Insurance Reform, a coalition of anti-tort-reform consumer groups, that showed the relationships among payouts, premiums, and the business cycle.[70] From 1975 to 2001, insurance company payouts for medical claims, including their costs of defense, increased at about the same rate as medical costs generally; in constant dollars, for example, payouts per doctor doubled between 1975 and 1983 and have increased by only 18 percent in the two decades since. Premium income fluctuated more dramatically, however, peaking in the mid-1970s and late 1980s and falling in between, with a more recent, steady decline from 1995 to 2000 and an upward trend thereafter, a pattern that tracks the national economic cycle.

The link between the business cycle and insurance rates lies in insurance company marketing practices. Insurance companies earn income from investments as well as gains on underwriting. When investment prospects are good—high interest rates and, to a lesser extent, a booming stock market—companies seek as many premium dollars as possible, by cutting prices to attract market share. This process is exacerbated by peculiar features of the malpractice market. Many of the insurers are mutual insurance companies, owned by the doctors and hospitals they insure, and so are under pressure to keep rates low; to retain market share, commercial insurers have to cut rates to compete.[71] And, as with other industries in the 1990s, the ability to take advantage of accounting peculiarities made malpractice coverage seem more attractive than it really was, and overinvestment in the stock market proved calamitous.[72] As a result, malpractice premiums respond to the business cycle perhaps more than to liability payments.[73] The General Accounting Office estimated that half of the increase in premiums between 2000 and 2002 was due to insurance companies' decreased investment returns.[74]

The lack of a strong relationship between liability costs and insurance costs is shown by the reaction in states that have enacted tort reforms. California is pointed to by both sides. Tort reformers argue that the 1975 reforms, including a $250,000 damage cap that has not been inflation-adjusted since, has resulted in lower premiums for California doctors. But the largest and most consistent cuts in premiums only occurred after 1988, as a result of stronger regulation by the state of insurance premiums.[75] More generally, a 2003 study by Weiss Ratings, an insurance-rating agency in Florida, reported that in states without caps on noneconomic damages, premiums for standard medical malpractice coverage rose 36 percent between 1991 and 2002—less than the 48 percent increase in states with caps. In nine states, premiums stayed the same or declined over the decade, but only two of those states had caps.[76] Therefore, capping damages provides no clear path to reducing insurance premiums.

In short, tort reform advocates, tort reform opponents, and independent scholars and researchers have produced a mountain of statistics on the liability crisis, the insurance crisis, and the actual and potential effects of reforms, but no firm conclusions about a crisis result. There are severe problems of access to health care in some places, but we do not know how much of the problem is attributable to an increase in malpractice premiums, nor do we know how much of that increase is due to an increase in claims. Draconian cuts in victims' rights logically would cut malpractice premiums, but they would not cut costs; instead, the costs would be borne by uncompensated victims. Reducing malpractice payments would have a trivial effect on the overall cost of health care, however. And the cost of diminished deterrence would be significant, because other regulatory systems, such as professional discipline or self-policing, are notoriously weak, but the amount of that cost is difficult to quantify, too.

The Rise and Fall of Tort Law

Tort law works, not perfectly, but reasonably, often better than other parts of government and society. Consider how it worked in the cases of the DES daughters. The illness of Joyce Bichler and every other DES daughter was individual and personal but not unique; each victim was also part of a large group of victims who suffered similar harm at the hands of the drug companies. The regulatory system had failed them; the FDA's conclusion that DES was safe turned out to be tragically wrong. As a result, Bichler and the other victims suffered catastrophic injuries that had physical, emotional, and financial consequences. For a victim without adequate insurance, the costs of immediate and continuing medical care alone could be staggering and presented the possibility of a lifetime without medical care to cover their DES-caused preexisting condition; added to those costs would be the lost income, especially for those whose lives were cut short by the diseases, and the incalculable emotional cost of being unable to bear children or have sexual relations and of living in fear that the disease would progress.

The DES cases embody the best of modern tort law. The cases presented a significant problem not just for the individual victims but for society at large. Other government agencies and social institutions had failed to remedy the problem, and the courts recognized that they had to decide to favor either the interests of the victims or, by doing nothing, the interests of the drug companies. In deciding the cases, they balanced the interests involved and applied the enterprise liability principle; the manufacturers that profited from selling DES should bear its true costs, including the costs of the harm it produced. Although unknown general effects of drugs, chemicals, and other products are not common, the DES cases provide a model of how to deal with them if they recur. And by establishing the principle that drug companies are liable for harm that spans generations, the cases provided an incentive for greater testing of drugs and other potentially harmful substances.

If the conservative campaign to transform tort law achieves its goals, the approach and results in cases like these would be very different. When the DES issue first arose, no one knew whether the courts would be receptive to the extensions of law required to give the victims a remedy, so their lawyers took a considerable risk in taking the cases on a contingent fee basis. If tort reforms that reduce the ability to retain a lawyer on a contingent fee contract are implemented, the potential reward might not be worth the risk in cases like these, so that victims could not get anyone to take their case. Changes in class action rules also would have prevented the victims from joining together to bring their suits where and as they did, again making it harder to sue.

If the conservative vision of substantive tort law is achieved, the DES daughters who managed to get to court would certainly lose. Because of the time lag between when their mothers took the drug and when their diseases appeared, the daughters could not tie any particular manufacturer to their harm, so they would be barred from recovery under conservative principles of fault and causation. Even if, by some miracle, they did win, their damages would be much smaller, and they would receive little compensation for the loss of their reproductive ability. And if it turned out that the manufacturers had knowingly concealed the risks of harm, the victims' ability to punish the drug companies and deter others from similar wrongful behavior would be diminished by the new restrictions on punitive damages.

Everyone except big business and big medicine would lose from a system like this. Anyone can suffer the physical and emotional harm of an accident, and all but the wealthy and the fortunate would be unprotected against its catastrophic financial consequences. But some groups are more at risk than others, especially homemakers, the elderly, and the poor, who would receive less compensation under a system primarily based on measuring financial losses. The DES cases are exceptional, but the same results would follow in many more ordinary cases. Moreover, the inability to get into court, the difficulty in winning when victims get there, and the limited damages available if they do win are only part of the story. The decline of tort law also would place less pressure on those who produce injuries— manufacturers of unsafe products and negligent doctors, for example—to invest in the safety of their customers. Finally, since the conservative campaign on tort law is part of the broader attack on government, no other institutions would be able to assume the responsibility of preventing harm and compensating victims. The FDA would have less authority and fewer resources to regulate drugs and would have to rely even more on the word of drug companies that their products are safe, and the Consumer Products Safety Commission, the National Highway Traffic Safety Administration, and other agencies would also be hamstrung. As the private market increasingly replaced public programs for health care and income support, avenues other than tort law to pay medical expenses and make up lost earning power would be reduced. The result would be more injuries, less compensation, and more people left unprotected by society.

4

Consumers, Workers, and the Tyranny of Freedom of Contract

Contracts—formal and informal, written and oral—are ubiquitous in our everyday life, including employment contracts, consumer purchases, automobile warranties, credit card agreements, insurance policies, health club memberships, Internet provider contracts, and thousands of others. Because of the pervasiveness of contracts, the conservative campaign to rewrite contract law holds the prospect of transforming many elements of our day-to-day affairs. Businesses, especially large corporations, will have greater power to use contracts to dictate the terms of the basic relationships that order people's lives as workers and consumers. They will be able to do so even if the terms are hidden, surprising, and inconsistent with what consumers expect. And the courts will have less power to review the contracts, either to determine that an agreement was really made, to assess the fairness of its terms, or to determine if it complies with the law.

Here are some commonplace examples: Rich and Enza Hill called Gateway and ordered a computer system, giving their credit card number in payment.[1] When the delivery arrived, the box included their new computer, the usual assortment of cables and manuals, and a sheet of paper with a set of boilerplate terms, including a statement that the Hills were bound by the terms unless they returned the computer within thirty days. When their computer did not work some months later and Gateway would not repair it, they sued. Gateway defended by pointing to one of the boilerplate terms that stated they had given up their right to sue Gateway and instead had to take any claims to arbitration.

Judge Frank Easterbrook of the U.S. Court of Appeals for the Seventh Circuit, a conservative professor at the University of Chicago Law School prior to his nomination to the bench by President Reagan, ignored the prevailing law and ruled the Hills had not really made a purchase when they called Gateway, ordered their computer, and gave their credit card number in payment, in return for which Gateway's representative promised to ship the computer. Instead, according to Gateway's boilerplate, the sale was really made and the Hills were bound by Gateway's terms when they failed to return the computer to Gateway within the thirty-day period. If they wanted to avoid the terms, including the arbitration clause, they would have had to pack up the computer and ship it back within thirty days, at their own expense. By validating the trick known as the "rolling contract," Easterbrook gave large companies a new tool for imposing surprising and often unfair terms on consumers.

A similar device is often applied by large employers to impose terms on unsuspecting workers. Eight months after Drake Albanza was hired as a fry cook at a Kentucky Fried Chicken restaurant in Honolulu, he was fired because, he alleged, he was African American.[2] He filed a complaint with the Hawaii Civil Rights Commission and then sued KFC. Like Gateway, KFC moved to block the suit because the job application Drake had signed contained a clause preventing him from suing, even for racial discrimination, and requiring instead that all disputes be submitted to arbitration. The application was a standard form with blanks for Drake to fill in his personal information and employment history. The ordinary applicant to be a fry cook at KFC would fill out the application without reading the fine print, or, if he did read it, would not assume that it was a contract, especially because it said as much: "Nothing contained in this application, any KFC manual, handbook, or other written materials shall constitute an implied or expressed contract of employment." However, the application contained a separate section called "Agreement," which included the arbitration clause, and the Hawaii Supreme Court held this was sufficient to prevent Drake from suing.

Under the Right's approach, courts also are less inclined to review the fairness of contract terms. The most important example concerns cases like the Hills' and Drake Albanza's. However a contract is made and whatever its terms, it has long been the rule that parties have to go to court to enforce their contracts, subject to generally applicable rules of law. But a key element of the conservative campaign on contract law is to allow big businesses to choose who will decide disputes, including deciding that no court will ever hear their disputes. Arbitration, a private dispute resolution procedure, has supplanted much contract litigation, and, as with the Hills or Albanza, arbitration is usually imposed on consumers and workers by a boilerplate term in a standard form contract that they probably were not aware of and did not know they were agreeing to. Since the 1980s, the U.S. Supreme Court has extended federal arbitration law to most classes of consumers and workers—customers of Shearson/American Express, employees of Circuit City, and homeowners asserting claims against a termite inspection company—and to all sorts of claims, from ordinary consumer disputes to statutory claims under the civil rights and age discrimination laws. The effect is to decrease the protections ordinarily available in court; companies like Gateway and KFC get to designate which arbitration system will be used or even set up their own system, there is no impartial judge or jury, discovery of information that would routinely be available in court may be unavailable in arbitration, and the consumer may be barred from participating in a class action or claiming punitive damages. Courts may not review the decision of the arbitrator to see if it was right, reasonable, or fair. The result is to allow businesses, through the illusion of obtaining the consumer or employee's agreement to a form contract, to remove their contracts from the legal system and from the law itself.

Visions of Contract Law

Contract law begins with agreements, and its traditional paradigm is an agreement freely bargained between two parties who hammer out the details in making their best deal. The Restatement (Second) of Contracts, an authoritative summary of the law by The American Law Institute, is full of austere examples of this type: "A offers to buy a book owned by B and to pay B $10 in exchange therefor. B accepts the offer and delivers the book to A."[3] A and B presumably have each figured out how much the book is worth to them, have haggled until they reached the $10 price, and have specified where and when the book will be delivered.

While the story of A and B makes a simple starting point for contract law, real contracts always have richer contexts. A and B never make contracts; real people and real businesses do. B is likely to be Barnes & Noble, which enters into millions of transactions like this each year. A (call her Alice) is likely to pay with a credit card, which involves a web of contracts and government regulations linking Alice, Citibank or another bank that issued her credit card, other banks, and MasterCard International. The express contract is never complete—Alice simply hands the book to the cashier and offers her credit card—but is supplemented by implicit expectations, such as that Alice has to pay before leaving the store with the book. And, as in most contracts, there is no bargaining on price or anything else; Barnes & Noble sells the book for a fixed price subject to its standard policies.

Moreover, many contracts are much more complex than the sale of a book. Alice's agreement with Citibank is not a simple, one-shot deal but is a relationship that extends over time and, in addition to the complexities of the credit card agreement itself (Citibank's includes twenty-eight numbered paragraphs presented in 6-point type), may include a checking account with overdraft protection, a debit card, a home mortgage, and financial planning and investment services. The cashier has a long-term employment relationship with Barnes & Noble that includes terms about compensation, supervision, conduct, termination, health benefits, and pensions; some of these terms may be stated in a written contract, others in an employees' manual, and still others arise from informal practices and conversations between the cashier and the store manager.

Contract law always responds in two ways to the wide range of contracts in society. It enforces the transactions the parties have made, enabling them to invoke the authority of law to enforce their agreement: if Alice charges the $10 book to her credit card, she cannot later decide that she only wants to pay $5. The law also regulates the transaction, determining what it takes to make a contract (is Alice obligated to buy the book if she just takes it off the shelf to look at it?), filling in gaps in the parties' agreement (if Alice reads the book and doesn't like it, can she get her money back?), and in some cases regulating the fairness of the deal (if the book is misprinted, does Alice have a right to return it for a replacement or a refund?). Therefore, contract law both empowers and restrains people; they can make agreements, but the law supplements and regulates those agreements.

Over the course of the twentieth century, contract law developed to give greater consideration to the real-world context in which contracts were made and greater recognition to the necessity of regulating market transactions. In the 1960s and 1970s, these developments culminated in a wave of consumer-oriented legislation and judicial decisions. Statutes mandated more disclosure of contract terms; if a product seller wanted to limit its implied guarantee that a product was what it appeared to be and would work as it should, the contract had to state that conspicuously.[4] Courts looked skeptically at standard form contracts; an insurance policy that covered loss by burglary only if there were visible damage to the exterior of the building would be read to cover any burglary, even in the absence of damage, in accordance with the reasonable expectations of the policyholder.[5] They also recognized the full complexity of contractual settings; Joseph Hoffman, a small-town baker, for example, won damages from the Red Owl supermarket chain for leading him on in the hope of getting a franchise, even though no franchise agreement was ever signed.[6] And courts felt able to review the fairness of contracts, especially between parties of unequal bargaining power, striking down a contract with extortionate credit terms between an inner-city furniture store and a poorly educated welfare recipient,[7] and a contract for 2,302 hours of dance lessons at a cost of $31,090 between Arthur Murray dance studios and a lonely widow.[8]

The conservative campaign challenges these developments, arguing that the law has departed from the true principle governing contract law: Courts should simply enforce the contracts people make. In this view, contract law's development over the twentieth century makes two mistakes.

First, conservatives say, it diminishes personal freedom, of which freedom of contract is an essential element in a market economy. As libertarian-conservative judge Alex Kozinski of the Ninth Circuit wrote:

> Perhaps most troubling, the willingness of courts to subordinate voluntary contractual arrangements to their own sense of public policy and proper business decorum deprives individuals of an important measure of freedom. The right to enter into contracts—to adjust one's legal relationships by mutual agreement with other free individuals—was unknown through much of history and is unknown even today in many parts of the world. Like other aspects of personal autonomy, it is too easily smothered by government officials eager to tell us what's best for us.[9]

Second, conservatives argue that because parties are the best judges of their own interest, and the market, left to its own devices, will produce the best results for society, courts are likely to produce detrimental results when they interfere with contracts. University of Chicago law professor Richard Epstein explains the superiority of the enforcement of contracts over legal intervention:

> [Contract] law can facilitate (not compel, but facilitate) sizable productive interactions which will continue to expand over time and transactions until they embrace all individuals who possess the minimum capacity to engage in contracting at all. The system goes forward in a benevolent fashion because the exchanges are mutually beneficial.... The background knowledge of the uniform incentives moving self-interested parties is a more reliable guide to their interests than any public vetting of their deal.[10]

For Epstein, then, interference with free contracting is damaging:

> It thus becomes unwise for the state to say that a certain minimum wage should be imposed as a matter of law, or that certain contractual forms, such as the contract at will, should be ruled out of bounds, or that certain institutional and organizational arrangements, such as mandatory collective bargaining and family leave arrangements, should be imposed as a matter of course.[11]

The solution to these problems is to revert to a simple model of contract based on an ideal market, strictly enforcing the bargains that parties make, not reading beyond the four corners of a document in enforcing a contract, and certainly not evaluating the bargains for fairness. The model is so simple that it can ignore the complexities of the modern world. As Epstein writes, "For all its minor differences, and with a little refurbishing at the edges, we could do as well with the [ancient] Roman law of contract as we do with any modern system dedicated to the principle of freedom of contract, as our system too often is not."[12]

The conservative approach applies across the entire range of contracts and contract law issues. Gateway can dictate a contracting procedure that binds the Hills to Gateway's terms if they do not ship back their computer. The boilerplate of KFC's form employment application is as binding on Drake Albanza as if he had sat down and hammered out a deal with the CEO of KFC. And if Gateway and the Hills, and KFC and Albanza, "agree" to submit their disputes to arbitration, then enforcement of their contracts demands that contract law has no other role to play at all.

Implementing the conservative vision of contract law would reinforce economic power with the authority of law by enabling big businesses to control relationships with their customers and employees. The new body of contract law would have four elements. First, businesses could dictate terms of dealing to consumers and small businesses. Second, they could avoid being legally bound except on their own terms. Third, they could avoid review by the courts of the fairness of those terms. Fourth, they could control how disputes are resolved under their contracts.

Form Contracts and Forming Contracts

The most common kind of contract today involves a standard form containing many terms, drafted by a business that enters into many such deals, that is presented to the other party on a take-it-or-leave-it basis.[13] Credit card agreements, employment contracts, insurance policies, online purchases, auto leases, and innumerable other transactions depart from the traditional model of hammering out the details of a deal face to face. Nearly a hundred years ago, contracts scholar Edwin Patterson imported the French term "adhesion contract" for this type of arrangement, because the party presented with the contract only has the choice to adhere to its terms or not, rather than negotiating.[14] A key step in the conservative campaign is creating rules about how contracts are made that make it easier for large businesses to bind consumers, employees, and even small businesses to contracts on their own terms through the use of standard forms—in Professor Charles Knapp's phrase, to treat adhesion contracts as "sacred cows" rather than "dangerous animals, likely to do harm unless confined and tamed."[15]

Ordinarily, the law presumes that a person who indicates agreement with the terms of a contract (by signing it, for example) has accepted its terms, whether the person has read them or not; one has a duty to read all the terms of a contract or run the risk of being bound by objectionable terms that were not read. But the rule may be subject to an exception when applied to form contracts, so a person is not bound to terms which are presented in such a way that the reasonable person would not have read, understood, and agreed to them. The exception applies where the terms are hidden in pages of fine print or in a place where contract terms are not usually located, such as in the back of catalogues, on baggage claim checks, on signs limiting liability in a parking lot, or on the packaging of a product.[16] The principle underlying the exception also is expressed in consumer disclosure laws; under state and federal warranty laws, for example, if a seller is not going to stand behind the quality of its goods, the disclaimer has to be conspicuous so it is likely to come to the attention of the ordinary consumer.

The combination of rule and exception are reasonable: Ordinarily, a seller does not know if a buyer actually read the terms on a sales document and can assume from the buyer's signature that the buyer either did read the terms or did not care about them. When the seller camouflages the terms, however, it is unreasonable to assume that the buyer has agreed to them. The conservative vision aims to elevate the rule and eliminate the exception, so any form contract terms, however presented and however surprising, become binding.

The U.S. Supreme Court illustrated the effect of this vision in a case that arose out of an ordinary slip and fall.[17] Eulala Shute, on a seven-day Carnival cruise with her husband, slipped on a deck mat during a guided tour of the ship's galley and subsequently sued Carnival for her injuries in federal court in Washington, her home state. Carnival successfully moved to have the case thrown out, pointing to a clause in the cruise contract requiring that all litigation be brought in Florida, where it was headquartered. On appeal, the majority of the Supreme Court felt no need to address whether the Shutes had actually agreed to the clause, because the Shutes "conceded that they were given notice of the forum provision and, therefore, presumably retained the option of rejecting the contract with impunity." Here, the rule about presumed agreement to form contracts is framed in terms of freedom of contract and the free market; the Shutes were provided with the contract terms and so were bound to the terms because they were free market actors, whether they actually did read the terms, easily could have read them, or could have bargained about them with Carnival.

Looking at the situation the Shutes were really in, instead of viewing them as abstract market actors, paints a different picture. What the Court viewed as the Shutes' concession, in their lawyer's brief, that they had notice of the terms was laden with sarcasm: "The forum selection clause [the term requiring them to sue in Florida] was reasonably communicated to the respondents, as much as three pages of fine print can be communicated." In this setting, as Justice Stevens stated in dissent, "only the most meticulous passenger is likely to become aware of the forum-selection provision," because it was included only in fine print as the eighth of twenty-five numbered paragraphs on the ticket, a means of presentation so obscure that he included a copy of the ticket in his opinion.[18] Moreover, the Shutes did not receive the official ticket with these terms until after they had purchased their cruise, and another of the terms stated that the price of the cruise was nonrefundable. Therefore, even if the Shutes actually read the ticket and understood its import, the only way they could avoid the forum selection clause would be to give up their vacation plans at the last minute and forfeit the price they paid, or at least go to court in Florida from their home in Washington in an attempt to get a refund.

The story of Drake Albanza, described earlier in this chapter, is an increasingly common example of how the rigid rule about the enforceability of form contracts traps employees even before they are employees. Recall that he filled out a standard job application, with blanks for his personal information, employment history, and the like, not expecting that it constituted a contract. Even if he had read it, the form stated specifically that it did not create an employment contract. Nevertheless, the Hawaii Supreme Court ruled that the included arbitration provision was enforceable because it demonstrated "both mutual assent ... and consideration for that mutual assent," an agreement and exchange by two free market actors—the fry cook Drake Albanza and the KFC corporation.[19]

The same rigid approach has been advocated for what are known as shrink-wrap, browse-wrap, and click-wrap contracts. Here sellers include the fine-print contract terms on the package or sealed inside it (shrink-wrap) or on a computer screen when loading software or obtaining access to a Web site where the user can see the fine print (browse-wrap), or the buyer must click on an "I accept" box before using the product (click-wrap). Conservatives have argued that the definition of what it means to agree to a contract should be pushed back to enable businesses to use any of these devices to dictate terms to consumers more easily, and some courts have agreed.

It is simple enough to require consumers to at least scroll through the terms of an agreement (without actually having read them) and then click "I agree" at the end, but conservatives argue that even this minimal demonstration of agreement should not be required, and some courts have acquiesced. MSN, for example, Microsoft's online service, displayed the terms of its user agreement on screen, but users could sign up for the service by clicking the "I agree" box without scrolling through the terms. A New Jersey court analogized this case to *Carnival Cruise Lines v. Shute,* in that in both cases the fine print was available to the customer (on the back of the ticket or on the screen), even though the user could easily avoid them.[20] Another court, in approving America Online's means of obtaining agreement, went a step further. Here, two boxes were presented; one said "I agree" and would subscribe the user to the service, and the other said "Read me" and would take the user to the terms. Because the terms were available elsewhere on the Web site, the consumer would be presumed to have read them, or have taken the chance on whatever they contained without reading them.[21]

The far shores of inferring agreement are reached by the procedures permitted under the controversial model statute known as the Uniform Computer Information Transactions Act (UCITA). Originally part of the revision process of the Uniform Commercial Code, and supported at various points by Microsoft and other software producers and opposed by Consumers Union, the Federal Trade Commission, and the attorneys general of more than a dozen states, UCITA went through many iterations before being enacted in only two states.[22] Under UCITA, Microsoft, for example, when operating MSN or providing downloadable software, does not have to present the terms and require the user to click "I accept" to control the transaction. Instead, agreement to any contract terms is presumed if, among sales pitches, product descriptions, advertisements, and other information on a Web page, there is a link to the information, a link to another Web site that contains the information, the address of such a Web site, or even instructions that a consumer who wants to see the terms can click a link or email for a copy. As a result, the consumer is bound to Microsoft's terms even if she does not know that they exist, does not have to scroll through the terms, does not have easy access to them, or does not know that using the service or downloading the software constitutes agreement to the fine print.[23]

The most controversial instance of the shrink-wrap/click-wrap/browse-wrap problem involves "rolling contracts," like the one involved in the Hill and Gateway case discussed earlier. A consumer purchases a product and later discovers boilerplate terms advantageous to the seller "shrink-wrapped" in the box, perhaps on a separate sheet or at the back of an instruction manual. And the later discovery may be much later; the typical consumer will not read the fine print until a problem arises, only then to discover that the fine print disclaims the seller's responsibility for a defective product or prevents the consumer from suing to assert its rights. A leading cases from the U.S. Court of Appeals for the Third Circuit had held that fine-print terms received after the deal had been made were not binding on the consumer,[24] but *Hill v. Gateway 2000, Inc.* and its companion case, *ProCD, Inc. v. Zeidenberg*, a pair of controversial decisions by Judge Easterbrook, were victories for the Right's vision of contract law because they held that the business controls the process of agreement, so that even terms disclosed only after the consumer has made a purchase are still binding.[25]

These decisions are strange because the court concluded, contrary to what consumers believe, that no contracts were made when the Hills ordered a computer from Gateway's telephone salesperson or when Matthew Zeidenberg took a box with software off the shelf, paid the cashier, and left the store. If there was no contract, Gateway, for example, could refuse to ship the computer and, when the Hills called back to inquire about the status of their order, tell them that the company had changed its mind and would only sell it at a higher price. The court assumed that Gateway was only offering to sell and specifying that the form of acceptance was the Hills' keeping the computer for thirty days, but that "offer" was not communicated to the Hills at a meaningful time and in a meaningful fashion—on the telephone, for example. To reject the offer, the Hills would have had to pack up their computer, take it to the post office, insure it, and ship it back to Gateway—at their own expense and inconvenience.

What is most significant about *Hill* and *ProCD*, however, is their status as landmark embodiments of the principle that large businesses can use standard forms and manipulate the mode of contracting and the rules of contract law to bind their customers without meaningful agreement, notice, or opportunity to pursue other terms. It transforms the normal into the surreal—giving a credit card number on the phone or, in *ProCD*, taking a box of software off the shelf, paying for it, and leaving the store—is not really a sale. Then, the surreal becomes normal; more and more, companies like Gateway can dictate the terms on which their products are purchased and used without revealing what is going on and with only the barest illusion of consent. As Wisconsin contracts professor Stewart Macaulay explained, under *Hill*, "misrepresentation is the oil that lubricates capitalism."[26]

A final, particularly problematic opportunity to bind consumers without their knowledge or consent arises when businesses change the terms of a contract. Businesses commonly include changes in terms as fine-print documents with monthly bills or as separate mailings, knowing that they will be disregarded. Prior to imposing mandatory arbitration on its residential long-distance customers, for example, AT&T conducted extensive market research that demonstrated that the customers would not pay attention to the new term. It knew, for example, that three-fourths of the customers were likely to throw the mailing away without opening it, and, for those who did open it, beginning the cover letter with a bold face statement "Your AT&T service or billing will not change under the AT&T Consumer Services Agreement; there's nothing you need to do" guaranteed that most customers would stop reading and throw the letter away. Under the Right's vision of agreement, customers would be bound even when AT&T knew few of them would read its terms.[27]

The initial agreement also may provide that the company can give notice of changed terms by posting the change on the company's Web site, putting the burden on the consumer to go to the Web site regularly to look for changes. Once the change is posted and the consumer continues to use the service, agreement to its terms is inferred. Comcast, for example, the largest provider of cable television service and a major provider of high-speed Internet access, has a barely visible link accessible by scrolling to the bottom of its home page entitled "Terms of Service." Clicking that link takes the user to a page with further links to the actual terms, and a statement that "the Terms of Service may be updated periodically without notice to you."[28] Comcast and other businesses may actually know how many of its customers take advantage of the opportunity to check for new terms—Web page counters are a familiar and simple operation—and know, therefore, that their changes go largely unseen. But under the conservative vision of contract, the initial agreement can specify how changes are made, so businesses can set up procedures that make it unlikely that consumers will know about the changes. UCITA, for example, specifically endorses this procedure, allowing the parties to a contract—realistically, the business presenting a form contract, in writing or online—to set standards applicable to future transactions, such as the standard that online disclosure is adequate notice.[29]

A direct, if limited, response to the problem of presumed agreement to form contracts was mounted in the revision process of Article 2 of the Uniform Commercial Code, the commercial statute that governs sales of goods in almost every jurisdiction. Business interests, however, arguing the Right's vision of contract law, beat back the response.[30] The reporter for the revision, Professor Richard Speidel of Northwestern University, and his drafting committee proposed that the law recognize the reality that there are two different kinds of contract: those in which the parties hammer out the details, and those made by standard forms incorporating standard terms. Under their proposal, a big business seller using a form contract would have a heightened obligation to bring its terms to the other party's attention, at the risk of otherwise having them excluded from the contract. In a consumer sales contract, for example, if a reasonable consumer would not have expected a particular term such as an arbitration clause to be in the contract, the term would be unenforceable, unless the consumer in the particular case had actually agreed to its inclusion.[31]

Gail Hillebrand of Consumers Union described this innovation as the "single most important improvement for consumers" in the revision process, but, under an attack from industry interests, it quickly was whittled down and ultimately discarded.[32] First, small businesses were removed from the protection of the section; a one-man landscaping business buying a truck is more like a consumer than like a large corporation, but excluding businesses from the scope of the section meant that the landscaper was still at the mercy of the adhesion contracts of strong sellers like General Motors (which was an active participant in the revision process). Then, the concepts of standard forms and standard terms were eliminated, a step that left the proposed section "hung out to dry," in Speidel's view; without defining standard form contracting as the source of the problem, it became impossible to agree on a standard for surprise or unfairness that the courts could use in reviewing contract terms.[33] The coup de grace came when even the limited version of the section was deleted from the revision. Industry groups, including the U.S. Chamber of Commerce and the American Automobile Manufacturers Association, opposed the proposed revisions and won the day.[34]

The effect of the defeat of the proposal and the spread of the conservative vision of contract law is the assumption that a transaction in which a consumer or a landscaper purchases a GM truck is just like a negotiated deal for a thousand cars between GM and Hertz. Small businesses and consumers are subject to surprising terms in standard form contracts, and businesses have little incentive to incorporate fair terms, to draft their forms clearly, or to draw their customers' attention to unusual, surprising, or one-sided terms in their contracts.

The conservative vision of contract begins with the power to set the terms of a relationship and proceeds to the power to contract only on the terms a business prescribes. From the 1920s through the 1970s, contract law became more flexible; that development enabled a court to find a contract even when the parties' behavior fell short of sitting down, hammering out the details of a deal, and signing on the bottom line, and it encouraged courts to recognize that a formal written contract often fails to contain all of the details of the parties' agreement. The Right's vision, which favors more formal, written contracts and disfavors imposing liability in other circumstances, has challenged this trend; under this approach, a court should find a contract only when the formalities of contracting have been observed, and, if there is an agreement, it should apply rigid rules to determine its meaning. Formal rules like these favor the more experienced and more powerful, who have the knowledge, the lawyers, and the leverage to use the rules to their advantage.

This shift is seen most dramatically in the weakening of one of the most widely discussed developments of the 1960s and 1970s, the use of reliance as a basis for the enforcement of promises. This doctrine offered a means of subverting the formal requirements of traditional contract law, making enforceable a promise on which someone relied even if the promise did not meet the traditional standards for forming a contract. In the famous 1965 case of *Hoffman v. Red Owl Stores, Inc.*, mentioned earlier, Joseph Hoffman and his wife owned a small bakery in Wautoma, Wisconsin, but aspired to build their piece of the American dream by becoming franchisees of the Red Owl supermarket chain.[35] Edward Lukowitz, Red Owl's divisional manager, led them on a two-and-a-half-year odyssey during which he encouraged them to sell their bakery, buy a grocery store, sell that store, purchase an option on land for a potential Red Owl store, move their family, and raise more and more money to invest in the new store, all in preparation for receiving a franchise. Ultimately, Red Owl's financial demands escalated beyond what the Hoffmans could meet, so they never received a franchise. The Wisconsin Supreme Court concluded, however, that despite the lack of a formal franchise agreement, the Hoffman's reliance on Lukowitz's promises, indistinct though they may have been, required a remedy. "Injustice would result here if [the Hoffmans] were not granted some relief because of the failure of [Red Owl] to keep their promises which induced [them] to act to their detriment."

Many judges and scholars embraced the principle underlying this decision, and a cottage industry arose among law professors in defining its scope.[36] Some synthesized the cases to assert that any credible promise made in furtherance of economic activity was enforceable; others pointed to the particular salience of the doctrine in cases in which the parties have different degrees of commercial sophistication (as with the Hoffmans), or are enmeshed in a broader relationship involving trust and confidence.[37] The conservative reaction that favors formal contracting and looks skeptically at claims of reliance on less-formal promises, however, limited the doctrine and turned it into "the revolution that wasn't," as characterized by Professor Sidney DeLong.[38]

Most striking is the way in which commercially sophisticated parties manage to renege on promises made to the unwitting and still avoid the reliance doctrine—exactly the setting for which the court in *Hoffman* thought justice demanded a remedy. One common situation involves workers who are promised long-term employment and then are disappointed to find that the promise is not enforceable. Conservative courts impose tough standards on what kind of employer promises are firm enough for the worker to rely on and how much reliance is required.

Dickens v. Equifax Services, Inc. is an example.[39] Roger Dickens had been employed by Equifax for thirty-one years in its Phoenix, Arizona, office when, in late 1991, he was asked to transfer to Denver, Colorado. To induce him to move, his supervisor, Frank Hinds, made promises to him that the court summarized as follows:

(1) he would continue to have a career with Equifax until age sixty-five, (2) he would be promoted if he moved to Denver, (3) he would receive annual pay increases and annual bonuses, (4) the amount of his bonus would compensate for his loss of his wife's income, (5) he would be a manager in Denver, (6) he would be taken care of by the company, and (7) he would remain employed by the company.

Relying on these promises, Dickens gave up his job in Phoenix, sold his home, and moved to Denver; his wife quit her job and moved, too. Six months later, Dickens's job in Denver was eliminated, and he was assigned to another position under the supervision of the Seattle office; six months after that, he was fired. Nevertheless, the court held that it was so clear that Hinds's statements were "vague assurances or unsupported predictions" that the case could not even go to a jury; in effect, the court was saying, an employee is foolish to trust his boss.

Dickens is not exceptional. Professor DeLong catalogued examples of other employer statements that do not rise to the level of promises and therefore leave employees in the lurch:

Employees have been held to have had no right to rely on language such as the following as a promise of permanent employment: "Don't worry about being fired"; "You will be here until you retire"; "I have no intention of firing you"; "You will not have to be concerned about job security because you have a job here as long as you want or until you retire"; "You will have continued and secure employment"; "You will have a job until you retire; we'll have you for the next twelve years"; "Your position will never be taken away and you can have it as long as you want it"; "You have full-time, permanent employment"; "I don't see a problem with you working until you are sixty-five"; "You will retire from this company"; "You will be the first person to work here for fifty years"; "You will never have to worry about your job"; "Should I look for another job?" "No, your job is secure"; "The only person that can eliminate you is yourself; you have a permanent job."[40]

In all of these cases, the lack of contractual formality preempted a remedy for reasonable reliance.

Interpreting and Policing Contracts, or Not

For a generation, courts also had become more flexible in their approach to issues of how to interpret contracts. If the purpose of contract law is to enforce the deal that people have made, the lodestar of interpretation ought to be the intentions of the parties, and the courts should be open to any evidence that sheds light on those intentions. It would be convenient for the courts if people always expressed themselves clearly and made their writings complete, but human weakness, the limits of language, and the exigencies of time and money guarantee that will not be so. Therefore, courts increasingly looked to all relevant evidence to find the meaning of contracts' terms and admitted more side agreements to supplement written contracts.

Conservatives have attacked this realistic approach. Judge Kozinski of the U.S. Court of Appeals for the Ninth Circuit, in an opinion criticizing the flexible law that California courts had developed, warned that the approach "casts a long shadow of uncertainty" over contracts, and even "chips away at the foundation of our legal system." "If we are unwilling to say that parties, dealing face to face, can come up with language that binds them, how can we send anyone to jail for violating statutes consisting of mere words . . . ? . . . Are all attempts to develop the law in a reasoned and principled fashion doomed to failure?"[41] Conservative activist lawyer Theodore Olson, later George W. Bush's solicitor general, concurred, warning that judicial intervention was required "if anything is to remain of the integrity of written contracts."[42] Even the editorial page of the *Wall Street Journal* chimed in, labeling the flexible approach "high weirdness."[43]

The alternative paradigm of contracting presented by conservatives is the complete written contract, and when a written contract exists, evidence of differing interpretations or varying terms are excluded. The effect is to give a business drafting a document the power to control terms and to refuse to honor any other promises it has made, and thereby to dramatically reduce the ability of courts to protect parties who reasonably rely on oral promises that are at odds with a written contract.

How far rigid rules of interpretation can go in frustrating expectations is shown by *Marketing West, Inc. v. Sanyo Fisher Corp.*[44] When the Sanyo and Fisher companies merged, sales representatives in the home appliance division were required to sign new contracts that provided that they could be terminated without cause on ninety days notice. When they were summoned to a meeting in New Jersey to sign the contracts, however, the company's senior vice president told them that:

> The New Jersey Agreements had been developed for use by Sanyo's other divisions, but that plaintiffs were being asked to sign only for the purpose of uniformity, and the New Jersey Agreements would have no effect on plaintiffs' division. Plaintiffs were further informed that the agreements "did not mean anything," did not change the terms of their relationship with Sanyo, were just part of the reorganization process involved in the merger, and that the execution of the New Jersey Agreements was a mere "formality" and was "just pro forma," and that the ... sales representatives would not be replaced by an in-house sales staff as long as [they] continued to perform.[45]

Subsequently Sanyo Fisher fired the sales representatives, claiming the right to do so under a ninety-day notice provision in the "New Jersey Agreements" without regard for their prior contracts, which permitted termination only for good cause.

The California court, illustrating a conservative shift after a change in the composition of the state supreme court, held that Sanyo Fisher was within its rights. The attack by Judge Kozinski and others, the court concluded, was well founded; strict rules of interpretation made written agreements conclusive, particularly where, as here, the agreement contained a clause stating that the writing constituted the parties' entire agreement. Therefore, the ninety-day termination clause governed, not the prior agreements or the reassurances. In the court's view, not only is an oral promise that is inconsistent with the written agreement unenforceable, but the oral promises may not be considered to show that there was not an enforceable contract; that is, the vice president's oral denigration of the New Jersey agreements as having "no effect" and "not meaning anything" had no value at all.[46]

The flexible approach to contracts also relied heavily on the idea that parties have an obligation to perform their contracts in good faith, an obligation that was recognized in every state and applied to every kind of case. What constituted good faith depended on the context of particular cases, but violations of good faith included such behavior as hewing to the letter of a contract while evading its spirit. In some settings, it became clear that enforcing the good faith obligation required remedies beyond those ordinarily provided, so, beginning in the 1960s, a tort action of bad faith breach of contract was created. The Right has mounted an attack on this use of tort principles to remedy bad faith breach.[47]

A classic type of bad faith case was dramatized in John Grisham's novel *The Rainmaker*, made into a movie starring Matt Damon as idealistic young lawyer Rudy Baylor and Danny DeVito as his street-savvy associate. Teen-aged Donny Ray Black develops leukemia, but Great Benefit Life Insurance Company, the family's insurer, refuses to pay for a bone marrow transplant that would save his life. After Donny Ray dies and Rudy sues on the family's behalf, the company offers to settle for $200,000, the cost of the transplant. This is what Donnny Ray's estate and parents are entitled to as a matter of contract law damages; if Great Benefit had honored the insurance policy, it would have paid this amount. But this is neither an accurate measure of the family's loss nor of the wrongfulness of the company's conduct. Because of its failure to pay, Donny Ray died. Worse yet, its failure to pay was part of a massive scheme to refuse rightful claims and save millions for the company. Donny Ray's mother refuses the settlement, Rudy uncovers the scheme, the jury, applying tort principles, awards compensatory damages of $200,000 and punitive damages of $50 million, and Great Benefit goes bankrupt.

Art imitates life; a substantial body of law reaches the same result. When a business wrongfully refuses to honor its obligations (by failing to pay for the transplant), it has breached the duty of good faith; ordinary contract remedies ($200,000) are inadequate to compensate the injured party and to deter similar conduct in the future, so a tort claim is in order (with punitive damages available). Courts extended this principle from insurance cases to other areas in which one party to a contract is vulnerable to the other's wrongdoing. The relationship of an employer to its worker or a bank to its customer are analogous, and the principle even was extended to commercial cases not involving people who were, like Donny Ray and his parents, humble and unsophisticated.

Conservatives attacked the bad faith doctrine as an example of tort law invading the proper sphere of contract. The colorful Judge Kozinski claimed that "nowhere but in the Cloud Cuckooland of modern tort theory" could such a doctrine have been concocted, a doctrine that was "so nebulous in outline and so unpredictable in application that it more resembles a brick thrown from a third story window than a rule of law," a doctrine "that gives judges license to rely on their gut feelings in distinguishing between a squabble and a tort."[48]

The attack quickly bore fruit, particularly in California and Montana, two states that had led the way in the formulation of the bad faith tort. Three liberal justices of the Supreme Court were removed by California voters in 1986, and conservative Republican governor George Deukmejian replaced them with conservatives and elevated conservative justice Malcolm Lucas to chief justice.[49] Shortly thereafter, the newly constituted court backtracked on the bad faith tort. In *Foley v. Interactive Data Corp.*, the court limited bad faith to the insurance context, in which it was established beyond dispute, and rejected a chain of precedent applying it in employment, banking, and other cases.[50] Accordingly, Daniel Foley, who was fired by Interactive, a subsidiary of Chase Manhattan Bank, for reporting to a manager that he had learned his supervisor was under investigation by the FBI for embezzlement, had no action for bad faith discharge. In dissent, Justice Allen Broussard labeled the opinion by the conservative majority "a radical attempt to rewrite California law" and "a radical contraction in existing remedies."[51]

Avoiding the duty of good faith is a step on the road to ensuring that once businesses make contracts on their own terms, their contracts are not subject to review by the courts on the basis that they are unreasonable, unfair, or in conflict with other requirements of law. The conflict between individuals' ability to contract on any terms that they want and the state's ability to control contracting behavior is inevitable; all but the most ardent conservatives and libertarians agree that a contract to commit a murder or a contract to enslave oneself should not be enforceable. But the Right's approach to contract law aims to remove virtually all restrictions on the ability to dictate contract terms short of those egregious examples. Under this view, contract is defined to include freedom from regulation, and contract trumps more obviously regulatory bodies of law.

One of those bodies of law is tort law, and the conservative campaign has advanced the idea that contract law should supersede the efforts of tort law to establish reasonable standards of conduct. The California Supreme Court defined the nature of contract and tort in a way that advances the idea: "The distinction between tort and contract is well grounded in common law, and divergent objectives underlie the remedies created in the two areas. Whereas contract actions are created to enforce the intentions of the parties to the agreement, tort law is primarily designed to vindicate 'social policy.' "[52] "Social policy," in scare quotes, is used as a pejorative term, denigrating the courts' interference with the working of the invisible hand of the market, through contracts. The fear of social policy, as the U.S. Supreme Court wrote in a products liability case, is that "contract law would drown in a sea of tort."[53] Therefore, when there is a contract, tort has no role.

Under tort law, a business engaged in an activity (a ski resort, for example) owes participants a duty of care to conduct the activity reasonably safely, but businesses have attempted to erode that duty through changes in tort and contract law. In tort law, as described in Chapter 2, they have sought the enactment of statutes that exclude them from the general principles of negligence liability; in contract law, they have required participants to sign boilerplate disclaimers and then have attempted to use the disclaimers to defend tort suits.[54]

Because disclaimers impinge on rights created by tort law, since the 1960s courts have limited the ability of a business to disclaim liability for its torts. The precedent-setting case is *Tunkl v. Regents of the University of California* (1963), in which the California Supreme Court struck down the UCLA Medical Center's standard form release that a patient was required to sign on admission relieving the hospital of liability for negligent treatment.[55] Many courts followed *Tunkl*, developing a body of law under which disclaimers are unenforceable if the activity involves a public interest (of which a hospital is the best example) or if the bargain is too one-sided or the language of the disclaimer is not clear.

Because the Right's vision of contract law holds that there should be few if any restrictions on contract, it rejects this body of law and argues that disclaimers should be enforceable.[56] Under this approach, disclaimers will be allowed in more circumstances, as fewer activities are considered to have a public interest, not only inherently dangerous recreational activities such as parachuting[57] and whitewater rafting,[58] but ordinary activities such as swimming at the YMCA[59] and going to the health club.[60] Indeed, conservative theorist Richard Epstein has argued that contract can supplant core areas of tort law such as medical malpractice; patients should be able to contract with their doctors for the level of care they want, or the level they can afford, he argues, including agreeing not to sue for negligent treatment, in direct opposition to *Tunkl*.[61] When disclaimers are allowed, they will be generously interpreted, barring tort liability not only for the inherent risks of an activity but for any risks, however unforeseeable; for example, a disclaimer against liability for injuries sustained in the pit area of a stock car race prevents recovery for injuries suffered through the negligent discharge of fireworks, and a disclaimer against liability of a health club includes not only the use of equipment but also the club's negligence in failing to have employees trained to deal with the heart attack of a user.[62]

Enforcing Contracts: Contract Law without Law

Whatever the law about how contracts are made, what their terms are, and how those terms can be regulated, in the end, parties have to go to court to enforce their contracts, subject to generally applicable rules of contract law. But not if the conservative campaign has its way. The final effort of the conservative trend in contract law is to allow businesses to choose which body of law they will be subject to—in effect, whether they will be subject to state regulation at all—and to choose who will apply that law, including deciding that no court will ever hear their disputes. In the commercial equivalent of a drug lord choosing not to be bound by the law against drug dealing, this effort involves validating "choice of law" clauses and "choice of forum" clauses in standard form contracts, particularly those that substitute arbitration for litigation.

A choice of law clause in a contract states that disputes arising out of the contract will be decided under a specified state's law. For example, Citigroup, the global financial conglomerate, sends everyone who signs up for a Citi-bank Visa card a form that constitutes the contract; whether the card holder lives in New York or Alaska, the holder has "agreed" by receiving a form with twenty-eight numbered paragraphs, in 6-point type, that "This Agree-ment and your account...shall be governed by and interpreted in accor-dance with Federal law and the laws of the State of Delaware." Delaware is the state of choice for Citibank and other credit card companies because it offers the most attractive legal environment, including lax regulations and high interest rates and late fees. Scholars call this phenomenon "a race to the bottom," in which states compete for business by offering the least restric-tive body of law, a race in which Delaware currently has pulled ahead of South Dakota, its principal competitor. For example, the Delaware legisla-ture helpfully enacted a statute permitting a credit card agreement to be modified if the company included a stuffer in the billing statement and the cardholder failed to close the account within fifteen days.[63]

In a choice of forum clause, the party drafting the form directs that all litigation arising out of the contract must be brought in a particular place or particular court. As discussed previously, in *Carnival Cruise Lines, Inc. v. Shute*, for example, Eulala Shute, a cruise passenger from the state of Wash-ington, was injured on a cruise from Los Angeles to Puerta Vallarta, Mexico, but the Supreme Court upheld a choice of forum clause that limited her to suing in Florida, the home of Carnival Cruise Lines. These clauses are sub-ject to review for reasonableness, but, as *Shute* illustrates, the review is not especially searching.

The effect of a choice of forum clause is not only to determine where a case must be brought but often to determine which body of law will govern it. Ordinarily, a court will apply its own law in deciding a case, and the law of the selected forum may differ in important respects from that of another state. Bruce Forrest, who lived in the District of Columbia, attempted to sue Verizon for breach of contract and fraud in failing to provide its DSL serv-ice as advertised.[64] Forrest brought the case as a class action; although many Verizon subscribers were damaged, no individual claim was worth litigating by itself. But the Verizon subscriber agreement (available through an online scroll box that equaled thirteen printed pages) specified that suits had to be brought in Fairfax County, Virginia. Virginia is one of only two states that does not allow class actions, so the effect of the provision was to bar Forrest's claim. Virginia is a popular jurisdiction in part for this reason; America Online also specifies that actions must be brought in Virginia courts, and it has successfully defeated class actions brought elsewhere on that basis.[65]

The most common forum selection clause is one that requires a consumer or employee to give up the right to sue and instead submit all claims to arbitration. Consumer advocates have resisted this device with occasional success; in early 2004, for example, Fannie Mae and Freddie Mac, the nation's two largest buyers of home mortgages, announced that they would no longer invest in mortgages containing mandatory arbitration clauses.[66] But mandatory arbitration has become all but ubiquitous in consumer transactions, employment agreements, and other types of contract. Bank of America, MBNA, Wells Fargo, American Express, and Capital One require their customers to arbitrate. Internet service providers Comcast, AOL, and Earthlink mandate arbitration, as do popular Web sites such as eBay, Amazon.com, and Hotels.com. Gateway computers has been notorious for its use of arbitration, resulting in high-profile litigation such as the Hills' case. Employers, including Red Lobster, Olive Garden, Circuit City, Chrysler, and Halliburton, require their employees to arbitrate claims, as did KFC in Drake Albanza's case; in the past five years, the number of employees covered by arbitration agreements has more than doubled. An increasing number of doctors and other health-care providers require patients to arbitrate claims, including Kaiser Permanente, the country's largest nonprofit HMO and health-care system. Buyers of new homes can be required to arbitrate disputes, even tort cases; nearly every major Texas home builder, for example, uses a standard form requiring arbitration.[67] Car buyers are typically subject to mandatory arbitration, even though car dealers went to Congress to seek relief from mandatory arbitration of their own disputes with the auto makers.[68]

Arbitration is a private mechanism of resolving disputes that is "litigation lite."[69] Unlike in litigation, the arbitrator is not a judge, there is no jury, there is limited discovery, the hearing is less formal, the arbitrator is not required to explain the basis for the decision, the remedies may be limited, and the results are not public. As originally practiced, arbitration was an expeditious means by which merchants could refer their disputes to an expert arbitrator for resolution; arbitration also is widely used for labor disputes under collective bargaining agreements. Arbitration can be a fair and effective substitute for going to court to assert a claim. Litigation is often expensive, time-consuming, and unpredictable, and a more efficient and more expeditious forum can more effectively vindicate rights.

But arbitration does not always live up to its billing; it can be costly, and it can fail to protect fundamental rights, both rights to fair process and the substantive rights granted by the law. The possibility of abuse is particularly high where the system is designed or selected by an employer, bank, or other business and imposed on a worker or customer. During the past twenty years, businesses and conservatives have transformed arbitration. Arbitration has moved from disputes between businesses to a wide range of issues that arise between individuals and businesses, even including claims by consumers and employees that statutory rights under consumer protection and civil rights laws have been violated. The parties do not refer disputes to arbitration after they arise, but consumers and employees are compelled to arbitrate by the fine print of a standard form contract entered in advance. And businesses and their supporters (such as the U.S. Chamber of Commerce) have litigated to guarantee that the terms they dictate in standard form arbitration clauses are enforceable as they stand, so arbitration clauses can limit consumer or employee rights, arbitration procedures go unchallenged, and courts have little opportunity to review the fairness of arbitrations.

Access to the courts is available at little cost (because the government pays judges' salaries and the other costs of the court system), but the expense of arbitration is borne by the parties, which can prevent consumers and workers from vindicating their rights. To initiate an arbitration, the disputing party has to pay a fee to the arbitration service provider, analogous to a court filing fee. Commonly, fees are in the same ballpark as court filing fees, up to a few hundred dollars. The American Arbitration Association, for example, limits fees charged to employees and consumers in small disputes to $125.[70] Sometimes, however, fees are set at a level that discourages consumers from filing; the Texas home builder's arbitration system requires a $3,000 filing fee, for example.[71] High arbitrator fees are not unusual, either. Tracy Christopher filed a sex discrimination complaint against her employer, WGNA radio in Albany, New York, which her employment contract required to be arbitrated. Her fees were $1,000 per day for the arbitrator, a $500 counterclaim fee, $150 per day hearing fee, and $150 per day postponement fee, so high as to deny her an effective forum.[72] In two arbitrations against termite control companies in Birmingham, Alabama, the home-owners' total costs (excluding lawyers' fees) came to $12,000 and $16,000.[73]

For these fees, the parties get a hearing before an arbitrator or panel of arbitrators. In theory, the arbitrator is disinterested in the particular dispute and unbiased with respect to the class of disputes; to draw an analogy to labor arbitration under collective bargaining agreements, the arbitrator should not be predisposed to find for union or management. Because labor arbitrators typically are selected by agreement of the parties from a list of potential arbitrators, one who consistently demonstrates bias will be struck by the other side. In consumer and employment arbitration, though, the parties do not have equal say. The company that drafts the form contract selects the arbitration system and, as a repeat player, has more experience with the arbitrators. Businesses choose arbitration for the same reason that they run sales for their customers or offer benefits to their employees: not out of the goodness of their hearts, but because it improves the bottom line, so it is in their interest to choose a favorable system and a favorable arbitrator. When large law firms began requiring their employees to submit claims of racial discrimination and sexual harassment to arbitration, they often specified that the arbitrators be selected from other large law firms, which would, as the *Wall Street Journal* reported, offer "a more sympathetic hearing."[74] And arbitrators and arbitration services also have to be concerned about the bottom line; in situations in which they answer equally to different interests (such as labor and management), it is in their interest to be truly neutral, but in cases where businesses are the only repeat customers, who pays the piper may call the tune.[75]

Arbitrators are not judges, and there is no jury in arbitration. Indeed, although many arbitrators are trained as lawyers, there is no requirement that they be lawyers or even have knowledge of the law or the specialized area in which they hear cases. Some times they are embarrassingly inexpert, or just embarrassing. In its series on arbitration, the *San Francisco Chronicle* reported the case of Renee Cecala, a former vice president at NationsBank whose employment contract required her to arbitrate her sex discrimination claim that she had been pawed, cursed, and subjected to obscene jokes. It was hard for her to get a fair hearing—or, literally, any kind of hearing at all—from the arbitration panel; one arbitrator was hard of hearing, the second slept through much of the session, and the third was a retired music teacher with no apparent expertise in a sex discrimination case arising from the investment banking industry.[76]

Individuals also are disadvantaged by the absence of information in arbitration. In court, for example, either party has access to relevant information controlled by the other party through the process known as discovery. Without full discovery, it may be difficult or impossible for a consumer or employee to prove her case. In Renee Cecala's employment discrimination case, for example, if she litigated she would have a right to obtain her personnel file and that of her abusers to document her claims and the pattern of abuse. If she alleged a company-wide pattern of discrimination, she could obtain information about other complaints that have been filed and how the company responded. Her lawyer also could depose her abusers, supervisors, and company managers, to establish what happened and what the company's policies were about dealing with complaints of harassment. In arbitration, all of these procedures are available only at the discretion of the arbitrator, leaving a victim with limited ability to prove the elements of her case.

Mandatory arbitration agreements also can limit the legal remedies that would otherwise be available to participants. Insurance companies' arbitration clauses bar damages for bad faith, which would leave John Grisham's *The Rainmaker* in the realm of fiction; this practice is so egregious that half the states have legislated some restrictions on arbitration clauses in insurance policies.[77] Other companies frequently bar punitive damages, and industry has sought legislation preventing arbitrators from awarding punitive damages in any case.[78] Because many arbitration clauses prevent consumers from participating in class actions, businesses can defraud many consumers in amounts so small that no individual case is worth pursuing. Civil rights and consumer plaintiffs can lose their statutory right to attorney's fees if they win, and they can be subject to a "loser pays" clause, putting them at risk of paying the company's attorney's fees if they lose.

Early in the twentieth century, arbitration was viewed skeptically by courts as ousting their authority to resolve disputes and, to that extent, supplanting the state's sovereignty. Over time, that view declined with respect to commercial arbitration, both as a matter of judicial policy and in response to the enactment of the Federal Arbitration Act in 1925. The expansion of consumer arbitration received its major endorsement by the U.S. Supreme

Court in a series of cases beginning in the 1980s. In *Moses H. Cone Memorial Hospital v. Mercury Construction Corp.* in 1983, the Court read the act as "a congressional declaration of a liberal federal policy favoring arbitration agreements, notwithstanding any state substantive or procedural policies to the contrary.... As a matter of federal law, any doubts... should be resolved in favor of arbitration."[79] In a dozen cases since, the Court has approved arbitration in different settings and has brought a wide range of issues within the federal arbitration policy. When 7-11 franchisees sued Southland Corporation for fraud and violation of California's franchise protection statute, the Court held that allowing the franchisees access to the courts under the statute conflicted with the Federal Arbitration Act and was void.[80] Customers of the Shearson/American Express stock brokerage firm were required to arbitrate their claims against the firm under an arbitration clause in the standard brokerage contract, even though their claims alleged violations of the securities laws and the racketeering statute.[81] An employee of another investment firm was required to arbitrate rather than sue on his claim that his employer had fired him in violation of the federal Age Discrimination in Employment Act, because New York Stock Exchange rules called for arbitration.[82] Other cases extended the rule to a Circuit City employee claiming employment discrimination, a homeowner asserting a claim against a termite inspection company, and a mobile home purchaser asserting a Truth in Lending Act claim against her lender, among others.[83]

Contrarily, the global trend as to the law and practice of arbitration is running in the opposite direction. Although arbitration between businesses is common in international commerce, mandatory arbitration by contract of consumer and employment disputes is almost unknown outside the United States. The European Union, for example, has a specific directive prohibiting its imposition in most consumer cases.[84]

The Court also has broadly empowered businesses to set the terms of arbitration and limited the ability of the states to regulate arbitration procedures. The danger that the costs of arbitration would be prohibitively expensive, effectively denying a borrower a remedy against the bank that financed her mobile home purchase when she alleged violation of the federal Truth in Lending Act and Equal Credit Opportunity Act, was not enough to avoid arbitration; somewhat incongruously, the Court held that the borrower could only overcome the federal preference for arbitration by litigating (at significant expense, no doubt) and proving that the costs of arbitration would be too high to overcome the federal preference for arbitration.[85] The court also has held that discovery in employment cases can be more limited in arbitration than in court without running afoul of principles of fairness or the public policy protecting employees against age discrimination.[86] A Montana statute required that an arbitration clause in a standard form contract be prominently displayed on the first page of the contract, so that the party subject to the clause (in this case, a Subway sandwich shop franchisee) would have adequate notice of giving up the right to sue. The Supreme Court in 1996 held that the disclosure requirement conflicted with the federal policy favoring arbitration; any special state rule governing arbitration contracts was invalid.[87]

The Court did leave open the possibility that some arbitration schemes are so unfair as to be invalid, or "unconscionable." Unconscionability is the most extreme limitation on freedom of contract, giving the court the power to refuse to enforce a contract or contract term that is too one-sided as a result of unequal bargaining power. There is a struggle in the lower courts over the extent of this power. Some cases are so extreme that courts strike down the arbitration clause. The most notorious involved a Hooters restaurant in Myrtle Beach, South Carolina. Annette Phillips, a bartender at Hooters, quit her job after allegedly being grabbed and slapped in a sexual manner by Gerald Brooks, a Hooters manager and the brother of the restaurant's owner. She filed a sexual harassment claim, which Hooters argued had to go to arbitration under her employment contract. Even the conservative U.S. Court of Appeals for the Fourth Circuit found Hooters' arbitration system was unconscionable because it was "so skewed . . . in its favor that Phillips has been denied arbitration in any meaningful sense of the word."[88] Phillips was required at the outset of the process to give the company notice of the specific acts that gave rise to her claim, a list of all witnesses, and a summary of the facts known to each; Hooters had no obligation to provide any information about its case to her. The arbitration was to be conducted by a panel of three arbitrators selected from a list created exclusively by Hooters, and Hooters could include on the list its own managers or others with a personal or financial interest in the case. Hooters, but not Phillips, could move to dismiss the case, raise any new issues during the proceeding, record the hearing, and appeal the panels decision to a court. The crowning touch: Hooters, but not Phillips, could cancel the agreement to arbitrate or change the rules governing the arbitration, in whole or in part, without notice to her.

There continues to be much litigation about the unconscionability of particular arbitration schemes, and courts do strike down some as too one-sided. In *Ting v. AT&T* in 2003, for example, the U.S. Court of Appeals for the Ninth Circuit invalidated the provision AT&T attempted to impose on its long-distance customers because it prohibited them from joining class actions, required them to pay excessive fees to arbitrate, and prevented them from disclosing the results of arbitrations.[89] Nevertheless, businesses press the issue. They have an intrinsic advantage in the process; the employee or consumer who does not want to arbitrate has to litigate to establish its right to litigate, and then litigate the substantive claim. And businesses continue to test new limits and support those limits with arguments about freedom of contract and the federal policy favoring arbitration. Arbitration clauses that have been defended against unconscionability claims include those in which the customer was bound to arbitrate but the company was not, clauses barring class actions and punitive damages, and provisions allowing the company to dictate the rules for arbitration and select the arbitrator.[90] The U.S. Chamber of Commerce, meanwhile, has argued that unconscionability has no role to play at all in these cases, because of a paramount federal policy favoring arbitration.[91]

The final indignity of arbitration is that an arbitrator's decision is essentially unreviewable by a court. Only if there is corruption, fraud, or the like can a court set aside an arbitration award; it is even questionable when an award can be set aside because the arbitrator exhibits "manifest disregard for the law."[92] Judge Richard Posner, commenting that parties are not entitled to an award that is "correct or even reasonable, since neither error nor clear error nor even gross error is a ground for vacating an award," explained the limits on courts' powers in a remarkable hypothetical:

> Maybe if the arbitrators said "We'd rather play golf today, so rather than consider the parties' claims we're simply denying all of them," the resulting award would not be considered a "mutual, final, and definite award," or, perhaps, any award at all;... Putting the golf hypothetical to

one side, therefore, if the district judge is satisfied that the arbitrators resolved the entire dispute and can figure out what that resolution is, he must confirm the award.[93]

Therefore, for example, when Raymond DiRussa won an arbitration against his employer, Dean Witter Reynolds, for violations of the Age Discrimination in Employment Act and received damages of $220,000, the arbitrator refused to award attorney's fees (claimed by DiRussa to be $240,000, more than his damage award), even though the Act specifically stated that the fees "shall" be awarded. Despite the clear violation of the statute, the reviewing court refused to upset the arbitrator's award. The court allowed review under the "manifest disregard" standard, but its deference to arbitration was so great that it would not set aside the award because the arbitrator had not intentionally refused to apply the statutory standard.[94]

The key to the debate about how far companies can go in depriving consumers of their rights through arbitration is not simply that consumers and employees will be able to pursue fewer complaints against businesses and employers, that they will win fewer of the ones they do pursue, or that the ones they win will remain secret, unlike judicial decisions. The push for widespread arbitration that supplants the court system is the ultimate triumph of the fantasy of freedom of contract and the reality of imposition on consumers and employees by big businesses and their form contracts. Here, contract replaces law. The enforcement of mandatory arbitration clauses prevents the courts from ever being able to judge the legality of any clause of the contract or the business's behavior under it. As Montana Supreme Court justice Terry Trieweiler stated, "Mandatory arbitration allows corporations to undermine the whole system by which we hold them accountable."[95]

The Decline of Agreement

The modern economy is largely characterized by contracts made through standard forms with standard terms promulgated by big businesses. The everyday affairs of the ordinary person are regulated by a job application, employment contract, and personnel manual while working at KFC or Kaiser, a fine-print contract amended by bill stuffers when using a Citibank credit card, boilerplate terms at the back of the instruction manual when buying a Gateway computer, and terms of service available through a series of links when using AOL. Standard form contracts are essential to the economy, and they can benefit both businesses and consumers if they are properly regulated.

If the conservative vision of contract law is fully adopted, however, the power of big businesses to dictate terms with their employees and customers would be magnified and reinforced with the law's authority. The worker at KFC or Kaiser and the customer of Citibank, Gateway, or AOL would be bound by contract terms that were presented in an obscure form or never presented at all at the time the contract was made, and to which he never agreed. The idea of agreement as the basis of contract would be submerged in a fictional concept of assent contradicted by the inability to know, understand, agree to, or decline the terms. The business could change the terms during the course of a relationship without notifying the customer or employee, and the new terms would be as fully binding as if they had been disclosed and negotiated. Because the standard form would be the sole basis for determining the substance of the contract, a customer who relied on the representations of a sales representative or an employee who relied on the assurances of her boss would be surprised and disappointed to find that the representations and promises were not enforceable; the effective deceit of hidden terms would diminish the ability of people to trust one another.

The problem presented by this vision is not just that contract would no longer be about agreement; the substance of the agreements would disadvantage individuals as well. Employees could be fired at any time for any reason or for no reason. Bank and credit card customers could be subject to exorbitant fees and charges. Product manufacturers would not have to stand behind the quality of their goods. And most outrageously, disputes arising out of contractual relationships would not be subject to law. Private systems of arbitration created and controlled by business would supplant the courts, so the idea of a consumer's or worker's "day in court" would become illusory. Even claims involving significant issues of public interest—claims that an employee had been subjected to sexual harassment or race or age discrimination—would be barred from the courts.

The claim of the conservative vision is that it would maximize individual freedom of contract and, through the operation of the market, increase social welfare. That claim is false, and its falsity is demonstrated by the history of contract law throughout the twentieth century. "Freedom of contract" was a political slogan touted by conservatives at the turn of the twentieth century, in the same manner as it is used by their successors at the turn of the twenty-first century, as a means of preventing the government from acting in the interests of ordinary people. From the 1920s through the 1970s, contract law became more attuned to the inequality and complexity of contracts in the real world. Courts, legislatures, and commentators came to reject that slogan and to develop a better understanding of contracting and contract law; the story of that rejection and understanding is told in the next chapter.

5

Freedom of Contract and Fair Contract

Sir Henry Maine, the nineteenth-century English historian, proclaimed that "the movement of the progressive societies has hitherto been a movement *from Status to Contract*." In medieval times, family and feudal relationships defined the social order, but in the nineteenth century, the development of modern economies and the destruction of traditional social ties led to a "social order in which all . . . relations arise from the free agreement of individuals."[1] American courts and lawyers in the era of classical legal thought, from the late nineteenth through the early twentieth century, embraced Maine's insight with enthusiasm. The market came to be seen as the principal mechanism of social organization; a body of classical contract law was fashioned to lubricate the mechanism. Today the Right aims to resurrect classical contract law, restore the primacy of the market, and so strengthen the power of big business to dictate contract terms. The campaign to do so rests on a false picture of freedom of contract and a rejection of a fair approach to contract law that developed over the course of the twentieth century.

Classical Contract Law

Classical contract law imagined a world in which parties created their own law by consenting to agreements; society was an extension of the market, in which free and independent individuals avidly pursued their individual self-interest. The job of courts was simply to enforce the rights created by the parties' contracts and otherwise to refrain from imposing obligation. They could do this job by mechanically applying abstract, formal rules of contract law. The result: freedom of contract, embodied in law and carried into practice.

Freedom of contract included the ability to enter into any contract on any terms. Here, contract law encountered the great social issues of the age with a singular, practical result: the courts protected the ability of big business to exert economic power with minimal government interference. One of its most notorious manifestations was *Lochner v. New York*, in which the U.S. Supreme Court, in 1905, invalidated a New York statute that limited bakery workers to a sixty-hour work week as an impermissible invasion of their freedom of contract. Under an ideal market—disregard the inequalities of the real world—"There is no reasonable ground for interfering with the liberty of person or the right of free contract, by determining the hours of labor, in the occupation of a baker."[2] A decade later, in *Coppage v. Kansas*, the Court struck down a Kansas statute that prohibited "yellow dog" contracts, or employment contracts that prevented workers from joining unions: "Included in the right of personal liberty and the right of private property—partaking of the nature of each—is the right to make contracts.... The right is as essential to the laborer as to the capitalist, to the poor as to the rich." Of course, as the Court recognized, the poor and the rich may not benefit equally from this right: "There must and will be inequalities of fortune. It is from the nature of things impossible to uphold freedom of contract and the right of private property without at the same time recognizing as legitimate those inequalities."[3]

Freedom of contract also included the ability to be free of contractual liability except where it had clearly been assumed. George Eddingfield, a physician in the small town of Mace, Indiana, was the family doctor for the Burks and cared for Charlotte Burk during her pregnancy. Charlotte went into labor and became seriously ill. Several times a family member went to Eddingfield, told him that Charlotte and the unborn child were in jeopardy and that no other doctor was available, and tendered his fee. Eddingfield refused to come to her aid "without any reason whatsoever," as the Indiana Supreme Court wrote, and Charlotte and her baby died for lack of medical treatment. Charlotte's heirs sued, but the court held that Eddingfield had no duty as a physician to come to her aid, and it could not even contemplate that he had a contractual duty to attend her. Their prior relationship as family doctor and patient and his position as the only physician available to aid a dying patient were irrelevant, because he had the freedom not to contract on this occasion.[4]

The entire body of contract doctrine flowed from the principle of freedom of contract. Rules about making contracts required that there be an identifiable moment at which the parties' consent exactly matched by a clear, definite agreement to create a contract. Prior to that moment, the individual had no contractual liability, and at that moment, liability attached and excuses for nonperformance were limited. The agreement embodied the terms of performance, so interpretation questions could be resolved by referring to its plain meaning. When a breach occurred, it violated a determinate expectation created by the agreement, and damages could be quantified by referring to that expectation.

These doctrines operated in modest and mundane cases as well as issues of great political moment and personal drama. C. J. Kershaw & Son, a Milwaukee salt dealer, wrote to J. H. Moulton, a dealer in La Crosse, Wisconsin, stating "we are authorized to offer Michigan fine salt, in full car-load lots of 80 to 95 barrels, delivered at your city, at 85¢ per barrel." Moulton immediately sent a telegram in response: "You may ship me 2,000 barrels Michigan fine salt, as offered in your letter." A contract? No, said the court, because the terms were indefinite. Kershaw's offer did not specify either a definite number of carloads that it would sell, or that it would sell any reasonable amount Moulton ordered. Moulton pointed out that both of them were dealers in the salt trade, and in that trade there was a well-understood meaning of Kershaw's offer, but the court declined to consider the practice because it "would introduce such an element of uncertainty"; the court believed it was "not at liberty to help out the written contract" by looking at evidence of additional facts outside the document.[5]

On the other hand, where a contract appeared to be completely expressed in a written document, the courts made the document the conclusive statement of the parties' agreement. In an 1885 Minnesota case, J. H. Thompson sold to Rowland Libbey a quantity of logs, giving a signed and dated document that stated:

> I have this day sold to R. C. Libbey, of Hastings, Minn., all my logs marked 'H. C. A.,' cut in the winters of 1882 and 1883, for $10 a thousand feet, boom scale at Minneapolis, Minnesota. Payment, cash, as fast as scale bills are produced.

When Libbey failed to pay and Thompson sued for the price, Libbey defended on the basis that Thompson orally had promised the logs would be of a certain quality, and the logs failed to measure up. The court refused to hear Libbey's evidence, though. Where the parties intended to put their complete agreement in writing, evidence of the supplemental oral promise was barred. But how did the court know that they intended the writing to encompass their complete agreement? By the application of an abstract, formal rule that writings always triumphed:

> The only criterion of the completeness of the written contract as a full expression of the agreement of the parties is the writing itself. If it ... contains such language as imports a complete legal obligation, it is to be presumed that the parties here introduced into it every material item and term.[6]

The Critique of Classical Contract Law

Classical contract law was built on an image of freedom of contract that was unrealistic to the point of being mythical. Critics attacked this image as stemming from the same two fundamental errors that infected classical tort law: the failure to attend to the social facts underlying the cases, and the use of abstract, unquestioned principles of right as the basis of decisions.

In *Coppage v. Kansas*, for example, the Court presented an image of worker and employer freely contracting for the worker not to join a union. If Hedges, a switchman on the St. Louis & San Francisco Railway, wanted to remain a member of the Switchmen's Union, he was simply exercising a free choice to do that rather than to stay employed, just as the railroad was exercising a free choice not to employ union members. This image was fantastic, ignoring the social context of the labor movement, in which workers achieved their goals not through individual contracting but through a decades-long struggle to organize and to confront employers; *Coppage* was decided in 1915, the midpoint of a two-year series of strikes for an eight-hour day by unionized railway workers like Hedges.[7]

Beyond ignoring social facts, such as the inequality of bargaining power between a railroad and its workers, classical law misstated the nature of contractual relationships generally. As the economy became more complex, the individual, bargained contract became dwarfed by standardized contracts. As Cincinnati and later Harvard law professor Nathan Isaacs pointed out in a 1917 article that anticipated today's debates about standard form contracts, Sir Henry Maine's dictum about the movement from status to contract missed the more important distinction between individualized and standardized relations, with the latter—employment in a large corporation, routine property and liability insurance, and business and consumer loans, for example—becoming predominant. "In ordinary transactions," he wrote, "people cannot or will not stop to make special agreements.... The effect is a making of contracts in wholesale lots."[8]

Critics demonstrated that the principle of freedom of contract was more than unrealistic; it could not provide a sound conceptual basis for contract law. In his restatement of the fundamental principles of contract law in the *Harvard Law Review* in 1932, George K. Gardner pointed out that contract law contained inconsistent ideas, not only that "promises are obligatory in their own nature," but also a concept of "economic justice." Then, he outlined the job of courts in deciding contract cases very differently than did classical courts that purported to deduce individual results from general principles.

> In a society exposed to an unending stream of revolutionary inventions and subjected to constant changes in economic structure, it is useless to suppose that justice can be made effective by rigid adherence to traditional forms.
>
> ...
>
> The task of the law of contract thus ceases to be the simple one of enforcing bargains and becomes the far more complex one of providing means for conducting a cooperative commonwealth on a voluntary basis, of reconciling group industry and economic justice with individual freedom and individual responsibility for results.[9]

The lawyer-economist Robert Hale went even further. Classical contract law assumed that all contracts are freely made, and that the law's task is simply to enforce transactions in which free choice has been manifested and to refuse to enforce those in which it has not. Hale took exactly the opposite position, pointing out that all choices are to some degree coerced and therefore unfree. "While there is no explicit legal requirement that one enter into any particular transaction, one's freedom to decline to do so is nevertheless circumscribed. One chooses to enter into any given transaction in order to avoid the threat of something worse—threats which impinge with unequal weight on different members of society."[10] The owner of a railroad, as in *Coppage*, can withhold payment from a switchman unless he works, and the switchman can withhold his labor unless the owner pays. But the choices may not be equal ones; Cornelius Vanderbilt, owner of the New York Central Railroad, could exercise more coercive power in the bargaining process than a switchman like Hedges.

Coercion, Hale said, is supported by law, which allocates bargaining power by establishing property and contract rights, particularly by favoring the interests of those who own things over those who own only their labor. In this way, the classical freedom of contract principle embodied what Anatole France described in another context as the "majestic equality" of the law, which "forbids the rich as well as the poor to sleep under bridges, to beg in the streets, and to steal bread."[11] As Hale pointed out, "by judicious limitation on the bargaining power of the economically and legally stronger, it is conceivable that the economically weak would acquire greater freedom of contract than they now have—freedom to resist more effectively the bargaining power of the strong, and to obtain better terms."[12] The issue in *Coppage*, therefore, was not whether the Court should endorse freedom of contract but which version it should endorse: An abstract version that favored the railroad or the version adopted by the Kansas legislature that gave more freedom to unionized workers.

The most dramatic attack on freedom of contract came through progressive legislation. At the height of the classical era, the Sherman Antitrust Act of 1890 limited the freedom to enter into contracts "in restraint of trade." *Lochner* struck down a maximum hours law, but shortly thereafter maximum hour and minimum wage laws became the norm. *Coppage* invalidated statutes prohibiting yellow dog contracts, but the New Deal's National Labor Relations Act put the power of law behind unions and collective bargaining, limiting employers' freedom to contract out of the collective bargaining process.

Of lesser visibility but greater importance for everyday transactions was the penetration of the critique into ordinary commercial law. In a case much like *Moulton v. Kershaw*, Heyman Cohen & Sons bought 200 pieces of tricotine fabric from M. Lurie Woolen Co., with "the privilege . . . to confirm more" if Lurie could get it. Lurie did get more fabric and gave Cohen some, but held back two hundred pieces, and Cohen sued. Lurie defended on the ground that the contract, having failed to specify an amount beyond the two hundred pieces, was too indefinite to enforce, just like Kershaw's offer to sell an unspecified number of carloads of salt. The court was willing to look to the commercial context of the deal and fill in the gaps and enforce the contract. The contract was indefinite as to quantity, but "We think the implication plain that the buyer is to fix the quantity, subject only to the proviso that quantity shall be limited by ability to supply." It also was indefinite as to when Cohen could order, but "We think a reasonable time is a term implied by law."[13]

The opinion in *Moulton v. Kershaw* was written by Benjamin Nathan Cardozo, chief judge of the New York Court of Appeals and later justice of the U.S. Supreme Court, whose contribution to the critique of classical law and the reconstruction of law based on the critique was so distinguished that upon his death, the Columbia, Harvard, and Yale law journals published unique, simultaneous tribute issues. As described by Yale contracts scholar Arthur Corbin, Cardozo's approach exemplified the developing contract law:

> Cardozo's opinions on contract law demonstrate his instinct for a justice that is human and practical. Himself a master of expression, both graceful and exact, he knows also how to understand and interpret the language of contractors, graceless and inexact, abbreviated and elliptical though it be. There is clear genius in his filling of gaps, his finding of promises by implication where none was put into clear words, his discovery and enforcement of the directing purpose for which a contract was made, not permitting that purpose to fail by reason of vagueness in details.[14]

Critics argued the need for a similar flexibility when confronted with written documents, demonstrating that the underlying social facts of cases were more important than abstract rules. Limiting the process of interpretation to the face of the writing is inconsistent with what Corbin described as the "cardinal rule": ascertaining the reasonable intentions of the parties. To understand that intent, the court must be "informed by extrinsic evidence of the circumstances surrounding the making of the contract. These include the character of the subject matter, the nature of the business, the antecedent offers and counter offers and the communications of the parties with each other in the process of negotiation, the purposes of the parties which they expect to realize in the performance of the contract."[15]

Following the "cardinal rule," courts looked beyond writings to ascertain the real agreement. In the Minnesota case discussed earlier, a buyer of logs could not introduce evidence of the seller's oral promise as to their quality because it was not included in the written contract. Nonsense, said Corbin. "If testimony is offered to prove that a party made an extrinsic promise or warranty, by which his duties, liabilities, or other burdens would be increased . . . [there is] ample support for admitting such testimony where justice requires it."[16] The court should look at the nature of the transaction in its setting (would it be customary to have a quality term, and could the contract reasonably be enforced without it?) and at the conduct of the parties (the fact that there was an oral promise itself suggests that the written document was incomplete).

Classical contract law was modeled on the ideal of the market, and through the doctrine of "consideration" presumed that only bargained transactions were worth enforcing. Critics argued that both simple justice and the everyday practices of business people called for enforcement even in the absence of bargain. Promises to make gifts often were enforced under the new doctrine, such as a promise by Mary Johnson to Allegheny College to endow a scholarship fund, where the only "consideration" was her "interest in Christian education."[17] More broadly, reliance emerged as a counterprinciple to bargain under which the recipient of a promise who reasonably relied on it could enforce the promise to prevent "injustice," as the vague formulation by the prestigious American Law Institute put it in its Restatement of Contracts. Representatives of the Ford Motor Company's credit subsidiary advised dealers that Ford would insure repossessed cars in the dealers' possession so the dealers did not need to procure their own insurance. When five cars were destroyed in a fire on a dealer's lot, it turned out that neither Ford nor the dealer had insured the cars. Ford argued that it had no obligation to do so, because even if it had promised, it had received nothing in return for the promise, which therefore lacked consideration. The Mississippi Supreme Court held that the dealer followed the "very reasonable course" of relying on Ford's promise, which made that promise enforceable.[18]

Contextual Contract Law

The critique of classical contract law led to a reconstruction of the subject that extended through much of the twentieth century; it is this reconstruction that conservatives aim to overthrow. Two landmarks of the reconstruction were the drafting and adoption, from the late 1940s through the 1960s, of the Uniform Commercial Code, the statute that governs sales of goods and related topics in nearly every state, and the American Law Institute's consideration and publication of its revised Restatement of the law of contracts, from the early 1960s through the late 1970s. This new body of law began where classical law began, with parties manifesting consent to a contract, but it did not stop there, recognizing the need to look at an agreement in its full context and to measure it against public standards of fairness. Where classical law regarded consent and regulation as opposed (in the classical view, the exercise of consent was the area of economic life free from state regulation), the developing law regarded consent and regulation as complementary, in which the law's regulatory role is necessary both to define consent in its context and to set limits on it.

The breadth of contextualization and regulation is illustrated by the way in which the Uniform Commercial Code rewrites the basic concepts of "agreement" and "contract":

> "Agreement" means the bargain of the parties in fact, as found in their language or inferred from other circumstances, including course of performance, course of dealing, or usage of trade.
>
> "Contract" means the total legal obligation that results from the parties' agreement as determined by [the Uniform Commercial Code] as supplemented by any other applicable laws.[19]

An agreement is not an abstract meeting of isolated wills, but a bargain *in fact.* The court defines the relationships of the parties by looking at what they said and did and the context in which they said and did it, including how they conducted themselves under the contract (course of performance) or under other contracts (course of dealing), and how others in their business typically perform (usage of trade). The agreement is not the end of the story, enforceable, as a classical contract was seen to be, of its own accord.

Rather, the parties' agreement is measured against the standards set by law, both the Code and other relevant bodies of law.

How far a court would go in looking for the true agreement is illustrated by a well-known case from Hawaii. Nanakuli Paving and Rock Company, a Hawaiian asphalt paving contractor, sued Shell Oil Co. for raising the price of asphalt sold to Nanakuli under a long-term contract from $44 to $76 per ton.[20] Nanakuli used asphalt in large road-paving jobs, and it argued that the contract required Shell to "price-protect" it by not raising the price of asphalt once Nanakuli had put in a bid for a job based on an existing price of asphalt. Shell pointed to the written contract, which specified that the price would be "Shell's posted price at time of delivery."

The court went into great detail in looking beyond the written document—in some ways, looking in opposition to it—and applying the Code to determine what the deal really was. On two prior occasions Shell had price-protected Nanakuli. Shell and Nanakuli had had close relations over the years, and their cooperation had helped both enhance their business; Shell had even given Nanakuli a discount as a means of financing a plant expansion. Price-protection was common in the asphaltic concrete paving trade in Hawaii; although asphaltic concrete was different than asphalt, Shell should have known about practices in related trades and have been bound by them. The apparent conflict between the words of the contract and Nanakuli's claim was not decisive:

> A commercial agreement, then, is broader than the written paper and its meaning is to be determined not just by the language used by them in the written contract but by their action, read and interpreted in the light of commercial practices and other surrounding circumstances.
>
> ...
>
> Astonishing as it will seem to most practicing attorneys, under the Code it will be possible in some cases to use custom to contradict the written agreement.[21]

The *Nanakuli* case exemplifies the view that the real deal is more important than the paper deal. This view diminished the respect given to written contracts that are inconsistent with the understandings of the parties or the surrounding circumstances, and it was particularly pronounced in cases in which a less-sophisticated or less-powerful party asserted the validity of an oral agreement in opposition to a written contract, often a standard form, imposed by a dominant party.

For example, in 1961 Elwin Brawthen, living in Minnesota, was invited to join the H & R Block tax preparation company by opening an office in California.[22] The standard form Articles of Employment he was presented stated that, after two years, he could be terminated on ninety days notice. After his wife expressed concern about selling an established business in Minnesota and moving to California under that provision, she and Elwin were told by Richard Bloch (the "R" in H & R Block; the family name, but not the corporate name, is spelled with a final "h") that they had "The word of Henry and Richard Bloch. We have never terminated a contract. We do not terminate contracts. Anybody who does a good job in the area will never be terminated."

The Brawthens moved to California and, over time, opened up offices in four cities. In 1967, the Brawthens were further reassured when the company sent out a newsletter to managers that stated, "No manager need worry about his contract if he is doing a good, honorable conscientious job to best serve the public and following the principles outlined in the Policy & Procedure Book." But the next year, after a dispute over compensation, the company terminated Brawthen's employment.

The employment contract clearly stated that Brawthen could be terminated. But the written contract was not the whole story. A trilogy of California Supreme Court cases in 1968 had taken the law to its fullest extent of focusing on the real deal even in the face of an inconsistent writing. The only way to tell if the parties intended the writing to be the whole contract to the exclusion of any oral promises was to look at all of the relevant evidence, including the oral promises themselves. Therefore, Brawthen could provide evidence of Richard Bloch's promise to him, similar promises made to other employees, and the company newsletter as proof that the writing was not conclusive. The court and the jury agreed with Brawthen's position, and he received $201,284 in damages.

Often the problem before the court is not that the parties have entered into an arguably inconsistent agreement but that they have entered into an incomplete agreement. Through limited time, limited resources, limited attention, or simple carelessness, contracting parties do not specify all the terms of their agreement. Classical law required an agreement that was complete on its face, but the law following the critique developed the position that where there appeared to be an agreement, the law should fill in the gaps using fair terms. The sales article of the Uniform Commercial Code, for example, provides more than a dozen gap fillers. If a contract does not specify when goods are delivered, they must be delivered within a reasonable time. The goods sold must be "merchantable"; that is, a car dealer is held to an implicit promises that a car will run properly and will not fall apart as soon as it is driven out of the showroom. If the parties intend to contract but do not specify the price, the court can even fill in a reasonable price. In all of these cases, the law holds people and businesses to community standards of fairness and reasonableness.

Even the core principle of freedom of contract—the ability to enter into any contract on any terms—was directly confronted by the new law. A court applying the doctrine of "unconscionability" would refuse enforcement to a contract that was unfair because of unequal bargaining power. There is always a tension here; unfairness is a part of life, and certainly part of market transactions, so courts do not want to push the doctrine too far. But in many cases, the courts used the doctrine to regulate contracts to protect consumers and even businesses.

A leading case involved Ora Lee Williams, whom the court described as "a person of limited education separated from her husband [and] maintaining herself and her seven children by means of public assistance."[23] Williams was a long-time customer of the Walker-Thomas Furniture Co., a store in inner-city Washington, D.C. From 1957 to 1962, she bought many items on the installment plan, including linens, rugs, chairs, beds, a washing machine, and, on her last purchase, a $514 stereo; the total of her purchases came to $1,800, and at the time of litigation she had paid $1,400, all on her monthly welfare check of $218, the amount of which was known to Walker-Thomas. The purchases were documented by form contracts, which purported to lease the items to Williams until she had fully paid for them, giving the store the right to repossess them in case of a default. It also contained a fine-print provision the court generously described as "rather obscure":

> The amount of each periodical installment payment to be made by (purchaser) to the Company under this present lease shall be inclusive of and

not in addition to the amount of each installment payment to be made by (purchaser) under such prior leases, bills or accounts; and all payments now and hereafter made by (purchaser) shall be credited pro rata on all outstanding leases, bills and accounts due the Company by (purchaser) at the time each such payment is made.

The effect of this clause was to allow the store to repossess all of the items if she failed to make a payment on any of them, which is what happened.

The lower court condemned Walker-Thomas's sales practices as "sharp practice and irresponsible business dealings," but it did not believe it had the authority to act. The appellate court was bolder, holding that an unconscionable contract could be refused enforcement and offering a definition of unconscionability:

Unconscionability has generally been recognized to include an absence of meaningful choice on the part of one of the parties together with contract terms which are unreasonably favorable to the other party.... When a party of little bargaining power, and hence little real choice, signs a commercially unreasonable contract with little or no knowledge of its terms, it is hardly likely that his consent, or even an objective manifestation of his consent, was ever given to all the terms.

...Corbin suggests the test as being whether the terms are "so extreme as to appear unconscionable according to the mores and business practices of the time and place."

Through unconscionability, courts explicitly policed the fairness of transactions. Instead of assuming market equality and value-maximizing choices, they inquired into whether the contracting process and its results were fair. Under this doctrine, the courts struck down security clauses like those in the *Williams* case, prices that were too high (a $300 freezer sold for $1,234.80[24]) or too low (a sixty-nine-year-old retired laborer, who was an alcoholic with a ninth-grade education, was prevailed upon to sell his home worth $12,000 for $1,800[25]), and exorbitant rent-to-own transactions (eighteen-month arrangement under which the buyer pays two and a half times retail price as rental payments).[26] Courts even extended the protection of unconscionability to less-powerful commercial parties. In an important case that provided authority for the incorporation of unconscionability in the Uniform Commercial Code, Campbell Soup Company contracted to buy carrots from George and Harry Wentz, the owners of a truck farm, on terms dictated by Campbell's. One of the terms excused Campbell's from buying the carrots when it did not need them but prohibited the Wentzes from selling the carrots elsewhere without Campbell's permission. This, the court said, is "carrying a good joke too far." Even though the parties freely agreed to the term—or as freely as the bakers agreed to work long hours in *Lochner* or the switchman agreed to not join a union in *Coppage*—the court would not enforce it.[27]

The extent of change in the law from the classical period to the incorporation of the critique is shown in the developing rights of workers. Workers' right to bargain collectively was established during the New Deal, but developments from the 1960s through the 1980s focused on the rights of individual workers. During this period, legislatures and courts recognized the complexity of employment relationships and the need to intervene to redress imbalances of power between employer and employee; intervention was necessary to shift from abstract freedom of contract to real, fair freedom of contract for workers. The law's growth here provides a particularly striking contrast to classical law (the era of *Lochner* and *Coppage*) and to the recent conservative trend, with its emphasis on using form contracts to cut back on employee rights and remove the right to sue by requiring arbitration.

The greatest expression of the need to regulate employment contracts lies in federal statutes. (Many states have related legislation as well.) The Equal Pay Act of 1963 requires that men and women doing equal work receive equal pay.[28] Title VII of the Civil Rights Act of 1964 prohibits employment discrimination on the basis of race, color, religion, sex, or national origin.[29] The Age Discrimination in Employment Act, enacted in 1967, prohibits discrimination against older workers.[30] The Rehabilitation Act of 1973 introduced federal protection for workers with disabilities,[31] and the level of protection was dramatically increased by the Americans with Disabilities Act of 1990.[32] The Employee Retirement Income Security Act of 1974 regulates employee benefit plans, including health insurance and pensions.[33] The Family and Medical Leave Act of 1993 requires employers to give workers leaves of absence for childbirth, adoption, illness, or the care of family members.[34]

From the late 1950s through the 1980s, courts also extensively engaged with the employment relationship, particularly the issue of the permanence of a worker's job. The old legal rule, a reflection of classical contract law and laissez-faire capitalism, was that where an employer and employee had not specifically agreed that the job was to be of a specific duration, it was presumed to be terminable at will; that is, the employee could quit or the employer could discharge him at any time, for any reason or no reason. The presumption was so strong that it operated even in the face of strong evidence that the parties had a contrary intention; if the parties agreed that the employment should be permanent, rather than for a specific duration, the court would nevertheless assume that they meant the least permanent type of relationship, that it would be terminable at will.

The courts that reconsidered the employment relationship created a series of exceptions to the employment at will rule, all of which rested on the concept of contract law that developed out of the critique of classical legal thought: in assessing employment contracts, the courts had to abandon the abstraction and individualism of the employment at will rule in favor of a realistic examination of the employment relationship and the social interests involved in its regulation.

Sometimes the exceptions rested on express or implied promises by the employer that the job would be long term. Wayne Pugh began working at See's Candies as a dishwasher and, in thirty-two years, worked his way up the corporate ladder to become vice president and a member of the board of directors.[35] Over that time, he had been told "if you are loyal and do a good job, your future is secure," and he had received raises and promotions, until the day he was called into the president's office and fired. The court held that if "the totality of the parties' relationship" indicated an implied promise to terminate only for just cause, then the presumption of employment at will would be overcome; factors to be considered included "the personnel policies or practices of the employer, the employee's longevity of service, actions or communications by the employer reflecting assurances of continued employment, and the practices of the industry in which the employee is engaged." (While the case established an important precedent of termination only for cause, Pugh himself was not so lucky; at trial, the jury was persuaded that See's had cause for terminating him, including being disrespectful to superiors and subordinates, disloyal to the company, and uncooperative with other employees over a span of twenty years.[36])

Courts also looked to employment manuals for promises of continued employment. The drug company Hoffman-La Roche, Inc. had a personnel manual that described reasons for termination, including "layoff," "discharge due to performance," "disciplinary discharge," "retirement," and "resignation." Because the manual did not provide for discharge without cause, Richard Woolley had a claim when he was discharged without cause and without the company following the procedures outlined in the manual. "All that this opinion requires of an employer is that it be fair," the New Jersey Supreme Court concluded; if the company intended that the manual not be binding, it had to make that clear.[37]

Many companies took up the court's suggestion and rewrote their personnel manuals to maintain employment at will. The employment application at Sears, Roebuck was amended to make clear that the job "can be terminated with or without cause, and with or without notice, at any time," and most courts upheld the provision.[38] But some courts still focused on the reality of the agreement rather than the form of the writing. Mobil Coal Producing Co. had a disclaimer in its employment application similar to Sears's and a further disclaimer in the employee handbook that the handbook was "not an employment contract." The Wyoming Supreme Court disregarded the disclaimer in the application and concluded that the disclaimer in the handbook was inadequate because it was only included in the general welcoming section of the handbook, was not set off by a border and was not capitalized, and would be unclear to "persons untutored in contract law."[39]

Other courts held that even a terminable at will contract entailed an obligation of good faith that could limit the employer's power to fire an employee. When NCR terminated Orville Fortune, a salesman, shortly after he was credited with a $5 million order, in order to prevent him from obtaining the commission, the Massachusetts court held that the firing was in bad faith and Fortune was entitled to his commission.[40]

And some courts shifted from contract to tort law to give employees a remedy for wrongful discharge. One means was by allowing employees to sue when they were discharged in violation of public policy. Some public policies had a clear basis in the law: an employee could not be discharged for performing his civic duty of serving on a jury,[41] a bartender could not be fired for refusing to serve an intoxicated patron who was going to drive home,[42] and an employee who refused to give perjured testimony to a legislative committee was protected.[43] Other courts read the right more broadly, finding a public policy that prevented discharge when, for example, Catherine Wagenseller was fired from her job as a nurse for refusing, while on a canoe trip with her supervisor and others, to participate in a parody of the song "Moon River" that would have required her to "moon" the audience by exposing her buttocks.[44]

Another avenue was through the tort of intentional infliction of emotional distress. Roger Dionne, the manager of a Ground Round restaurant, summoned all the waitresses to a meeting, announced that "there was some stealing going on" but that he did not know who was responsible, and said that until the guilty party was found he would fire waitresses in alphabetical order.[45] The unfortunately named Debra Agis, the first fired, began to cry, was greatly upset, and suffered severe emotional distress from her arbitrary dismissal. Although her employment was terminable at will, it could not be terminated in a way that was so outrageous, and she had a claim for emotional distress.

Less Freedom of Contract

The conservative campaign to rewrite contract law places its faith in an idyllic vision of free and equal parties transacting in an open market. By strictly enforcing the apparent deals parties make, not looking beyond the four corners of a document that embodies an agreement, and not judging the fairness or reasonableness of a transaction, conservatives assert, courts will maximize individual freedom and the social good.

The history of contract law through the twentieth century gives the lie to the claim that the conservative vision can ever achieve its goals. For nearly a hundred years, critics and courts have demonstrated that the idea that freedom of contract is a basic principle that can give rise to a simple body of contract law is illusory. Contract law inevitably regulates economic transactions and must take account of complexity and inequality. The enactment of the conservative vision into law would not achieve the objective of increasing either individual freedom or social welfare. Instead, by magnifying the power of big businesses to impose one-sided relationships and removing those relationships from review by courts and the law, it would diminish the freedom and welfare of consumers and workers.

6

Property Rights and the Right's Property

A key part of the conservative effort to rewrite the common law is to transform property law into a roadblock that makes it cumbersome, expensive, or impossible for government to control land development, protect the environment, and rein in big business. The campaign was inspired by strange academic ideas about the absolute protection of private property and framed in the Reagan administration; Ronald Reagan himself was an early advocate of substituting "the law of supply and demand operating in the free market" for government protection of the environment.[1] Originally designed to thwart the enforcement of environmental laws and land development controls, it has expanded to a general attack on the ability of the federal government and the states to protect the public.

If this campaign achieves its objectives, America would be very different. The Clean Water Act, the Endangered Species Act, state smart-growth legislation, Superfund cleanup rules, historic preservation laws, and public-lands management all would be jeopardized. Housing developers could, on environmentally sensitive land, cut down all the trees, fill in all the wetlands, or build on oceanfront dunes because the government would be barred from requiring developers to preserve fragile parts of their land. Growth management to prevent suburban sprawl would be impossible, because government planning agencies would be unable to preserve open space or prevent the construction of tract housing. Government could not enact any rule preventing pollution, zoning strip clubs out of residential neighborhoods, or requiring workplace safety measures without paying every person who suffered the smallest economic loss because of the regulation. Indeed, government as we know it could hardly function at all—which is exactly the point.

Understanding and Misunderstanding Property

The conservative campaign to rewrite property law transforms a child's concept of property into a political ideology. Children have a simple understanding of property. Billy's favorite toy car is his property, and that's the whole story. He can pretend the car is a police car or a NASCAR racer, or he can leave it lying in the toy box. He can keep it, give it away, or trade it to his friend Sam for an action figure. Although he could not put it in those words, Billy's relationship to his toy is, as Sir William Blackstone, the eighteenth-century redactor of English law, stated it, "sole and despotic dominion . . . in total exclusion of the right of any other individual in the universe."[2]

As children grow up, they acquire a more sophisticated understanding of property. It doesn't take long; Billy quickly learns that sole and despotic dominion doesn't extend to leaving his car on the dining room floor or hitting his sister over the head with it. A regulatory authority—his parents—limits his ability to use his property.

That more sophisticated understanding is held by lawyers and legal scholars. Property ownership is never absolute. The government—the regulatory authority—defines what it means to own property by prescribing what an owner can and cannot do, and what others can and cannot do in relation to the owner. Billy's parents' house is their property. They can exclude others from entering, but not all others; even though they own the sidewalk, they cannot prevent pedestrians from using it. They can invite in whomever they like and hold Satanic rituals in the kitchen. But they cannot let garbage pile up on the lawn, or, if they live in a residentially zoned area, they cannot operate a slaughterhouse. They can plant marigolds in the garden but not marijuana.

In these and a thousand other ways, government properly restricts the use of property. But the Fifth and Fourteenth Amendments to the Constitution, and comparable provisions in state constitutions, define a limit: The government may not "take" property without "just compensation" to the owner. If the government wants to use the property itself, say to build a highway through the backyard, it can do so, but only by taking and paying for the property, through eminent domain. That seems fair; not only is government using the property, but it is taking the property away from the former owner. The same logic applies to what are known as "regulatory takings," government regulations that so restrict the use of the property that they are equivalent to taking it away from the owner. Suppose, for example, that to preserve open space, the city said that Billy's parents could not build any kind of structure on their land, temporary or permanent, and could not use it for any purpose other than admiring the scenery. Even though the city has not physically taken possession of the land, it has regulated the land's use so severely that the result is the same, and the city should have to pay for it.

This is all simple in concept, but the devil is in the details. Ordinarily, government does not have to pay for regulating the use of property, but when a regulation becomes too restrictive, it functions as a taking, and the government either has to remove the regulation or pay for the loss in value of the land. But how to determine when a regulation is too restrictive? In the *Penn Central* case in 1978, involving historic preservation regulations that protected New York City's Grand Central Station, the Supreme Court, in a rare moment of honesty reminiscent of Justice Potter Stewart's comment that obscenity defies definition but "I know it when I see it,"[3] recognized that drawing the line between permissible regulations and takings involves "essentially ad hoc, factual inquiries."[4] Like any other question of how much is too much, the boundary is fuzzy rather than firm.

The conservative attack on property law rejects almost everything serious that has been said about property law and the takings clause for at least a hundred years, and probably since the time of the framers, whom conservatives claim to revere. The attack rests on two points. First, property ownership *is* absolute. In the conservative vision, a property owner is like Billy clutching his favorite toy, throwing a tantrum when his parents try to make him put it away and go to bed. Property is a natural right, granted by God, John Locke, or Adam Smith, and includes every incident of property ownership, including the right to use, maximize economic value, sell, or pollute. Second, this understanding of absolute ownership is enshrined in the Constitution. *Any* government action that restricts the use or reduces the value of property in any way is a taking, and the owner must be compensated. Only very narrow exceptions exist to these rules, and the exceptions almost never include modern forms of government regulation.

Why take this extreme position? The conservatives call it the "property rights movement," protecting long-established rights of owners. But the "Right's property movement" is a better name, because it aims to advance the agenda of the Right in limiting the size and power of government at every level, especially limiting the power to prevent big business from having its way.

Here are some examples of what property rights advocates want. To protect the environmentally sensitive Norhouse Dunes in the Huron-Manistee

National Forest in Michigan's lower peninsula, the state Department of Natural Resources refused to permit oil companies to damage the lakefront dunes and marshes by drilling for oil. The oil companies claimed a taking of their mineral rights and won, requiring the state to pay more than $50 million to compensate them for their loss.[5]

A land development company acquired 250 acres on Long Beach Island, a barrier island at the New Jersey shore. After filling in wetlands and building houses on 199 acres, the company wanted to develop the rest of the tract. To protect the environmentally sensitive wetlands, the Army Corps of Engineers required the company to keep in its natural condition 12.5 of the remaining 51 acres on the 250-acre tract. The developer sued and the court, adopting a strategy argued by conservative advocates, focused only on the 12.5 acres, holding that the government had taken that property by depriving the developer of all economically beneficial use of it, even though the developer already had built on four-fifths of the tract.[6]

The City Council of Oakland, California determined that run-down motels and rooming houses were frequent venues for unsanitary and dangerous conditions, prostitution, drug use, and other illegal activity, so it enacted ordinances that required minimum standards of recordkeeping, security, housekeeping, and maintenance. A group of motel owners sued, claiming that requiring them to adhere to the standards constituted a taking, so the city would have to pay them for requiring that they keep up their property.[7]

In the wake of the *Exxon Valdez* oil spill in Prince William Sound, Alaska, Congress required that single-hull oil tankers either be retrofitted with double hulls to prevent future spills or be retired within twenty-five years. Tanker operators sued, claiming that even in the heavily regulated oil shipping industry, imposing such a requirement diminished the value of their tankers and constituted a taking.[8] In a related case, in a display of chutzpah that would make Alan Dershowitz blush, the owner of the *Valdez*, since delicately renamed the *Mediterranean*, argued that legislation that prevented the tanker from returning to the scene of the crime also constituted a taking.[9]

The ultimate ambition of the property rights movement is illustrated by the campaign for Measure 7, one of a mind-numbing twenty-six ballot measures in Oregon during the election of 2000. Conservative groups conducted a successful, low-visibility campaign for this amendment to the

Oregon constitution, which required the state or local government to pay compensation when a regulation restricts the use and reduces the value of real property to any degree. Until it was struck down by the Oregon Supreme Court on procedural grounds, the amendment mandated compensation to all affected landowners when a new zoning regulation prevented construction of a factory in a residential neighborhood or a restriction protected historically significant buildings, open space, or wildlife habitat, whether the reduction in property value was $1 or $1 million dollars, 1 percent of the value or 90 percent.[10]

Together, these and other elements of the Right's property movement add up to a wholesale attack on government regulation. The aim is clearest in the seminal scholarly work of the movement. In 1985 Richard Epstein, professor at the University of Chicago Law School, published *Takings: Private Property and the Power of Eminent Domain*, with financial support from William Simon and Irving Kristol's conservative foundation, the Institute for Educational Affairs.[11] Epstein's idiosyncratic views have been propounded in scores of articles and books that make him among the dozen most-cited legal scholars. He argues, for example, that labor laws are unwise and unconstitutional, that racial discrimination in employment can be cured through the workings of the market rather than through antidiscrimination laws, and that the entire body of federal regulations, which now numbers some two hundred volumes, could be reduced to the size of a single paperback that would fit in the glove compartment of a car.[12]

Takings proceeds from a simple assumption: The law reached a golden age around 1900, or maybe even 1800, and it has been all downhill ever since.[13] In the golden age, as Epstein imagines it, freedom of contract and property reigned supreme, and public regulation of the economy and public support for the disadvantaged—from Progressivism and the New Deal to Medicare and the minimum wage—were blessedly absent. As applied to takings and government regulation, this vision rests on the core assumptions that would be adopted by the Right's property movement: There is a single correct understanding of what it means to own private property, an understanding that is in effect always and everywhere, clear and unchanging, and, miraculously, that understanding is enshrined in the U.S. Constitution.

Epstein proclaims that there is a "natural and unique set of entitlements that are protected under a system of private property." What is contained in this set of entitlements? "My answer is the traditional one, that is, one gets the full bundle of rights, both in the physical domain (earth to sky) and all the standard incidents of ownership—possession, use, and disposition." Citing sources from Roman law to modern Supreme Court cases, Epstein asserts that there are "no gaps in the fabric of rights. For things reduced to ownership, the rules of property uniquely specify the rights of all persons for all times. The rights so specified are internally consistent." Disputes between neighbors, pollution cases, ownership of sites on the World Wide Web, and the validity of every action by every level of government, from local ordinances requiring homeowners to shovel snow off their sidewalks to Social Security and Medicare taxes, all can be resolved by deduction from general principles and ancient sources.[14]

Epstein's conception of property is embodied in his understanding of the takings clause of the Constitution. The ordinary usage of words such as "take" and "property" at the time they were written, buttressed by assumptions about the Lockean philosophy that motivated the framers and an inference about the structure of the Constitution as a whole, establishes broad restrictions on government action.[15] The courts can divine the clear understanding of those words in 1789, and their meaning has not changed over time. Any time the government infringes on the absolute rights of possession, use, or disposition of property, it has taken the property. "*All* regulations, *all* taxes, and *all* modifications of liability rules are takings of private property prima facie compensable by the state."[16] When the taking is an exercise of the "police power," the state's traditional ability to protect the health and safety of its citizens from harm, no compensation is required. But Epstein rejects the broad modern understanding of the police power in favor of allowing the state only the power that would otherwise be available to individual citizens in suits under the old common law, suits for force, fraud, or nuisance. All other takings require just compensation, either in cash or in kind.[17]

Inexorably, inevitably, his analysis of property and the Constitution leads Epstein to conclude that the twentieth century should be repealed. "The basic rules of private property are inconsistent with any form of welfare benefits." "Tax deductions . . . for charitable contributions . . . are generally prohibited." Indeed, "the case for progressive taxation is not 'uneasy.' It is wrong." "There is no real cost to reading the eminent domain clause as requiring the flat tax." "Is there any reliance interest that prevents the immediate invalidation of the minimum wage?" "Why then stop with the minimum wage? The National Labor Relations Act could be struck down." "It will be said that my position invalidates much of the twentieth-century legislation, and so it does. But does that make the position wrong in principle?"[18]

Stanford Law School professor Thomas Grey called Epstein's *Takings* "a travesty of constitutional scholarship" that "belongs with the output of the constitutional lunatic fringe, the effusions of gold bugs, tax protesters, and gun-toting survivalists."[19] Even Epstein's archconservative fellow traveler, defeated Supreme Court nominee Robert Bork, noted that Epstein's "conclusions are not plausibly related to the original understanding of the takings clause."[20] And Epstein's musings and their trumpeting by property rights advocates would be comic if they were not so threatening. Like reruns of *The Andy Griffith Show* on TV Land, they exhibit a pining for a simpler time, recreating a mythological age in which individual freedom reigned, the law was clear, and we were untroubled by annoyances such as Progressivism, postmodernism, and poverty. That such a time never existed, that property and freedom were never unconstrained, is not relevant to the fantasy any more than the realities of racial segregation and Appalachian destitution intruded on idyllic tele-Mayberry.

Rewriting the Law

Unfortunately, all of this is not harmless fantasy. The corruption of property law is part of the broad conservative campaign to reshape the common law, and it rests on the same foundations as the rewriting of contract and personal injury law. Individual ownership of property is all but absolute, infringing on the rights of ownership is a taking, and taking demands compensation. The rules are simple because they flow from principles that are self-evidently true, probably God-given, or at least obvious to anyone who thinks about social organization.

For a quarter century a movement has been afoot to enact this vision of property into law, through an aggressive campaign of public misinformation, litigation, and legislation that environmental activists Douglas Kendall and Charles Lord of Community Rights Counsel call "the takings proj-ect."[21] The campaign has been mounted by the ideologically committed and the economically self-interested, with ideological commitments often shaped by economic self-interest. Land developers, home builders, min-ing companies, right-wing foundations, and a network of litigation centers such as Defenders of Property Rights and the Pacific, Mountain States, and Washington Legal Foundations are key campaigners in the property rights movement.

Charles Fried, solicitor general in Reagan's second term, best summed up the ambition of the campaign. Fried was a scholar rather than a political activist, before and after his government service a professor at the Harvard Law School who specialized in moral and social philosophy. Nevertheless, Fried's notably conservative views and brilliance as a lawyer brought him to Washington, where he ably carried the administration's ball before the Supreme Court on such conservative staples as attacking affirmative action. But the takings issue presented Fried with "the most severe tests of loyalty, the incidents that tested not just character but judgment":

> Certainly economic liberty, deregulation and the fight against unprin-cipled, ad-hoc, sentimental redistributive adjudication in the federal courts were among the projects that had brought me to government and the administration in the first place. But Attorney General Meese and his young advisers—many drawn from the ranks of the then fledg-ling Federalist Societies and often devotees of the extreme libertarian views of Chicago law professor Richard Epstein—had a specific, aggres-sive, and, it seemed to me, quite radical project in mind: to use the Tak-ings Clause of the Fifth Amendment as a severe brake upon federal and state regulation of business and property. The grand plan was to make government pay compensation as for a taking of property every time its regulations impinged too severely on a property right—limiting the possible uses for a parcel of land or restricting or tying up a business in regulatory tape. If the government labored under so severe an obliga-tion, there would be, to say the least, much less regulation.[22]

The Right has mounted a three-pronged attack in using its expanded definition of the takings clause to end government regulation. First, increase the red tape required before an agency can promulgate a rule or take another action that might affect property owners. Second, make it easier to challenge actions of all levels of government in the federal courts that have been newly stocked with conservative judges. Third, require compensation in a far broader range of cases than ever has been contemplated before.

The first element of the attack is to prevent government officials from regulating land development and other business activities by making the process of issuing regulations more cumbersome. In 1988, Ronald Reagan issued Executive Order 12,630, still in force, which requires agencies to evaluate every proposed rule to determine that no unnecessary infringement of property rights would occur that could subject the government to takings claims, and to evaluate the risk of takings judgments and their potential cost to the government. Since the issuance of EO 12,630, the states have picked up the ball. Under prodding from property rights groups, more than a dozen states have enacted statutes that require "takings impact assessment" requirements of the kind first prescribed in the Executive Order.[23]

The aim of the broadest takings impact assessment requirements is to hamper the government's ability to regulate in two ways. First, although advocates call them "look before you leap" measures, opponents correctly characterize them as "red tape" requirements. Before adopting a rule or policy, an agency is required to engage in detailed fact-finding about the effect of the rule on businesses and individuals, whether that effect would constitute a taking, and how much compensation might be required. This is cumbersome, complex, and the opposite of what rule making usually is—the adoption of rules of general application to large groups, considering their costs and benefits as a whole. If rule making is more difficult, fewer rules will be made. Second, the assessment requirement is not restricted to takings as they have been defined by the courts. Instead, the requirements define a scope for takings beyond what any court has considered, requiring agencies to consider as takings actions that affect the value of property, even if they only affect its value temporarily or only affect some interest in the property. Many government actions—almost any government actions—can be considered takings by that standard.

Although trumpeted as a major shift in regulation, the effect of impact assessment has been more symbolic than real. In the federal government, even under guidelines issued by Reagan's own attorney general and not amended since, many government actions are excluded from its ambit, such as actions of the Environmental Protection Agency enforcing the environmental laws. In the absence of aggressive monitoring by its advocates in the administration, and with no private means of enforcing it, Executive Order 12,630 is routinely satisfied by formulaic expressions that proposed rules do not raise takings implications or do not require a takings impact analysis. In 2003, property rights advocates attempted to resuscitate the mechanism, leading to a Congressional hearing, but no changes were made.[24]

The effects of state legislation have mostly been symbolic, too. The statutes, proposed with enthusiasm, have been enacted and applied with limitations that undercut their real ability to hamper the government. Many of the statutes only require an informal assessment of the takings effect of a proposed action; others do not specify what is to happen to the assessment, and rarely do they provide for any kind of public notice or judicial review.

The second means of undercutting regulation is to provide for more extensive judicial review before sympathetic courts. Several procedurally complex but potentially far-reaching bills have been promoted in recent Congresses. The titles of the bills, none of which has been enacted, are framed in innocuous terms: The Private Property Rights Implementation Act and the Citizens Access to Justice Act, for example.[25] While the details of the bills raise the kind of technicalities only a lawyer could love, their purpose can be summed up in the least technical of language: a shift of power from state and local government to the federal courts, especially the most conservative courts, the relatively obscure Court of Federal Claims and Court of Appeals for the Federal Circuit. (The National Association of Homebuilders and proponent of some of the bills said the legislation would be "a hammer to the head" of state and local government.[26]) This purpose is inconsistent with widely held beliefs about federalism and separation of powers, which are usually espoused by conservative Republicans, under which courts do not intervene until the other branches of government have had a chance to do their work, and federal courts do not intervene in state affairs until the state law has been finally decided and applied.

These proposed statutes would make two dramatic changes in federal law. The first change would allow takings advocates to bypass state and local administrative procedures and state courts to pursue their claims in federal court. The Supreme Court has long held (and in a 2001 takings case, reaffirmed) that a landowner asserting a takings claim can resort to federal court only after the state has made a final decision on the matter, denying the landowner compensation.[27] The statutes would change this situation, permitting landowners to invoke the power of federal courts even when state agencies were still considering the matter. In a typical case, this would remove the local or state government as primary decision maker in land use matters, substituting the federal court; zoning decisions would be made in federal courts, not town halls. It also would hugely increase the potential litigation costs of underfunded local governments, placing tremendous pressure on them to settle with developers to avoid the litigation. Given this, virtually every organization representing local and state government, such as the National Association of Counties, National Conference of State Legislatures, National League of Cities, and the U.S. Conference of Mayors has joined environmental groups in opposing these measures.

The second change advocated by conservatives would expand the jurisdiction of specialized federal courts. The Court of Federal Claims and the Court of Appeals for the Federal Circuit are, unlike the U.S. District Courts and circuit Courts of Appeals, wholly creatures of Congress. They have more limited authority, and their judges do not have life tenure and the degree of insulation from political influence that goes with it. Traditionally, only the district and circuit courts have had the authority to review the actions of federal agencies and to invalidate those actions where they exceed statutory or constitutional grounds; the claims court's authority has been limited to awarding money damages against the government. The takings statutes would expand that court's jurisdiction, allowing it to review agency actions and issue injunctions, as well.

The shift in jurisdiction has a broader purpose than giving law school teachers of civil procedure something to talk about. The claims court and federal circuit court were reconstituted during the Reagan era and have become the home for activism in favor of expanded takings law. The claims court hears suits for damages against the United States, including suits asserting regulatory takings. As Clint Bolick, director of the conservative Institute for Justice, commented, liberals were "asleep at the switch and the [Reagan and Bush] Administrations [were] extremely sophisticated in their selection and placement of judges on the court." As a result, the court was packed with judges such as Loren Smith, counsel to Reagan's presidential campaigns and a vocal supporter of the Right's property movement. Among his other activities, Smith contributed an introduction to a property rights tract coauthored by property rights advocate Nancie Marzulla and published by the conservative National Legal Center for the Public Interest, and he has been a frequent speaker at Federalist Society gatherings. The Court of Appeals for the Federal Circuit is best known for its role in developing patent law, but as the appellate court in claims cases, it has a significant role in takings jurisprudence, too. Many of its judges are patent specialists, but its takings expert has been S. Jay Plager, a Federalist Society member and former head of the Reagan administration's Task Force on Regulatory Relief, which was designed to provide industry with relief from the burden of onerous government regulations.[28] More recently, President George W. Bush's appointments to the Court of Federal Claims include Lawrence J. Block, who worked on property rights and tort reform legislation as counsel to the Senate Judiciary Committee; Victor J. Wolski, a former attorney with the Pacific Legal Foundation, a property rights litigation center; and George W. Miller, formerly a member of the Defenders of Property Rights advisory board.[29]

Putting procedural roadblocks in the path of government officials adds red tape and expense to the regulatory process and may discourage it, but the Right's goal of gumming up the works of government can best be achieved by the third prong of its strategy: broadening what constitutes a taking. If any government action that affects property—a development plan that limits suburban sprawl, a prohibition on building on beachfront dunes, or protection of an endangered species—is potentially a taking, either the government must halt the action or it must compensate the affected property owner. Because governments have been financially strapped for a generation as a result of the Reagan-Bush tax-cutting mania, most will be unable to afford to pay compensation and will have to abandon regulation instead. Property rights advocates have pursued this goal in Congress, in the state legislatures, and, most prominently, in the courts. Their ability to achieve the goal depends on their success in peddling the two core ideas of the Right's property movement: property rights are virtually absolute, and absolute property rights are enshrined in the Constitution.

The *Penn Central* case in 1978 was the leading modern takings decision in the Supreme Court until the Court's recent conservative transformation.[30] The majority opinion by Justice William Brennan summarized the law as it had developed for a century, and the dissent by then associate justice William Rehnquist drew the roadmap for the expansion of takings. Under New York City's historic preservation law, the Landmarks Preservation Commission designated Grand Central Station, owned by Penn Central, as a landmark and rejected Penn Central's plans to construct a mammoth office building atop the architecturally significant station. "To balance a 55-story office tower above a flamboyant Beaux-Arts façade seems nothing more than an aesthetic joke," the Commission concluded.[31] Instead of appealing the Commission's decision as provided in the preservation law, Penn Central sued, claiming that the rejection constituted a taking without just compensation.

Justice Brennan's majority opinion recognized the balancing inherent in property law. "This Court, quite simply, has been unable to develop any 'set formula' for determining when 'justice and fairness' require that economic injuries caused by public action be compensated by the government." Resolutions depended on the particular circumstances in each case and were "essentially ad hoc, factual inquiries." In reaching that resolution, the Court balanced the harm to Penn Central and the character of the Commission's action, giving deference to the commission's view of what would promote "the health, safety, morals, or general welfare."[32] In the case of Grand Central Station, the Court concluded that the benefits of the historic preservation scheme and Penn Central's ability to continue to use the terminal for other purposes did not yield a taking.

Justice Rehnquist dissented and articulated a stark vision of property that would be adopted by the property rights movement. For him, property ownership was an absolute, consisting of "every sort of interest," including "the right to possess, use and dispose of it." Penn Central's right of ownership had been invaded in two ways. Penn Central's inability to erect an office tower on top of the existing terminal took away its "air rights" (in an old phrase, the right to build "up to heaven"), and invasion of any piece of the right of ownership constituted a taking. Moreover, the designation of the terminal as a historical landmark imposed an obligation on Penn Central to maintain the façade in good repair, limiting its power to change the building or allow it to decay, a power that it otherwise would have as owner.

Justice Rehnquist recognized, as he had to in light of a chain of precedents, that not every government action is a taking. As in a 1915 case, a city could prohibit the operation of a brickyard in a residential neighborhood. Every landowner in a residential neighborhood benefits from the restriction and, more important, the restriction is one that prevents harm to others. But such instances, he argued, were exceptional, and limited either to cases of mutual advantage or to a historically defined class of cases in which the state regulation was preventing harm and protecting the public health and safety by preventing a nuisance. In Penn Central's case, though, the city was not protecting public health or safety but only preserving the design of the building for "sightseeing New Yorkers and tourists."[33]

Justice Rehnquist's opinion contains the core of the property rights movement's campaign to render takings law an effective bar to government regulation. Property law is an absolute, defined to include all of the potential incidents of ownership. When any one of those incidents, such as air rights, is limited, a taking has occurred and just compensation is required. The only significant exceptions are defined historically, by the common law of nuisance, to prevent actual injury to others. And for Rehnquist the takings question does not require balancing and ad hoc inquiries, but flows from the definitions of "property," "taken," and "compensation"; what Justice Brennan's opinion treats as fuzzy standards—factors to be considered and interests to be weighed—Rehnquist treats as clear, fixed rules.

Takings in the States

The property rights movement has followed the Rehnquist roadmap in the legislatures and in the courts. Takings compensation statutes in a number of states define what constitutes a taking more clearly and more severely than the courts do, and thereby attempt to increase the costs of government regulation by making many more regulations subject to a compensation requirement.[34] The statutes set a threshold above which any reduction in value of property is automatically a taking: 20 percent of the property's value in Louisiana, 25 percent in Texas, 40 percent in Mississippi, and an "inordinate burden" on the property in Florida.

The Florida and Texas compensation statutes are the most notable. Florida has had a strong property rights movement since the 1970s, with numerous commissions and proposals. In 1994, the movement mounted a petition drive to amend the Florida Constitution so that any government action that diminished the value of property would entitle the owner to compensation determined by a jury without requiring him to resort to administrative remedies. The conservative Florida Legal Foundation was a prime mover behind the $3 million petition drive, supported by corporations that owned huge amounts of land subject to environmental and development regulation, including the St. Joe Paper Company and the U.S. Sugar Corporation. The Florida Supreme Court struck down the proposed amendment because it did not meet constitutional requirements.[35]

The movement in Florida gained renewed power after the 1994 elections, in which Democrat Lawton Chiles barely defeated Jeb Bush (while brother George W. was winning election as governor of Texas) and the Republicans gained control of the Senate for the first time since Reconstruction. The Florida Legal Foundation and large corporations were joined in pushing for legislation by farmers and developers who were increasingly subject to regulations designed to protect wetlands and the oceanfront. In an attempt to forestall more radical measures, Governor Chiles convened a working group to develop a compromise proposal. The group's proposal was eventually enacted, with one last-minute addition written by lobbyist Wade Hopping for large landowners and big businesses. Instead of protecting "existing uses" of property, the statute provided compensation measured against "reasonable, foreseeable, nonspeculative" uses of land, a major change that dramatically increased the compensation available to owners.[36]

The Florida statute has chilled the adoption of some new environmental protections. Palm Beach County, for example, halted its plan to limit development of a 20,000-acre agricultural reserve near the Everglades, fearing a wave of litigation under the statute. Dade County officials refrained from extending the Ocean Beach Historic District to prevent the construction of a thirty-story condominium, under threats from the developer's attorney.

Texas, too, has had a longstanding, active property rights movement. In 1995, Governor George W. Bush signed legislation under which a landowner is entitled to compensation when a governmental action reduces the value of the owner's property by 25 percent or more. This strict standard allows property rights advocates to trumpet the statute as a model. As elsewhere, though, without a public reporting requirement for agencies or reported cases applying the statute, its effects are hard to measure. The statute itself contains many exclusions, leaving outside its scope actions taken to fulfill an obligation mandated by state or federal law such as environmental and coastal zone protections, regulation of nuisances, and a variety of special-interest exceptions such as certain rules about water safety, hunting, fishing, and protecting oil and gas resources and groundwater.

Despite the Right's claims to populism and protecting the small farmer and individual landowner, until the 2000 election, every takings provisions put to the voters had been rejected. Rhode Island voters adopted a constitutional amendment in 1986 that limits the application of takings law to prevent environmental regulation. The Washington legislature was one of the first to adopt legislation pushed by the property rights movement, enacting a takings impact assessment law in 1991 and a compensation statute in 1994, but environmentalists quickly amassed 231,000 signatures to put the issue to a referendum. Although the statute's supporters spent twice as much as its opponents, the referendum defeated the statute by a 60–40 margin. The key to the victory was the predicted expense of the measure. One study estimated its cost to the state at $11 billion, with municipalities having either to spend 10 percent of their budgets compensating landowners or to abandon land use regulations. "The thought of hard-earned taxpayer money going right into the coffers of shopping-mall developers really galled people," said Ed Zuckerman of the Washington Environmental PAC. Following the 1992 enactment of a takings law in Arizona, environmentalists gathered 71,000 signatures to put the measure to a public vote. Takings advocates raised a $600,000 war chest from real estate brokers, developers, cattle ranchers, and the mining industry, again outspending environmentalists two to one, but grassroots support for environmental protection led to the defeat of the takings measure.[37]

Oregon's Measure 7 is the most extreme version of a compensation provision.[38] An amendment to the Oregon constitution adopted in 2000 and struck down by the state supreme court on procedural grounds in 2002,[39] Measure 7 would have required the payment of compensation whenever the state or local government adopted a regulation that restricted the use and thereby reduced the value of real property to any degree. Thus, a new zoning regulation that prevented the construction of a factory in a residential neighborhood, or a restriction to protect historically significant buildings, open space, or wildlife habitat would have required payment to the affected landowner, whether the reduction in value was one dollar or one million dollars, 1 percent of the value or 90 percent. Oregon attorney general Hardy Myers's opinion about the scope of the bill ruled that grocery stores that had to accept returns of recyclable bottles under the state's Bottle Bill would have a takings claim, because they had to set aside part of their store property for the storage of the bottles. A municipality could require the owner of a store or office building to provide parking spaces only by paying for the requirement. Ditto restrictions on building height to protect scenic views of Mount Hood, or a ban on the construction of cell phone transmission towers. Even the measure's sponsors admitted that it would cost the state and municipalities $5.4 billion a year.

In the November 2000 election, Measure 7, one of a stupefying twenty-six initiatives on the Oregon ballot, passed by a 53 to 47 percent margin. How did such a measure pass in tree-hugging Oregon, a state devoted to protecting salmon, wilderness, and bike trails? "This definitely slipped in under the radar," according to Randy Tucker of 1000 Friends of Oregon, a citizens' organization promoting land use planning. Opponents of the measure, from the Sierra Club and the American Farmland Trust to Democratic governor John Kitzhaber, only engaged in a last-minute publicity blitz during the final week of the campaign, when polls showed a slim margin of voters favoring the measure.

The primary sponsors of Measure 7 were two conservative activist groups, Oregon Taxpayers United (OTU) and Oregonians in Action. Oregon Taxpayers United is the project of conservative tax activist and radio host Bill Sizemore. Sizemore also runs a company that promotes ballot measures for OTU and others, for a fee; aside from Measure 7, their proposals in 2000 included provisions to allow unlimited deductions for federal income taxes on state returns (thereby cutting the state's tax revenues by a billion dollars a year) and to limit union payroll deductions. After the supreme court invalidated Measure 7, its sponsors drafted a new version, Initiative 36, slated for the November 2004 ballot, which would require payment to property owners when a land use regulation restricts the use of property or reduces its value, again to any extent or in any amount.

Takings in the Courts

The legislative record of the property rights movement is mixed. When put to the voters in a visible and understandable way, takings compensation proposals are almost always rejected. Even in the legislatures and executive branch, the to-and-fro of interests and the practical accommodation to the work of government produces statutes or enforcement that are less sweeping than their advocates would like. These problems could be solved by making absolute property rights a constitutional requirement, so the movement has engaged in aggressive litigation campaigns to achieve that goal.

With the conservative wing of the Supreme Court bolstered when Clarence Thomas replaced Thurgood Marshall, in 1992 the new majority of the Court followed the Rehnquist roadmap and issued its major takings decision of the new conservative era, *Lucas v. South Carolina Coastal Council*.[40] David Lucas was a contractor, manager, and part owner of the Wild Dunes Development on the Isle of Palms in Charleston County, South Carolina. When the development was mostly finished, he purchased two of the four remaining lots for his own account. Lucas's oceanfront land had been variously part of the beach, on the dunes, or under water during the previous forty years, although at the time of litigation it was on dry land. To protect the beach from erosion, to maintain the natural dune barriers that provide storm breaks, and to prevent beachfront homes from damaging inland property when swept away in storms, the state prohibited construction on tidal areas such as Lucas's. Lucas sued, claiming that the regulation constituted a taking. The South Carolina Supreme Court held that the state had the power to protect its public resources in this way, under a line of Supreme Court authority through *Penn Central* mandating deference to the legislative judgment of the public need and the reasonable exercise of the police power.

In the U.S. Supreme Court, the case attracted enormous attention. Briefs in support of Lucas were filed by U.S. solicitor general Kenneth Starr, the American Farm Bureau Federation, the American Mining Congress, the U.S. Chamber of Commerce, Defenders of Property Rights, the Pacific Legal Foundation, and other property rights warriors. The attorneys general of more than half the states, the American Planning Association, the National Trust for Historic Preservation, the Sierra Club, and the U.S. Conference of Mayors lined up behind South Carolina.

In an opinion by Justice Scalia, a majority of the Court held that South Carolina's coastal zone management plan had taken Lucas's property. The core of the opinion was the finding that the state's action had denied the developer "all economically beneficial or productive use of the land," and that denial constituted a taking. The ruling was a major departure and conservative victory for three reasons.

First, it rested on the reinstatement of the concept that ownership was absolute, a concept that had long been abandoned until it was revived by Professor Epstein and Justice Rehnquist. Lucas was not barred from all use of his land, only from building houses on it. But denying that one element of the bundle of rights of ownership was sufficient to be a taking, especially because under the economically oriented conservative approach, making a profit is the primary value of property.

The reinstatement of absolute ownership is especially striking in comparing *Lucas* to *Andrus v. Allard*, a pre-Scalia/Thomas decision.[41] To protect eagles and other endangered birds, federal statutes prohibited the purchase or sale of their feathers and of products made with them. Allard and others involved in the merchandising of Indian artifacts sued, claiming that the statutes caused a taking. Although the statute had extinguished the right to buy or sell, which are the key elements of maximizing value through ownership, the Court found no taking. "Government regulation—by definition —involves the adjustment of rights for the public good. Often this adjustment curtails some potential for the use of economic exploitation of private property. To require compensation in all such circumstances would effectively compel the government to regulate by purchase."[42] In *Andrus*, although the statute had rendered the artifacts almost worthless, it had not extinguished all of the rights of ownership. The owners still could look at the artifacts, give them away, or put them on display; in contrast to *Lucas*, the fact that their economic value may have been destroyed did not give rise to a taking.

Second, the *Lucas* court gave short shrift to the state's interest in protecting the coast. The police power—the government's traditional power to protect the public health, safety, and welfare—could only prevent a taking in the tautological situation in which the property owner did not have a right to do what it proposed to do anyway. "Any limitation so severe cannot be newly legislated or decreed (without compensation), but must inhere in the title itself, in the State's law of property and nuisance already in place upon landownership."[43] In short, the law of property and nuisance was frozen at some point in the hypothetical past, and any attempt to impose new regulation, especially in the interests of environmental protection, would be invalid.

Third, the result was stated as a "categorical rule." The traditional posture, expressed in every case through *Penn Central,* required that the owner's interest be balanced against the state's interest. No more; following then-justice Rehnquist's suggestion, Justice Scalia substituted a rule for the traditional case-by-case adjudication. Where there was a denial of the economically productive use of the land, there was a taking, with no need to consider the state's interest.[44]

As with most important constitutional decisions, the reaction to *Lucas* was mixed. A disappointed Richard Epstein, who had coauthored a brief in support of Lucas, criticized the justices for being "afraid to face the broad implications of the Takings Clause ... [that would] bring many more forms of land use regulation within the Takings Clause, where they could receive the close scrutiny and swift dispatch most of them so richly deserve."[45] Glenn Sugameli of the environmental group the National Wildlife Federation optimistically read the case as limited to the situation in which "land use statutes or regulations ... deny *all* economically beneficial or productive use of an *entire* parcel of land."[46] The best prediction may have come from Daniel Popeo and Paul Kamenar of the Washington Legal Foundation, also participants in the case: "While the *Lucas* decision may not be everything hoped for, the tide is clearly turning toward the judicial protection of property rights. If the government continues to enact and enforce confiscatory land-use controls, that tide will most surely bring a flood of new litigation."[47]

That prediction turned out to be too modest; a tsunami of litigation by the Right's property movement has followed *Lucas.* The strategy was suggested by Justice Rehnquist in *Penn Central* and refined by Justice Scalia in *Lucas,* and it has been pushed aggressively by advocates and judges since: establish a vision of absolute ownership, limit the state legislature's sphere for infringing ownership, and cast the resulting doctrine in hard-to-avoid rules.

The Supreme Court's own response to this litigation has been ambivalent. The three most conservative justices (Rehnquist, Scalia, and Thomas) have only occasionally been able to enlist their less-extreme colleagues (particularly O'Connor and Kennedy) in the cause. Results in other courts have been mixed, too, with the specialized federal courts being the most congenial to property rights arguments. Nevertheless, the property rights movement has continued in case after case to pursue the Rehnquist-Scalia roadmap. If the Army Corps of Engineers required a developer to preserve 5 percent of its tract as fragile wetlands, that 5 percent had been taken and had to be paid for. If the Tahoe Regional Planning Agency imposed a temporary moratorium on development to allow time to develop a comprehensive environmental and development plan, landowners could claim that the months during which they could not build were taken from them, requiring compensation. Under the conservative view, these cases are not issues of policy to be fairly debated with the public benefits and private burdens balanced. Instead, they can be easily decided by the deductive application of ineluctable rules, flowing from the definition of property itself.

The Right's strategy has been most successful in the Court of Federal Claims and the Court of Appeals for the Federal Circuit, which hear claims against the federal government and are heavily populated with property-rights-friendly judges. Under the Clean Water Act, the Army Corps of Engineers has authority to issue permits for development projects on wetlands. In a series of cases, these courts used takings rules to limit the Corps' ability to stop development that would harm the environment.

The easiest way to convert a partial taking into a total taking is to change the amount of property considered as part of the taking—the so-called "denominator problem." Suppose that a developer has a 100-acre parcel to develop, and the Corps, to protect wetlands, requires the developer to leave 10 acres untouched. Looking at the entire parcel, the requirement has taken 10 percent of it (10/100). But if the court looks only at the land subject to the restriction, the denominator changes (10/10), and the partial taking magically becomes a total taking.

The *Penn Central* court expressly rejected this trick. The Court refused to consider the air rights over Grand Central station separately, instead looking at all the uses to which Penn Central's land might be put, including its current use as a railroad station. In *Lucas* the denominator issue was not relevant, because South Carolina had prevented development on all of Lucas's land. Many courts have been unreceptive to this approach, but the specialized federal courts have seized on this device as a means of expanding categorical takings.

An early case involved a development on Long Beach Island, a barrier island at the New Jersey shore known for its upscale summer homes and limited commercial development.[48] Loveladies Harbor, Inc. acquired 250 acres of undeveloped, virgin wetlands. Over time, it dredged and filled 199 acres and constructed 375 houses. The corporation proposed to fill in the remaining 51 acres, which were all wetlands or shorefront tidelands, to build another 108 houses. The Corps of Engineers and state regulators rejected the proposal and suggested instead that Loveladies fill in 12.5 acres, enough to build 35 houses, and leave the remainder undeveloped. After initially rejecting the compromise and litigating, Loveladies eventually accepted it, but the Corps and the state finally concluded that development should not proceed. Loveladies challenged the denial of a permit under the Clean Water Act, but the courts ruled that the permit had properly been denied. The corporation then went to the Court of Claims, asserting that the permit denial had taken its land.

Under the new law of *Lucas*, (but not under *Andrus* or *Penn Central*) the permit denial could be seen as a denial of all economically beneficial use. Whether it constituted a total taking depended on the denominator. Ultimately, Loveladies was denied permission to develop 12.5 acres, but what was the relevant fraction: 12.5/12.5, 12.5/51, or 12.5/250? If the first, the Corps action was a total taking; if the last, likely there was no taking at all; if the middle, it would be a question of degree.

At trial in the claims court, Judge Loren Smith focused on the 12.5 acres, found that its value had been diminished by 99 percent, and awarded Loveladies $2,658,000. After the trial had occurred, the Supreme Court decided *Lucas*, so the appeal in the Federal Circuit attracted considerable attention. The National Association of Home Builders, the Pacific Legal Foundation, and the Washington Legal Foundation filed briefs in support of the developer, and the Environmental Defense Fund supported the Corps. Judge Plager—like Judge Smith, his court's most fervent property rights advocate—wrote an opinion for the court finding a total taking. The discussion of the denominator issue was minimal. The opinion purports to rely on the trial court opinion, but that opinion had not considered the issue. Plager simply concludes that the parcel regulated is the only relevant parcel; the corporation's ownership and development of the other 199 acres over the preceding years was simply not pertinent. By narrowly focusing the issue, the court dramatically expands *Lucas*'s categorical rule.

In the *Loveladies* case, the government warned that the court's approach creates the opportunity for strategic behavior by developers: buy a large parcel, develop most of it, and claim a taking when the government bars development on the remaining slice of environmentally fragile land. The government's prediction has been realized. In *Palm Beach Isles Associates v. United States*, a developer originally purchased a 311-acre tract, sold 261 acres, then claimed that the denial of a permit to fill in 49 submerged acres of the remaining 50 constituted a taking. The developer argued, and Judge Plager again agreed, that the denominator was the portion of the parcel regulated, rather than the entire parcel originally owned.[49] In another case, which was decided on procedural grounds, the Boise Cascade Corporation owned a 1,770-acre tract of commercial timberland in Oregon. Several pairs of spotted owls (an endangered species) were seen nesting on the land, and the Oregon forestry department required that a 70-acre area be maintained to preserve the nesting sites. Boise Cascade sold 1,706 acres from the tract and subsequently sued, making a takings claims, with the support of the Pacific Legal Foundation.[50] By preventing it from logging on the 64 remaining acres, the company argued, Oregon was taking its property, even though the 64 acres were part of the original, much larger tract.

If parcels of land can be split into ever smaller pieces by size to invoke the categorical rule, what about splitting them up by time? Advocates developed the theory that since an owner has the absolute right to use land at any time for any purpose, if the government prevents any use for a period of time, that is a taking, even if it later allows the use. The theory was tried in 2002 in *Tahoe-Sierra Preservation Council, Inc. v. Tahoe Regional Planning Agency*, but the Supreme Court balked.[51]

Lake Tahoe was described by Mark Twain as a "noble sheet of blue water,"[52] but its crystalline clarity was threatened by overdevelopment. In response, California and Nevada created the Tahoe Regional Planning Agency to regulate development and preserve the environmental qualities that make the lake such a popular vacation spot. The Agency imposed a moratorium on development while it was creating a plan for the lake, a moratorium that eventually extended for thirty-two months, and, by court injunction, for more than an additional two years. The Tahoe-Sierra Preservation Council, a group of landowners, sued, challenging both the moratorium and the resulting plan.

Tahoe-Sierra was an opportunity by property rights advocates to grab for the brass ring in the Supreme Court, an opportunity that ultimately backfired. The Preservation Council was represented in the Supreme Court by leading property rights lawyers Michael Berger and Gideon Kanner and were supported by briefs from the National Association of Home Builders, Defenders of Property Rights, the Washington Legal Foundation, and the American Farm Bureau Federation. On the other side, amicus curiae briefs were filed in support of the planning agency by the National League of Cities, the National Governors Association, the Sierra Club, the Natural Resources Defense Council, the National Audubon Society, and twenty-one states. In something of a surprise, Solicitor General Theodore Olson, formerly a board member at Defenders of Property Rights, argued in support of the Agency. The question posed for the Court was the purest, most extreme issue for property rights advocates: whether the moratorium was per se a taking —whether a delay in development automatically required the agency to compensate landowners, without considering either the need for the moratorium to protect the lake during the planning process or the actual injury that it might have caused the landowners. A ruling that the moratorium automatically equated to a taking would have been dramatic. It would have wrecked planning processes across the country, potentially making it too expensive for cities, states, and regional agencies to engage in careful planning. Even more broadly, it would have solved the denominator problem in a spectacular way. If a property could be sliced in time for takings purposes, it also could be sliced by geography, as in *Loveladies Harbor, Inc.,* and by legal interest, effectively overruling *Penn Central*'s refusal to consider air rights separately from the rest of the rights of ownership.

The Court refused to go this far. In an opinion by Justice Stevens, the Court reaffirmed its view in *Penn Central* that the denominator question is to be resolved by looking at the property as a whole. "An interest in real property is defined by the metes and bounds that describe its geographic dimensions and the term of years that describes the temporal aspect of the owner's interest."[53] Accordingly, the Court would not look at thirty-two months of use as a right distinct from the ability to use the land before and after, and it suggested, but did not hold, that it would regard with similar disfavor attempts to divide parcels as the *Loveladies* and *Palm Beach Isles* courts had done.

Justices Rehnquist, Scalia, and Thomas dissented, arguing that *Lucas* and not *Penn Central* controlled. The landowners had been totally deprived of the right to develop their land, as had David Lucas. It did not matter that the deprivation here was temporary, rather than permanent. Under an absolute view of property, any deprivation was a taking.

The Court also thwarted, at least for the moment, one of the major conservative campaigns concerning Interest on Lawyers Trust Accounts (IOLTA). Federal and state funding for legal services for the poor and other public interest activities has declined in recent decades, in part because of direct conservative attacks and in part because of tax cuts putting pressure on state and federal budgets. To make up the shortfall, every state adopted an IOLTA program. Lawyers who hold small amounts of client funds are required to deposit the funds in special IOLTA trust accounts. Ordinarily the amounts and the time periods are so small—a few hundred or a few thousand dollars held for days or weeks—that they would not generate any interest for the client. In the aggregate, though, the funds of all of a lawyer's clients can add up, and the interest in the account is accumulated and paid to an agency that distributes it to legal services and other nonprofit organizations.

Conservatives mounted an attack on IOLTA programs, ostensibly because paying interest to the state agency rather than to the client was a taking of the client's property. The effect of invalidating the programs, however, would not have been to benefit clients, because the amounts involved are so small that banks would not pay them as interest, or would assess transaction fees that exceed the amounts earned. Instead, the principal effect would have been to starve legal services programs, preventing poor people from getting lawyers and diminishing the threat of class actions against landlords, predatory lenders, and other businesses that exploit the unrepresented. The Washington Legal Foundation was a named plaintiff in one leading case, and Defenders of Property Rights, the Pacific Legal Foundation, the Mountain States Legal Foundation, the National Right to Work Foundation, and the National Association of Home Builders supported the cause with amicus briefs. Recognizing the threat to legal services, the Conference of Chief Justices, the American Bar Association, the Council of State Governments, and forty-nine state bar associations opposed the campaign.

In *Phillips v. Washington Legal Foundation*, the Court held that the interest generated in IOLTA accounts was the property of the clients.[54] In *Brown v. Legal Foundation of Washington*, however, the Court held that even if the interest is "taken," no compensation is required.[55] Because the bank would not have paid any interest to the client on the small amounts in the IOLTA account, the client has suffered no loss. "Just compensation" is measured by what the client lost, not by what the IOLTA agency gained. Otherwise, as the majority notes, the result would be the absurdity proposed by Justice Scalia in dissent: The client should receive $.55 interest on a two-day deposit even if the payment would be subject to a $2 transaction charge.

Although *Brown* was a defeat for the property rights movement, it represents a new breed of takings cases that advocates have pressed with increasing fervor. Traditionally, takings cases concerned government regulation of land. In the past few years, advocates have attempted to expand the doctrine to cover anything that can be described as a property interest, whether it involves real property or not.

In *Rose Acre Farms, Inc. v. United States*, a 2003 decision of the Court of Federal Claims, the property was chicken and eggs.[56] Rose Acre is one of the three largest egg producers in the country. In 1990, the U.S. Department of Agriculture (USDA) established emergency regulations to try to control the increasingly frequent salmonella outbreaks attributed to contaminated eggs. Three outbreaks were attributed to Rose Acre's eggs. On August 11, forty-two guests became ill at a wedding party in Versailles, Kentucky, when they ate eggs benedict with hollandaise sauce. On September 30, four hundred people became ill from salmonella-infected bread pudding at a True Value Hardware convention at the Hyatt Regency hotel in Chicago. Finally, on October 25, seven people in Tennessee became ill when they consumed banana pudding with meringue. In each case, health officials traced the infected eggs to one of Rose Acre's farms.

All aspects of salmonella infection in eggs are still not completely understood, but the USDA logically believed that the presence of salmonella in the hen houses or the chickens themselves indicated an increased likelihood that the chickens would produce contaminated eggs. When each of the outbreaks occurred, the hen houses at the Rose Acre farms were tested and found to contain salmonella. The inspectors also removed 6,741 hens for testing, and 2 percent of them tested positive for salmonella. As a result, Rose Acre was required to clean and decontaminate its hen houses. Until the process was completed, Rose Acre was barred from selling its eggs for fresh consumption; instead, it had to sell them for uses, for example as ingredients in cake mixes, in which they would be pasteurized, killing any salmonella present.

Rose Acre sued, asserting that the government had taken its property by killing its chickens for testing, forcing it to sell eggs in the less-lucrative pasteurized market, and shutting down its operation during the cleaning of the hen houses. According to the court, the government's plan to control salmonella was deficient because it did not actually test the eggs. Finding the offending bacteria in the hen houses and testing the chickens and finding it in them did not provide strong enough evidence for the court of the reasonableness of the department's plan. As a result, taking the hens for testing and limiting the sale of eggs to pasteurized use was a taking of Rose Acre's property.

Rose Acre shows the movement from real property to tangible personal property (the tested chickens) and economic losses associated with tangible property (the lost opportunity to sell the eggs as fresh). Property rights campaigners have been industrious in trying to extend these boundaries. When South Carolina banned video gambling machines in 1999, advocates sued on behalf of two gambling houses, arguing that the state's action constituted a taking of their property—not just the now-useless machines themselves, but also the goodwill value of the businesses, which had been greater when the land was used for gambling. If the state wanted to prohibit gambling, it had to buy the machines from the owners and also pay them for the diminished value of their land and businesses. The South Carolina Supreme Court rejected the argument, pointing out that the machines were contraband, like illegal drugs or guns, and prohibition or even forfeiture of such items has long been accepted. As to the businesses, even under the *Lucas* view of takings, at least so far, prohibiting illegal activity on land does not mean that the government has taken it.[57] Nevertheless, Defenders of Property Rights made a similar argument in opposition to a Missouri referendum that would ban billboards in scenic areas; if the state wanted to preserve the landscape, let it buy the billboards, not ban them.[58]

DPR also filed objections to a proposed Securities and Exchange Commission rule to regulate accountants. Under the rule, accounting firms in a post-Enron world would be limited in their ability to sell collateral services to their audit clients, to prevent conflicts of interest in conducting the audit. The rule may be good or bad public policy, but Defenders made a novel constitutional argument, which was ultimately rejected, that the rule would be an unconstitutional taking of the accountants' business.[59] Here the doctrine floats untethered. Not only is a regulation a taking if it imposes any restriction on the use or value of land, but any regulation that affects the economic value of any business interest can be a taking, too.

Some cases like this, asserting purely economic interests as property that can be taken, have been more successful. For example, Massachusetts enacted a statute requiring tobacco companies to disclose the additives they place in cigarettes, such as sugars, glycerin, propylene glycol, preservatives, "plasticizing" agents, and flavorings. Philip Morris sued, and, after protracted litigation and attempts by the Massachusetts legislature to modify the statute, the U.S. Court of Appeals for the First Circuit ruled that the disclosure requirement constituted a taking of the company's secret formula.[60]

To fulfill their statutory obligation to protect endangered species, the U.S. Fish and Wildlife Service and National Marine Fisheries Service issued opinions that the chinook salmon and delta smelt were jeopardized by excessive pumping of water from the Feather and Sacramento Rivers in California. Accordingly, the state Department of Water Resources limited pumping, and recipients of the water sued, claiming that the reduction constituted a taking of their expectation of receiving water. The Court of Federal Claims held that a contractual right to receive water is property, which the government's action took from them, and awarded $14 million to the water users.[61]

The most striking case along these lines is the Supreme Court's 1998 decision in *Eastern Enterprises v. Apfel*.[62] In 1946, the United Mine Workers of America called a strike against the nation's bituminous coal companies, pushing President Harry S. Truman to nationalize the mines and direct Secretary of the Interior Julius Krug to negotiate a settlement with union leader John L. Lewis. After a week of negotiations, the two produced an agreement that ended the strike and created benefit funds, financed by royalties on coal produced and payroll deductions, to provide medical care and disability, retirement, and death benefits for miners and their dependents. That agreement was superceded periodically by a series of national compacts between the miners and the companies to similarly fund benefits. Beginning in the

1970s, a decline in the amount of coal produced, a rise in health-care expenses, and an increasing number of retired miners threatened the financial viability of the system. By 1992, Congress had to intervene, creating a system to guarantee benefits by allocating expenses to coal companies and to companies still in business but no longer operating mines.

Eastern Enterprises was one of those companies that had left the coal business, at least nominally, by transferring its coal operations to EACC, a subsidiary that it wholly owned and managed. Eastern received more than $100 million in income from EACC between 1965 and 1987, when it sold the subsidiary to Peabody Coal. Under the 1992 Coal Act, Eastern had responsibility for the benefit payments of a thousand retired miners, as the company for which the miners had worked for the longest period of time. Eastern sued, asserting that this arguably retroactive obligation violated substantive due process and constituted a taking.

The Court decided the case 5–4, with Justice O'Connor writing a plurality opinion joined by Chief Justice Rehnquist and Justices Thomas and Scalia, and with Justice Kennedy providing a fifth vote but writing a separate opinion. The four plurality justices decided the case on takings ground, and Kennedy on due process grounds, all agreeing that the Coal Act's retroactive imposition on Eastern was unconstitutional.

The plurality justices recognized that the takings argument was an odd one. Not only was no physical property taken, but no identifiable property interest at all was taken—not even an intellectual property right, as in the Massachusetts cigarette case, or a contract right, as in the California water rights case. Their theory was that company assets had been taken, because assets that could have been used for other purposes now had to be committed to the retired miners' benefits. Unlike any prior case, the Court could not point to a specific piece of property or legal interest that the government had acquired or destroyed, but for the plurality justices, the creation of a new obligation was equivalent to a taking of the company's property.

Although Justice Kennedy agreed with the result, he found the takings analysis unprecedented. "Until today," he noted, "one constant limitation has been that in all of the cases where the regulatory taking analysis has been employed, a specific property right or interest has been at stake."[63]

A majority of the justices in *Eastern Enterprises* rejected the takings analysis, but the possibility of adding a fifth vote to the four plurality justices or persuading lower courts to extend the case's reasoning has opened bold new fronts for takings challenges. The essential problem with the Coal Act was its alleged retroactivity, imposing a current burden for past benefits. Retroactivity also is frequently used to fund environmental cleanups. Since *Eastern Enterprises,* challenges have been brought against CERCLA, the Superfund statute that imposes the costs of cleaning up toxic sites on parties who owned the contaminated property or transported or disposed of the toxic materials even prior to the effective date of the statute. Other cases have challenged the Energy Policy Act, which requires power companies that had purchased uranium to pay into a fund for the cleanup costs of radioactive processing facilities. So far, both of these challenges have been unsuccessful, but the threat from property rights advocates continues.[64]

Even more broadly, the *Eastern Enterprises* reasoning poses a threat to all government fees and even taxes. As Justice Breyer noted in his dissent, "If the [Takings] Clause applies when the government simply orders A to pay B, why does it not apply when the government simply orders A to pay the government, i.e., when it assesses a tax?"[65] Conservative scholar and former solicitor general Charles Fried raised a similar question: "Uncompensated takings of individual isolated holdings . . . are an evil, to be sure, but the generalized confiscation implicit in very high marginal tax rates puts the individual's property at least as much at the mercy of the state."[66] Is every tax a taking? If so, the conservatives' two means of emasculating the power of government—starving it through tax cuts and barring regulations as takings—would coincide in perfect political and legal harmony.

Deregulating Property

As individual property owners, we might like to be able to use our property any way we want, but we know we cannot, because we are affected by the actions of other property owners who would like to do the same thing. A landowner in a residential neighborhood cannot construct a slaughterhouse, the owner of beachfront property cannot level the dunes and erect a condominium, and a factory cannot dump toxic waste on its land or into a nearby stream. Government always and pervasively regulates the use of property.

If the Right's property movement has its way, local, state, and national governments would be unable to regulate effectively the use of property, and the interests of the individual owner will trump the interests of everyone else. Federal environmental protection and municipal land use planning would be endangered. Open space, fragile wetlands, and smart growth would be threatened by commercial development and tract housing. Property rights would be extended beyond land, too, making it difficult to fund programs that provide legal services, health-care, and retirement benefits.

Property rights advocates argue that not only would these results be good, but that they are demanded by the concept of property itself and by the protection the Constitution affords to property. Those claims are absurd. Once before, at the end of the nineteenth century, the rich and powerful made these claims, and the history of property law ever since has been a rejection of them. Judges, lawyers, and scholars for most of the twentieth century understood that property ownership is never absolute. Property requires a balancing of the private desire of the property owner to use his property as he wants and the public interest in regulating the use of property, and the Supreme Court embodied that understanding in an established body of case law. The next chapter describes the development of property law and explains why the claims of property rights advocates are false.

7

Takings and Transcendental Nonsense

The core idea of the property rights movement—the need to protect private property from government invasion—resonates with American values, from the ancient "A man's home is his castle," to freed slaves' "Forty acres and a mule," to, less ringingly, Gordon Gecko's proclamation in the 1987 film *Wall Street* that "Greed is good." Professor Epstein and Justice Scalia may have carried things too far, many might say, but there is a basic principle at stake. As the conservative Cato Institute puts it:

> America's Founders understood clearly that private property is the foundation not only of prosperity but of freedom itself. Thus through the common law and the Constitution, they protected property rights— the rights of people to freely acquire and use property. With the growth of the modern regulatory state, however, governments at all levels today are eliminating those rights through so-called regulatory takings.[1]

But this property rights story is a distortion of history, a misstatement of the nature of property, and a fabrication of the role of government. Property rights are fundamental, but the broad concept of fixed property rights and the narrow scope for government action argued for by conservatives is not justified by our history or by any coherent conception of property law. Instead, their unsound claims about history and theory only serve to rationalize their attack on government's ability to protect the public good.

The Right's property movement has mounted a comprehensive attack on government regulation, based on the absolute rights of property and its constitutional dimension. Their first proposition, the absolute right of ownership, is nonsense—"transcendental nonsense," as the legal philosopher Felix Cohen labeled it in 1935.[2] The proposition is manufactured out of thin air, inconsistent with almost everything that has been said and written about property law for a hundred years and more. Their second proposition, constitutionalizing absolute property, is nonsense taken wing, without a basis in the Constitution or its history and inconsistent with generations of Supreme Court precedent, a peculiar position for conservatives who otherwise espouse strict construction and judicial restraint.

Classical Property Law and Its Critics

The conservative argument on takings aims to resuscitate a long-discredited concept of property as part of the broader project of moving to resurrect the classical vision of the common law and to restore the age of the Robber Barons and laissez-faire government. As the scale of economic enterprise exploded in the late nineteenth century, new types of property that overwhelmed the value and importance of land were created by entrepreneurs and their lawyers: Corporate charters, negotiable instruments, trust indentures, preferred and common stock, oil and gas drilling rights, and business good will, among a myriad of others. Owners of dynastic landholdings were dwarfed into insignificance by the new industrial magnates in railroads, oil, and steel; J. P. Morgan, John D. Rockefeller, and Andrew Carnegie were the new titans of the economy, more important than the economic heirs of farmers such as Washington and Jefferson. In this context, what was property, and what did it mean for government to take it?

This was not solely, or even primarily, an academic question. The essential issue, at the turn of the twentieth century as at the turn of the twenty-first, was the relationship between property and power. How much power would the owners of great concentrations of industrial might, those whom Teddy Roosevelt called "the malefactors of great wealth," have over society? How much power could government exercise over them? The issue was debated in the courts, the legislatures, and the streets, underlying movements from the Granger laws, which sought to protect farmers against the life-and-death power of the railroads, to the Haymarket riot and the great May Day strike of 1886.

One answer came in the definition of property. This conservative answer, then as now, was political and economic as much as intellectual, coming in response not only to the conceptual question but also to the fear of "anarchy, socialism and communism,...foreign workmen bringing with them socialistic ideas which prevail among the laboring classes of Europe, ...raving fanatics, emotional and misdirected philanthropists, and blatant demagogues," as president and chief justice William Howard Taft described it.[3] Property was dephysicalized and generalized. Increasingly, lawyers recognized that property was not a thing—not, for example, land itself—but a relationship between people with respect to a thing. Therefore, anything could be the subject of property; if property was not a physical object, an interest in the Standard Oil trust was as much property as was a farm.[4] And if the purpose of property was the growth and accumulation of wealth, almost any interference with its use by the state could become a taking.

To enshrine this idea in law, Supreme Court justice Stephen Field articulated an absolutist conception of property as a commodity that promoted individual wealth. Field stated the case frankly: "If there be no protection, either in the principles upon which our republican government is founded, or in the prohibitions of the Constitution against such invasions of private rights, all property and all business in the State are held at the mercy of a majority of its legislature."[5] To avoid this danger, Field and others defined property as consisting of anything of value and including the right to use the property as one might, to derive profit from that property, and to realize its full value. Any government action that interfered with the full scope of enjoyment and profit—building a dam that flooded land, reducing railroad rates, preventing employers from forcing their workers to sign yellow dog contracts—was forbidden.[6]

At this point one of the cornerstones of the edifice of classical legal thought had been laid. The vision of property that had not existed heretofore but that would in our time animate the ideas of the property rights movement had been constructed. Anything could be the subject of property—not only the new vehicles of corporate wealth, such as trust certificates, stock, and debt instruments, but also, in one court decision after another, the right to run a railroad, an employer's power to operate a plant free from union organizing, a tax exemption, the use of the mails, news one has gathered, and so on. Once made into property, the right was absolute, creating a sphere of autonomy for owners, which the government could neither infringe by regulation nor take away without compensation. As Taft instructed the graduating class of the University of Michigan Law School, "not only have we had broad constitutional guarantees of property and contract rights, but there has been present in the breasts of our whole people a firm conviction of their sacred character."[7]

The critics of classical property law demonstrated that this conception of property was absurd. Property rights are not a self-evident category; rather, property rights are defined by law to balance the interests of owners and non-owners. In a series of articles published between 1913 and 1917, Stanford and Yale law professor Wesley Newcomb Hohfeld exposed the fallacies of classical property. He carefully defined the kinds of legal interests, or "entitlements," a person can have with respect to property. For example, a landowner is "privileged" to use the land without interference from others (others may not invoke state power to prevent him from doing so). Each entitlement has a correlative interest that defines a relationship between two people with respect to a certain issue; when the landowner has the "privilege" to use the land, his neighbor has a "no-right," or the legal inability to do anything about the owner's privileged use.[8]

Hohfeld's construction of legal interests completed the dephysicalization of property. Land and other physical objects may be the subject of property, but they are not property; property is a relationship among people, with the extent of the relationship defined by the entitlements and their correlatives. Moreover, each legal entitlement with respect to property ownership is distinct from the others. A landowner's right to exclude others from her land is conceptually independent from the privilege to use the land as she wants, and the privilege to use the land to build a house is independent of the privilege to use it to build a factory. In the traditional metaphor, property is a bundle of rights, like a bundle of sticks, and in different settings the bundle can be composed of different entitlements.

Hohfeld's analysis of legal correlatives also demonstrated that property relationships are two-sided, consisting of a positive legal interest on one side (such as a landowner's privilege to use the land) and a correlative negative interest on the other side (her neighbor's no-right to interfere with the owner's use). Therefore, although classical judges used *rights* as the basis of property, the system could as easily be described as one of *obligations*. As later scholars would describe it in a metaphor from physics, property is governed by the law of reciprocity of entitlements and exposures—"for every legal entitlement there is an equal and opposite legal exposure"—and the law of conservation of exposures—"the sum of legally determined exposures is a constant."[9] The law determines who has which interests in the property, and there always are winners and losers in the process. This means that the claim of the property rights movement that it aims to expand private rights and limit government regulation is incoherent. Expanding the property rights of one owner simply constricts the rights of others. When the government cannot prevent a developer from filling in wetlands and building condominiums, the rights of non-owners to enjoy the wetlands are limited accordingly.

Property rights, as described by Hohfeld, define relationships among people. The lawyer-economist Robert Hale pointed out that the relationships always involve the application of state power. Having a right means that a property owner can summon the power of the state to compel the performance by someone else of the correlative duty; having a privilege means that the owner can summon state power to compel the correlative holder of the no-right not to interfere in the exercise of the privilege. Therefore, because property involves state power and state power is a form of coercion, property is about coercion as much as liberty.

By the 1930s Hohfeld, Hale, and other critics had demonstrated that property rights necessarily involved choices by the government about how interests should be allocated, so the only relevant question was what choices the government should make. And over the next fifty years, their insight would be incorporated into the law.

What is utterly bizarre about the conservatives' current attack on property law is that they not only reject this body of law, but they also ignore the underlying insights, which have been accepted by virtually all serious thinkers about property for a half-century and more. Professor Epstein claims that "for things reduced to ownership, the rules of property uniquely specify the rights of all persons for all times."[10] George Mason University law professor Steven J. Eagle writes for the Cato Institute that "property is a natural right of free persons."[11] Other Right's property advocates claim that property is an individual right, not a social or political relation. Hohfeld exposed these errors in 1917.

Shortly after the critique of classical property became established in the academy, the Supreme Court knew better, too. The Court addressed a series of takings cases that brought to light the contradiction that always had been inherent in classical thought and then absorbed the reformers' critique. That story is part of the tale that gives the lie to the equally preposterous conservative assumption that the Constitution embodies a concept of absolute property in the takings clause.

The Takings Clause in the Fifth Amendment: Strict Construction

Because conservatives usually emphasize the need for strict construction of the Constitution and adherence to the original understanding of the framers, the story begins, as most stories about American law begin, at the time of the founding. According to property rights advocates, the colonists, the framers of the Constitution and the Bill of Rights, and the leaders of the early republic had a vision of government and property that was "liberal" in the classical sense and that lead them to enact a constitutional limitation on the regulation of property. Liberalism rested on two fundamental tenets: First, rights are individual and prepolitical, held by people by the law of nature and not by the will of the state. Second, the function of government is to protect those natural rights. (Beginning in the late nineteenth century, liberal individualism would take a less-religious, more materialistic form, particularly among economists, who emphasized the power of grasping self-interest as the prime mover and greatest good of society.)

The patron saint of liberalism for property rights advocates is the political philosopher John Locke. As seen by conservatives, Locke believed that all people are "naturally in ... a state of perfect freedom to order their actions, and dispose of their possessions, and persons as they think fit, within the bounds of the law of nature, without asking leave, or depending upon the will of any other man." In exercising that freedom, people acquire property, not through the grant of government but through their own appropriation of the world of nature. "God, when he gave the world in common to all mankind, commanded man also to labour.... He that in obedience to this command of God, subdued, tilled and sowed any part of it, thereby annexed to it something that was his property, which had no title to, nor could without injury take from him."[12]

The conservative account caricatures Locke. The deeply religious Locke would have rejected the later liberal view that property is merely a means for looking out for Number One. Property was a gift from God to be used and not wasted and to benefit all humanity, not just those who can grab the most of it. Locke explained in words that would place him in the left wing of today's Democratic Party: "But though this be a state of liberty, yet it is not a state of license." The fruits of labor become property, "at least where there is enough and as good left in common for others." Moreover, "charity gives every man a title to so much out of another's Plenty, as will keep him from extream [sic] want, where he has no means to subsist otherwise."[13] (Religious values still count in the property rights debate. The national Conference of Catholic Bishops, the United Methodist Church's General Board of Church and Society, and the Religious Action Center of Reform Judaism all have opposed takings legislation; the Methodist Social Principles, for example, state "We believe private ownership is a trusteeship under God...but is limited by the overriding needs of society.")[14]

Locke's religiosity and expression of the limits of property undermine the view of him as an advocate of unfettered, absolute private property rights, so they are often ignored or discarded by conservatives. Epstein, for example, presumes to correct Locke, by dispensing with the idea of divine justification for private property, a correction akin, as law professor Thomas Ross noted, to claiming that Christianity is consistent with Judaism, with a modest correction recognizing Jesus Christ as the Son of God.[15]

The problem runs much deeper than misreading a particular writer. The political philosophy known as "republicanism" was at least coequal with liberalism and probably dominant in the founding era. Republicans viewed rights as constructed by the state, not as natural artifacts, and constructed for a particular purpose: to advance the common good. Property, therefore, is not a natural right, nor should it serve the selfish interests of individuals. Property is created, defined, and limited by law to promote the general welfare.[16] The most noted republican in theory and action, Thomas Jefferson, pushed measures in Virginia to revamp the inheritance and landholding laws to reduce dynastic wealth and to allow emigrants to the undeveloped western territories to acquire land, principles that subsequently were adopted for the Northwest Territories and the lands of the Louisiana Purchase. "Legislators cannot invent too many devices for subdividing land," he wrote, making clear that property was a social construct the purpose of which was collective, not individual benefit.[17]

The diverse attitudes toward property at the time of the founding are reflected in the law of eminent domain and the history of the takings clause. Two essential points undercut conservative mythmaking about the long-standing, fundamental nature of property rights. First, from colonial times through the drafting of the Fifth Amendment's takings clause and for decades after, the law did not generally prohibit government from taking property without paying for it. Second, "taking" meant then what it means today —to take, not to regulate—so there was no requirement of compensation when government action diminished property rights short of physically taking away the subject of the property.[18]

In English law, the supremacy of Parliament enabled it to decide whether and how it would compensate owners for property taken. This power was carried over to the colonial legislatures. Only two of the colonial charters— Massachusetts and Carolina, the latter drafted by John Locke but never fully implemented—provided for compensation, and Massachusetts's provision was limited to goods, not land. None of the state constitutions enacted in 1776 included a compensation requirement, and by 1820 a majority still did not include such a provision. Even though states were not constitutionally obligated to do so, they did often provide some compensation when land was taken for road building or to be given to entrepreneurs for the construction of canals or other improvements. Often but not always: Several states did not compensate the owners because they presumed that the original grant from the colonial proprietors to the owners included an excess amount of property to account for any that should be taken by the government in the future. And the amount of compensation was up to the legislature or executive officials and was not reviewed by the courts; if the compensation was given in land unrelated to the cash value of the loss, or if the compensation for an industrial site was based only on its value as uncultivated agricultural land, so be it.[19]

In addition, any requirement of compensation could not have applied when property was regulated, because government regulation of property was ubiquitous. Another great conservative myth is that big government was a creation of Franklin Roosevelt, that prior to the New Deal the economy hummed along without interference. (Thus the Reaganite metaphor of "lifting government off our backs," to restore us to a pristine past of rugged individuals unfettered by the state.) In fact, government regulation of economy, morality, and everyday life was pervasive for decades before and after the framing of the Constitution. Land use was tightly controlled. From its founding, for example, Virginia limited the amount of tobacco landowners could plant and required them to grow other crops. During and after the Revolution, legislatures obliterated the property interests of British citizens and American loyalists. Virginia allowed American debtors to pay money owed to English creditors into the state treasury, and to pay it in paper money even though the paper had depreciated to 2 percent of its original value. Land use controls that rival modern zoning ordinances in their rigor regulated the use of property for slaughterhouses, bakeries, candle makers, and cemeteries. Many elements of economic life were closely regulated. Between 1781 and 1801, the New York legislature passed statutes regulating lotteries, peddlers, lenders, beggars, landlords, ferries, apprentices, dogs, fishermen, physicians, tavern owners, bakers, and (presumably in separate categories) bastards, idiots, lunatics, and lawyers.[20] And none of this required any compensation of those whose economic interests were diminished or even extinguished by the government action. Both property law and theory and republican politics dictated the result: "The general good is to prevail over partial individual inconvenience," said the New York Supreme Court.[21] Therefore, even when a city regraded a street and undermined the foundation of an adjoining house, or changed the course of a river resulting in its overflowing private land or obstructed access to private docks, no compensation was required.[22]

Then, why was the takings clause included in the Fifth Amendment, and what did it mean? Given the context, it could not be a crucial provision and integral to the constitutional scheme. Certainly, there was no great demand for it. The state conventions ratifying the Constitution proposed over eighty amendments to be included in the Bill of Rights, but the takings clause was not among them.[23] If it was debated at all in the Congress that proposed the Bill of Rights or the states that ratified it, no record exists of that debate.

One thing that is clear from the contemporary commentaries is that the clause applied only to cases in which the government physically takes over a person's property. Even Justice Scalia, author of the leading contemporary property rights decision, admits that "early constitutional theorists did not believe that the Takings Clause embraced regulations of property at all."[24] Madison's original draft used a term that is as clear as "take": "No person shall be . . . obliged to relinquish his property, where it may be necessary for public use, without a just compensation." Beyond that, the clause only may have been designed to prevent particular confiscatory abuses, especially seizure of personal property by an army in the field. St. George Tucker, author of the first published legal commentary on the Bill of Rights, opined that the clause "was probably intended to restrain the arbitrary and oppressive mode of obtaining supplies for the army, and other public uses, by impressment, as was too frequently practiced during the revolutionary war, without any compensation whatever."[25]

Takings in the Supreme Court

It is a very long way from the original understanding that the takings clause, not central to the constitutional scheme, applies only to cases in which the government actually seizes possession of property, to the Right's property advocates' claim that it applies on its face to every instance in which the government impinges on the use or value of any kind of property. The Right's claim is only understandable as a reflection of classical property law.

But the classical period was a brief interlude in the otherwise unbroken understanding that extensive regulation was not a taking, and even it entertained exceptions. Even under its preferred mode of analysis, "substantive due process," the Court permitted severe restrictions on land use. If Peter Mugler lawfully constructed a brewery on his property in Salina, Kansas, which had little value for any other purpose, a subsequent state statute prohibiting the brewing of alcohol did not constitute a taking.[26] If a state outlawed margarine, ostensibly to prevent fraud and protect the public health (but implicitly to protect the dairy industry), a margarine manufacturer such as W. L. Powell of Harrisburg, Pennsylvania, had no claim, even if the value of his factory and machinery was destroyed and the means of his livelihood lost.[27] If a Los Angeles ordinance that prohibited the operation of a brickyard was applied to an area newly incorporated in the city, the application did not cause a taking, even if the way the brickyard was constructed prevented the land, worth $800,000, from being used for any other purpose.[28] In the 1920s, the Supreme Court—even though it was still generally a conservative court, prior to its transformation during the New Deal—

merged this understanding of the takings clause with the new Hohfeldian academic understanding of property, as shown by *Miller v. Schoene*, a key case that involved apple and cedar trees.[29]

Miller owned a grove of red cedar trees that had become infected with cedar rust, a disease that is not harmful to cedar trees but that can spread and cause fatal damage to apple trees. To protect the state's apple industry, therefore, the law authorized the destruction of cedar trees within 2 miles of apple orchards, and the state entomologist ordered Miller to cut down his trees.

Under the classical and modern conservative approaches, the entomologist's action would have been a taking unless the existence of the cedar trees was a nuisance permitting the exercise of the police power. In the *Rose Acre* case discussed in Chapter 6, for example, the conservative judges of the Court of Federal Claims held that removing hens from salmonella-infected hen houses for testing constituted a taking. But the Supreme Court in *Miller* saw things differently: "We need not weigh with nicety the question whether the infected cedars constitute a nuisance according to the common law." Why not? Justice (later Chief Justice) Harlan Fiske Stone, who, as former dean of Columbia University's law school would have been well acquainted with Hohfeld's scholarship and the debates about property theory, explained:

> The state was under the necessity of making a choice between the preservation of one class of property and that of the other wherever both existed in dangerous proximity. It would have been none the less a choice if, instead of enacting the present statute, the state, by doing nothing, had permitted serious injury to the apple orchards within its borders to go on unchecked.[30]

Property rights are relational; the legal interests of the cedar tree owner could be protected only at the expense of the apple grower, and vice versa.

How should the court decide who gets the entitlement? In most cases, it should not decide but should defer to the legislature's judgment. "When forced to such a choice the state does not exceed its constitutional powers by deciding upon the destruction of one class of property in order to save another which, in the judgment of the legislature, is of greater value to the public."[31] The key phrase is "in the judgment of the legislature." The government must allocate property rights on the basis of social policy, and the allocation is essentially a legislative function.

During the next fifty years, the uniform position of the Supreme Court was that it should not be in the business of invalidating regulations adopted by the legislature by applying the classical property regime and its expansive view of the takings clause. The court upheld virtually all government actions against takings challenges, handing down landmark opinions in the process. In 1926, the Court upheld the recently developed practice of municipal zoning in *Village of Euclid v. Ambler Realty Co.*[32] Euclid, Ohio, a suburb of Cleveland, adopted a comprehensive zoning plan that divided the village into six districts specifying permitted uses, three districts regulating building height, and four districts regulating the size of lots. The effect of the plan was to limit prospective uses of property, often drastically. Nevertheless, the Court found no constitutional problem. The experts who devised the plan and the local officials who adopted it had considered safety, security, noise, and other consequences of building for the social fabric, and their "reasons are sufficiently cogent to preclude us from saying, as it must be said before the ordinance can be declared unconstitutional, that such provisions are clearly arbitrary and unreasonable, having no substantial relation to the public health, safety, morals, or general welfare."[33]

Indeed, the Court established the principle so firmly that the cases virtually dried up. The *Penn Central* case in 1978 discussed more fully in Chapter 6, synthesized the Court's position. There, the majority of the Court continued to express deference to government regulation and to take a flexible approach in assessing when a regulation constituted a taking. Justice Rehnquist, turning aside from the established law, set the course for the Right's property movement in arguing that because ownership is absolute, the infringement of any interest in the property constitutes a taking, with only rare, traditional exceptions.

Radical Property Law

The conflict in *Penn Central* epitomized the current conflict in property law. It is a very short journey from Justice Rehnquist's dissent to Justice Scalia's majority opinion for a changed Court in *Lucas*, Judge Plager's extreme positions in *Palm Beach Isles*, and the even more-radical positions taken by Defenders of Property Rights, Mountain States Legal Foundation, and other conservative property warriors. A short journey in terms of legal doctrine, and short in terms of effects. If air rights over a train station are a distinct element of property that can be taken, so are the right to fill in wetlands, build on every inch of a development tract, exploit the highest economic value from land, cut all its timber, and mine all its minerals. If historic preservation is not sufficient to justify limiting the use of property, then neither is protecting migratory birds, endangered species, clean water, oceanfront dunes, open space, or scenic vistas. Even beyond the regulation of land, conservative activists claim the right to be free of any kind of regulation that impinges on the ability to operate a business or extract the highest profit from any property. As with the other claims of the conservative attack on the common law, that claim is, in fact, not conservative at all, but a radical attack on our society, our system of government, and more than two hundred years of American law.

8

The Movement to Un-Make the Law

Art, music, architecture, clothing, and literature exhibit changing fashions —classicism to romanticism, simple to ornate, and back again. So, too, we might consider the changes in the common law to be little more than a reflection of political fashion in the current, more conservative era that follows the liberalism of the 1960s and 1970s. In fact, the un-making of the common law is part of a comprehensive campaign to reshape American government, law, and society to benefit the rich and powerful at the expense of the common people.

Ronald Reagan proclaimed the principal item on the conservative agenda most baldly in his first inaugural address: "Government is not the solution to our problems; government is the problem."[1] If government is the problem, then the solution is to reduce the reach of government. Anti-tax activist Grover Norquist declared the movement's ambition to be cutting the size of federal, state, and local government in half, to "get it down to the size where we can drown it in the bathtub."[2] Many government programs can be cut or killed altogether; others will be reduced or eliminated by shifting responsibility from government to the market, and from the federal government to the states. Publicly supported retirement and health care will be replaced by private investment accounts instead of Social Security, and HMOs and private prescription insurance instead of Medicare. Public support of education will be replaced by voucher-funded school choice. Public welfare, already reformed "as we know it" under centrist Democrat Bill Clinton, will be supplanted by voluntary, faith-based initiatives. Tax cuts will starve government (as well as rewarding campaign contributors); the attack on liberal policies has been "tax and spend," not just "tax."

In this vision, government is the problem because it interferes with individual freedom, particularly the individual freedom to pursue self-interest through the market. Conservatives idealize and worship the market as the single social institution that produces efficient, just, and democratic results: "One market under God," as Thomas Frank has styled it.[3] Accordingly, government has a minimal role to play. "The mantra," according to Mortimer B. Zuckerman, owner of the market cheerleader *U.S. News and World Report*, "is privatize, deregulate and do not interfere with the market."[4]

As in any movement this diverse, there are tensions between the self-interested and the true believers. For example, the ideal of free markets yields to political expediency in imposing protectionist tariffs on steel imports, the desire to shrink government did not prevent a 25 percent increase in federal spending during the second Bush administration, and the belief in nonintrusive government still makes room for assertion of control over reproductive rights and civil liberties. But the occasional (or more) manifestation of hypocrisy or self-interest should not obscure the essential thrust of the movement, which is ideological as well as instrumental. It comes from and advances a belief system that attempts to convince people that inequalities of wealth and power are natural and good, and that government should not intervene to correct those inequalities.

There is, of course, a close fit between the conservative attack on government and the campaign to transform the common law. Commentators and activists, including William Greider and Bill Moyers on the left and Grover Norquist, Richard Posner, and Karl Rove on the right, have seen that conservatives are "rolling back the twentieth century," returning America to the Gilded Age (with George W. Bush playing the part of William McKinley), and it was in the Gilded Age that classical legal thought reigned.[5] Along with the celebration of wealth and the reduction of any impediment to its accumulation, individual rights defined by a conservative common law will trump the public interest. The power of government to control business on behalf of the common good will be diminished, and courts will see their regulatory function reduced in favor of a role of protecting broadly defined economic rights.[6]

Politics and Interest Groups

The association between the conservative campaign to change the common law and its broader project of gutting the government makes clear that the origins of the campaign lie not solely in economic and political self-interest, and its effects are not only the transformation of legal rules. The new conservatism is also an ideological movement with ideological effects. Indeed, not since the age of McKinley has there been such a totalizing conservatism. Every arena of government and politics is simply another vehicle to advance the conservative cause. State court elections and federal court appointments are no different from congressional campaigns or presidential elections, and changes in the common law by legislation or judicial decision are as eagerly sought as tax cuts or reductions in environmental regulations. And networks are in place to coordinate efforts of politicians, businesses, and intellectuals across all these areas.

The story of the conservative attack on the common law begins with conservatism's redefinition of the mainstream of American politics. From Goldwater to Reagan to Gingrich to George W. Bush, what once was the extremist fringe of our political life has increasingly defined the center. By the time Bush became president in 2001, conservatives had developed an effective organization that combined the ideologically committed and the purely self-interested into a totalizing movement, subjugating all elements of the government to the advancement of the conservative agenda. With a conservative Supreme Court, a Republican majority in the House and Senate, more Republican than Democratic governors and state legislative majorities, and increasingly conservative state courts, the second Bush presidency has marked the zenith of conservative accomplishment.

The conservative political victories of the last quarter century were propelled by equal measures of interest and ideology, with interest backed up by money and influence. George W. Bush became the leader in the Republican presidential race a year in advance of the convention when about sixteen lobbyists, "the Washington representatives of corporate America," sat down to dinner and, according to the *Washington Post*, "declared their allegiance" to him. When the oil producers, chemical companies, electric utilities, paper companies, and others lined up behind Bush, the money, the votes, and the presidency would follow.[7] For the 2004 campaign, President Bush—the president most closely allied with business interests since Herbert Hoover, according to historians Alan Brinkley and Robert Dallek—counts on a war chest similarly funded by business; the 391 "Pioneers" and "Rangers" who have raised $100,000 or $200,000 each for the campaign include seventy individuals from the finance industry, twenty-seven from energy, twenty-five from telecommunications, sixteen from transportation, and seventy corporate lawyers or lobbyists.[8]

The campaign on the common law is likewise founded on interest and ideology, with money from big business playing a prominent role. The organizational strengths of the campaign lie in the proliferation of groups that lobby, litigate, and propagandize, and the ability to coordinate and concentrate efforts among many of the groups. The combination of industry pressure groups and direct action litigation and lobbying centers to work in the trenches; think tanks and academics to provide ideas, ideology, and respectability; foundations to bankroll the operation; and formal and informal networks to tie it together has been successful in advancing the conservative agenda.

Industry groups are a natural bulwark of the movement. The Pharmaceutical Research and Manufacturers of America (PhRMA), for example, has tried to protect drug companies, often the deepest pockets in tort litigation, through legislation limiting punitive damages and establishing FDA approval of drugs as a bar to liability of manufacturers.[9] The Shooting Sports Foundation, the gun industry trade group with a $100 million war chest, has backed the Protection of Lawful Commerce in Arms Act, which would immunize gun manufacturers from most lawsuits.[10] The Civil Justice Reform Group, known as the "$100,000 club" because that is the minimum contribution required to join, is made up of general counsels of Fortune 500 companies such as DuPont, Aetna, Ford, Metropolitan Life, and Johnson & Johnson; Solicitor General Theodore Olson handled much of the group's lobbying and legal work while in private practice. Its aims have included enactment of federal legislation limiting the liability of manufacturers of defective products and curbing punitive damages.[11]

The American Tort Reform Association (ATRA) is the political heavyweight of the movement to reduce injury victims' rights. Founded shortly after the release of the Reagan administration's Tort Policy Working Group's report in 1986, ATRA is a coalition of hundreds of corporations and trade associations, including leaders from the drug, gun, tobacco, insurance, auto, chemical, and oil industries. ATRA's president is Sherman Joyce, formerly the Senate Republicans' staff expert on products liability; its board chairman is Ralph Wayne, co-chair of the Bush presidential campaign in 2000, and its general counsel is Victor Schwartz, Washington lawyer and a key node in the network of tort reform groups. Although it touts its broad base of support, ATRA receives most of its funding from the largest corporations, including, in one year, more than half its funding from tobacco companies.[12]

A principal vehicle for ATRA's efforts is its support of supposed grass-roots lobbying groups throughout the country. In more than a dozen states, ATRA and its affiliates have organized and supported groups with public-spirited names such as Michigan Lawsuit Abuse Watch and Mississippi for a Fair Legal System. These groups portray themselves as local coalitions of ordinary citizens, but much of the money and expertise is provided by ATRA and by APCO & Associates, a beltway lobbying and communications firm that specializes in creating what appear to be grassroots campaigns. For example, the Michigan group received so much financial support from ATRA that the IRS questioned its tax-exempt status. Neal Cohen of APCO boasted that the Mississippi group used "every campaign tactic we had" to enact state tort reform legislation in 1993, and because Mississippi had no disclosure requirements, their opponents "didn't really know who was at the heart of everything."[13]

The U.S. Chamber of Commerce is the most broadly based business group involved in transforming the common law, representing thousands of large and small businesses. In the property area, it has been active in opposing regulations "that unnecessarily restrict the free exercise of private property rights." In contract law, it has litigated extensively to allow businesses to restrict consumer rights through arbitration clauses. Its broadest activities have come in tort reform; after Thomas J. Donohue, former head of the trucking industry's trade group, became president of the chamber, he targeted trial lawyers as a convenient common enemy that could rally the diverse interests of its small business and huge corporation members. In this effort, the chamber has litigated and lobbied to restrict punitive damages, class actions, and the rights of medical malpractice victims. The chamber also has focused on state supreme court elections as a key pressure point in the system. In the 2000 election, the chamber and its Institute for Legal Reform spent $10 million on pro-business court candidates, most of it in Alabama, Illinois, Ohio, Michigan, and Mississippi, totaling about one-fourth of all the money spent in judicial campaigns nationwide. While unions and trial lawyers supported their own candidates, their contributions were dwarfed by the chamber's; it spent $1.9 million on television ads alone, more than twice as much as unions and trial lawyers combined.[14] In 2002 it worked to influence eighteen state supreme court races, and for 2004, it considered underwriting and working with groups to support candidates in forty races.[15]

Changes in the common law also have been promoted by groups that both have ties to industry and have broader political programs. The National Rifle Association, of course, has been a major opponent of regulation of the gun industry, whether the regulation comes through legislation or suits against manufacturers for overproducing guns that they know will end up in the hands of criminals. The property rights movement includes the "Wise Use" movement, an umbrella term for groups that oppose federal acquisition and ownership of land; favor opening up federal wilderness and other resources for commercial use and development, from logging and mining to invasion by off-road vehicles; and generally oppose environmental and land use restrictions.[16] Asserting that traditional environmentalism of the Sierra Club stripe is radical "in the sense of demanding fundamental change ... in present political systems, in the reach of the law, in the methods of agriculture and industry, in the structure of capitalism (the profit system), in international dealings, and in education"[17] and calling themselves the "true environmentalists," Wise Users organize under such tree-friendly names as Environmental Conservation Organization, National Wetlands Coalition, and Wilderness Impact Research Foundation.[18] Citizens for a Sound Economy works to pass "the freedom agenda for America," which includes a flat tax, deregulation of the energy industry, a "free-market" approach to environmental protection, and privatization of Social Security, in addition to tort reform. CSE's co-chairmen are former House majority leader Dick Armey and C. Boyden Gray, counsel to the first President Bush; its other leadership includes billionaire David Koch, a major funder of right-wing causes and Libertarian Party candidate for vice president in 1980.[19]

Many of these groups tout their broad membership and grassroots origins but are actually supported or directed by corporate interests or right-wing funders. Although hailing its grassroots appeal, CSE receives multi-million dollar funding from the beneficiaries of its causes, including $1 million from Philip Morris and $1 million from telephone company U.S. West.[20] While it bills itself as a grassroots movement, Wise Use's roots have been heavily fertilized by companies affected by government regulation, including Chevron, Kennecott, and Homestake Mining.[21]

Particularly valuable to the campaign against the common law is a collection of well-funded, well-organized litigation centers that are the right-wing equivalent of the ACLU or the NAACP Legal Defense Fund, Inc. A few of these, such as Defenders of Property Rights, focus on a particular issue. Others, innocuously given regional designations such as the Mountain States, Pacific, and Washington Legal Foundations, pursue changes in property, contract, and tort law as well as charter schools, welfare reform, and other issues, all, of course, from the conservative point of view.

Advocacy on behalf of the Right's property law agenda is a family business at Nancie and Roger Marzulla's eponymous law firm and their organization, Defenders of Property Rights, self-described as "the only national public interest legal foundation dedicated exclusively to protecting property rights." Roger Marzulla headed the Mountain States Legal Foundation and was assistant attorney general in charge of the Lands and Natural Resources Division in the Reagan administration, where he spearheaded the administration's efforts to reshape the takings clause. Nancie Marzulla worked at Mountain States while attending the University of Colorado law school, and also later joined the Justice Department. After the 2000 election, Nancie Marzulla advised the Bush transition team on environmental matters.[22]

DPR engages in education, litigation, and legislative work "to ensure that the property rights contained in the Constitution be given the full effect of the law." "Government's appetite for more private property without paying for it is seemingly unlimited," so "property rights has become the line drawn in the sand between tyranny and liberty."[23] The Marzullas or their nonprofit alter ego DPR have filed amicus curiae briefs in a dozen Supreme Court cases, including the major decisions on takings and environmental statutes, and have participated in more than a hundred cases in lower courts.

The Marlboro man of right-wing public interest law firms is the Mountain States Legal Foundation. (With the cigarettes; Mountain States head William Perry Pendly, a Wyoming native, former Marine, and director of minerals policy in the Interior Department under James Watt, President Reagan's controversial interior secretary, denounced litigation against the tobacco companies as based on the idea that we are all "mind-numbed robots" who can't resist advertising.[24]) Founded by Watt, Mountain States produced not only the Marzullas but also Reagan's EPA administrator Anne Gorsuch Burford, Bush administration interior secretary Gale Norton, and other property rights advocates.[25]

The core of Mountain States' crusade is to fight back against what it sees as "the war on the West." Banning the sale of low-grade, polluting coal, closing federal lands to mining, and protecting endangered species and national monuments all threaten the Western way of life.[26] And the Western way includes freedom from impediments to rugged individualism such as affirmative action; one of Mountain States' notable successes was *Adarand Constructors, Inc. v. Pena,* in which the Supreme Court held that racial preferences for minority contractors must be strictly scrutinized.[27]

The Washington Legal Foundation, one of the largest right-wing litigation centers, engages in an aggressive program of litigation and public advocacy across a range of issues. A particular forte is filing briefs in major cases in the U.S. Supreme Court and state supreme courts; it has supported gun manufacturers, HMOs, and insurance companies on liability issues, opposed the use of class actions by injured victims and other consumers, tried to limit the fees of victims' lawyers, argued for the enforcement of form contracts that mandate arbitration and limit consumer rights, and claimed that Interest on Lawyers Trust Accounts, which are a major source of funding for legal services for the poor, violated property rights.

The legislative branch of the conservative campaign is headed by the American Legislative Exchange Council, which bills itself as "the nation's largest bipartisan, individual membership association of state legislators." ALEC was founded in 1973 by conservative activist Paul Weyrich, also a founder of the Heritage Foundation, "to advance the Jeffersonian principles of free markets, limited government, federalism, and individual liberty."[28] To supplement its legislative membership, ALEC has a Private Enterprise Board headed by Kurt L. Malmgren of the drug manufacturers' group PhRMA and including members from ExxonMobil, R. J. Reynolds Tobacco, Pfizer, Coors Brewing, and Koch Industries. In the property rights area, it sponsors model legislation that would require compensation for any reduction in value of property, no matter how small, as a result of changes in a land use or zoning law or any other government regulation. ALEC's Civil Justice Task Force concentrates on tort reform under the leadership of the ubiquitous Victor Schwartz, also counsel to the Product Liability Coordinating Committee and the American Tort Reform Association. Its proposed legislation limits class actions, protects HMOs from tort suits, and prevents the use of statistical evidence to assess the harm caused by tobacco companies and gun manufacturers.

The Conservative Movement: Ideas and Ideology

Actions flow from ideas as well as self-interest, and an important segment of the conservative campaign has been the development and support of a right-wing information industry. The most visible wing of this industry is the mass media, including conservative talk radio hosts such as Rush Limbaugh, the "fair and balanced" Fox News Channel, Internet news and commentary sources such as The Drudge Report, and the stream of liberal-bashing books claiming *Treason* and *Slander* (by Ann Coulter), *Arrogance* (by Bernard Goldberg), and *The Death of Common Sense* (by Philip K. Howard).

Ideas must be generated before they can be propagated, and one of the key elements of the conservative movement is a network of think tanks and academics that provides ideas, ideology, and an aura of intellectual respectability for the movement. The Manhattan Institute for Policy Research, for example, with its slogan of "turning intellect into influence," has succeeded in selling the crisis in tort law and the need for tort reform as weighty ideas that deserve to be taken seriously. The Institute was founded in 1978 as the International Center for Economic Policy Studies by William J. Casey, soon to be head of Ronald Reagan's election campaign and then director of the CIA.[29] The renamed Manhattan Institute executes a well-conceived program of selecting promising conservative authors, supporting the publication of their books, and aggressively marketing the authors and their ideas to journalists, commentators, politicians, judges, and other opinion makers.[30] As its first president, William Hammett, said to contributors, "any funds made available to the Judicial Studies Program will yield tremendous returns at this point—perhaps the highest return on investment available in the philanthropic field today."[31] Its notable successes in packaging conservative ideas as social science include Charles Murray's attack on welfare policy, George Kelling's "broken windows" theory of policing, Linda Chavez's critique of multiculturalism, and Stephan and Abigail Thernstrom's attacks on affirmative action.

Manhattan's tort reform efforts are spearheaded by Walter Olson and Peter Huber. Olson has criticized the "litigation explosion" and has taken particular aim at laws that protect the disabled and prevent race and sex discrimination. He also edits the "overlawyered.com" Web site, jocularly reporting alleged tales of outrageous lawsuits that feed the demand for tort reform.

Huber was discovered by the Manhattan Institute after writing an attack on tort law in the scholarly *Columbia Law Review*, which tort reform leader Victor Schwartz called "the intellectual underpinning of the tort reform effort"; after joining Manhattan, Huber wrote *Liability: The Legal Revolution and Its Consequences*, which Schwartz described as having an "unparalleled influence on how people think."[32] Along with Richard K. Willard, author of the Reagan administration's *Tort Policy Working Group Report*, Huber was featured at a New York City forum launching Manhattan's tort reform project. Following the forum, Manhattan's marketing machine went into full gear, mailing tens of thousands of copies of the proceedings to opinion makers, hosting lavish events for commentators, academics, and corporate executives at the Harvard Club of New York and elsewhere, cultivating journalists, and placing opinion pieces in major newspapers. The tidal wave of promotion overcame the weaknesses of Huber's scholarship. To take only the most famous example, discussed earlier, Huber manufactured the idea that the excesses of the tort system impose a "liability tax" of $300 billion annually on the American economy. The idea was quickly picked up and spread by politicians, lobbyists, and advocates, despite the fact that, as an MIT professor described it, the figure was the undocumented product of statistical "slick sleight of hand."[33]

For a long-term transformation of the intellectual climate, shifts in even the most abstract and abstruse academic subjects can eventually resonate throughout the society. Although the Right denounces universities as havens for radicals and liberals, there has been a conservative turn in academe that has contributed to the conservative campaign on the common law.

By far the greatest conservative success in the legal academy, and one that is directly associated with the support of conservative money, has been the ascendancy of the law and economics movement. The intersections between law and economics have long been obvious, and the early economists addressing legal issues were progressives, such as Robert Hale at Columbia in the 1920s and 1930s, who questioned the underpinnings of classical contract and property law. But modern law and economics dates from the 1960s and the 1970s, and its heart is conservative in approach and influence. Since its relatively recent founding, modern law and economics has grown exponentially, becoming what Anthony Kronman, former dean of the Yale Law School, labeled "the most powerful current in American law teaching today."[34]

The Chicago approach to law and economics, named for its strong ties to the University of Chicago, has at its core an application of the principles of microeconomics to legal questions.[35] A fundamental principle, according to its leading practitioner Richard Posner, federal appeals court judge and part-time (formerly full-time) Chicago law professor, is that "man [Posner's footnote: "And woman too, of course."] is a rational maximizer of his ends in life, his satisfactions—what we shall call his 'self-interest.' "[36] From this proposition, economists deduce that people respond to price incentives: some grocery shoppers buy steak instead of hamburger, because the higher price is worth it to them; others make do with hamburger, because they would rather spend the extra money on ice cream; still others, who are too poor to have "effective demand," as the economists say, are unable to afford either steak or hamburger.

From here law and economics branched in two directions. One branch is descriptive: "The common law is best (not perfectly) explained as a system for maximizing the wealth of society."[37] The dynamics of litigation —self-interested individuals suing to overturn rules that inhibit their economically rational behavior, judges seeking reputation, influence, and good results (i.e., wealth maximizing results)—drive individual legal rules and the common law as a whole in the pursuit of efficiency. The corollary, implicit or explicit, is that traditional rules are usually the best, and legislatures are likely to muck things up if they intervene.

Over time, emphasis shifted from the descriptive theory to a normative theory: Not only does the law tend toward efficiency, but it should do so. Economists evaluate legal rules and results according to the efficiency of the outcomes they produce, and find some laudable and other wanting.[38] For conservative economists, this branch became more attractive as the actions of liberal courts and legislatures became more prominent; unattractive decisions expanding the rights of injury victims and unsophisticated consumers could then be criticized as normatively improper without facing the inconsistency that they were the product of common law development that was supposed to be efficient, according to the descriptive theory.

As with any academic discipline, there is more to law and economics than this: scholastic disputes, criticism by outsiders, and higher mathematics, among other features. The movement has become much more diverse at it has grown in size. For present purposes, though, what is significant is the tendency among the mainstream of the discipline to use its results in ways that accord with the agenda of the conservative campaign against the common law. Basic principles support the primacy of market transactions. Judge Posner, for example, argues that "contract law cannot readily be used to achieve goals other than efficiency," thereby excluding fairness measured in other ways.[39] Harold Demsetz, economist at Chicago and then UCLA, argues the virtues of private property regimes and the dangers of community control of property rights.[40] This is hardly surprising: the economists' rational maximizer is brother to the Reaganesque icon of the independent person who should be able to manage his affairs free of government regulation. And on particular common law rules, economists often conclude that the conservative position is the best: courts should not use contract law doctrines of duress or unconscionability to remedy onerous terms in form contracts imposed by unscrupulous merchants on welfare recipients or by monopolists on unknowing consumers,[41] for example, and juries' power to award punitive damages against corporations for egregious wrongs should be restricted.[42]

Funding and Networking

Legal philosopher Brian Bix found it "mysterious" that law and economics has become a pervasive and even dominant subject in American legal scholarship but not in other countries.[43] It is not mysterious at all, any more than the success of the rest of the conservative movement is mysterious. A fundamental assumption of law and economics is that people act as rational maximizers of utility, and the behavior of its advocates illustrates the principle. Specializing in law and economics, rather than consumer law or French literature, carries more than the traditional academic rewards, because the law and economics movement, like the rest of the conservative campaign to transform the common law, has been richly funded. A core of right-wing foundations has supported law and economics from its early days; Media Transparency, a foundation watchdog group, estimates that the total contributions to universities and other institutions in support of law and economics exceeded $36 million between 1985 and 2002. Research centers, conferences, institutes, academic chairs, fellowships, and book writing and publication that spread conservative ideas are all bought and paid for by the foundations. In a single year (2001), for example, the John M. Olin Foundation, the principal promoter of the law and economics movement, supported law and economics programs by grants of $200,000 to George Mason University, $442,000 to the University of Chicago, $490,571 to Stanford, $530,503 to Yale, and over $1 million more to other universities.[44]

The funding of the law and economics movement is only one instance of the centrality of coordinated funding to the campaign to transform the common law. If money is the mother's milk of politics, it is also the lifeblood of conservative activism. The figures, like the $36 million for law and economics, are dramatic, but the strategy is more important. A small number of foundations have developed and implemented a program of producing and marketing conservative ideas with the long-term goal of changing law and public policy by shaping the debate on public issues.[45] As described by Richard Fink, president of the Charles G. Koch and Claude R. Lambe Foundations, these funders have adopted a market approach to changing the world: developing intellectual raw materials, converting them into specific policy products, and marketing and distributing the products to citizens and lawmakers as consumers.[46]

Fewer than a dozen foundations are the principal funders of this conservative movement. Richard Mellon Scaife, heir to the Gulf Oil and Mellon banking and industrial fortunes, controls the Scaife Family Foundation, the Sarah Scaife Foundation, the Allegheny Foundation, and the Carthage Foundation. In addition to funding the "Arkansas Project," the multiyear, multimillion-dollar project to dig up dirt on President Clinton (*Time* magazine described Scaife as the ultimate patron of Clinton-haters), Scaife and his foundations have funded many of the conservative think tanks and litigation centers:[47] A million dollars to Defenders of Property Rights and to the American Legislative Exchange Council, more than $2 million to the Pacific Legal Foundation and George Mason University, and more than $17 million dollars to the Heritage Foundation. The Coors family foundations, including the Castle Rock foundation, were originally funded by profits from the Coors brewing fortune. Conservative activist Joseph Coors was instrumental in founding the Heritage Foundation, and the foundations have supported Defenders of Property Rights and the Pacific, Southeastern, and Mountain States Legal Foundations. The Lynde and Harry Bradley Foundation, the Koch family foundations, the Earhart Foundation, the Smith

Richardson Foundation, and the Claude R. Lambe Charitable Foundation are likewise large funders.[48]

Looked at from the other end, the principal players in the movement that espouses free markets and protection of the individual are largely supported by grants from wealthy foundations. The Manhattan Institute has received millions from the Scaife, Coors, and Olin foundations, among others. Although groups such as Defenders of Property Rights and the Mountain States Legal Foundation claim broad membership, a core element of their support comes from a coterie of right-wing foundations. For DPR, for example, Scaife and Coors foundations have been early and regular contributors. Mountain States Legal Foundation claims over 70,000 donors but acknowledges that a third of its budget comes from fewer than fifty donors, with Scaife and Coors foundations again providing a major share.[49] The power of this funding is not just the money. Typically, funders give substantial grants year after year for general operating support. This not only funds projects but it builds institutions. Think tanks, litigation centers, and publicists have a consistent source of funding to build a conservative movement over time.

And this type of sustained funding is only part of the institution building that is the strength of the conservative campaign. If the campaign is not a cabal, "a vast right-wing conspiracy," to use the Clinton-era phrase, it is at least a network, with a common ancestry, shared aims, coordinated efforts, and overlapping players.

The genealogy begins with Ronald Reagan, the revered ancestor, and more directly with Edwin Meese, III, the paterfamilias. Meese was White House counselor to Reagan from 1981 to 1985 and then attorney general until 1988, when he resigned after an investigation concluded that he had violated tax and ethics rules in giving preferential treatment to military contractor Wedtech.[50] As attorney general, Meese brought a cadre of right-wing activists into the Justice Department, particularly lawyers who were recruited and sponsored by the Federalist Society.

For example, Roger and Nancie Marzulla of Defenders of Property Rights both came out of the Meese Justice Department. Roger Marzulla, a former California real estate lawyer, headed the Mountain States Legal Foundation and, despite opposition from environmentalists, joined the Reagan-Meese Justice Department. Nancie Marzulla worked at Mountain

States and also joined the Justice Department. Meese now sits on DPR's Board of Advisors, along with rejected Supreme Court nominee Robert Bork; former members include Bush interior secretary Gale Norton and Solicitor General Theodore Olson.[51]

Mountain States, in turn, was founded by James Watt, Reagan's controversial interior secretary, and it produced not only the Marzullas but also Anne Gorsuch Burford, Reagan's EPA administrator, and Gale Norton, who took Watt's job in the second Bush administration. Mountain States is now headed by William Perry Pendly, who was head of minerals policy in the Interior Department under Watt.[52]

Meese is now ensconced at the Heritage Foundation as the Reagan Distinguished Fellow, chairman of its Center for Legal and Judicial Studies, and member of the board. He is also a member of the Board of Visitors of the Federalist Society and Rector and Chair of the Executive Committee of the Board of Visitors at George Mason University, home to the law school's Law and Economics Center. From these positions, Meese convenes monthly meetings of conservative lawyers and activists to plot and coordinate strategy in litigation, lobbying, and public activities.[53] Meese's meetings are an example of what has become a standard practice of the conservative movement. Tax activist Grover Norquist convenes "the Wednesday meeting" every week at 10 a.m., bringing together a hundred or more representatives of business, social, and religious groups and Bush administration officials to coordinate plans to advance the conservative agenda. Then, many of the attendees head to a lunch organized by right-wing organizer Paul Weyrich for even more plotting.[54] Norquist has created a network of similar meetings in major cities and state capitals around the country; New York's right-wing leaders, including major Republican donors and members of the *Wall Street Journal*'s editorial board, meet once a month on a Monday in midtown Manhattan.[55]

The agenda for tort reform also was crystallized in the Reagan-Meese Justice Department, in the Tort Policy Working Group chaired by Richard K. Willard, assistant attorney general in charge of the Civil Division.[56] More recently, Willard has been an advisor to conservative think tanks and litigation centers, including the Washington Legal Foundation. In recent years, Victor Schwartz has become the voluble ringmaster of the tort reform movement. Schwartz is currently a partner at the Washington, D.C., law firm

Shook, Hardy & Bacon, which offers clients "the whole package" of litigation, public relations, and lobbying services through the firm's "Public Policy Group."[57] Schwartz, a one-man network, also has served as counsel to the Product Liability Coordinating Committee, chair of the Civil Justice Reform Committee of the American Legislative Exchange Council, and general counsel to the American Tort Reform Association. Reaching out to wider audiences, he has served on the Advisory Committee for the American Law Institute's Restatement (Third) of Torts and chairs the American Bar Association's legislative subcommittee on products liability. Meanwhile, as a former law professor at the University of Cincinnati, he has maintained his academic ties as coauthor of a leading law school torts text and as the author of numerous articles spreading the tort reform ideology; one well-known article, "Menu for the New Millennium," outlined the tort reform lobby's agenda for the second Bush administration.[58] For his efforts, in addition to lobbying fees reported in the tens of thousands of dollars per month,[59] Schwartz has been named one of the top lobbyists in Washington and one of the most influential attorneys in the country.[60]

A few more examples: In the executive branch, Theodore Olson, solicitor general in the second Bush administration, was assistant attorney general for the Office of Legal Counsel in the Reagan administration. Before and between government stints, he practiced at the Los Angeles and D.C. law firm Gibson, Dunn & Crutcher, where he handled much of the legal and lobbying work for the Civil Justice Reform Group, made up of general counsels of Fortune 500 companies such as Dupont, Aetna, Ford, and Johnson & Johnson. Other Bush II appointments favored industry lobbyists as regulators of their former clients. J. Steven Griles, mining industry lobbyist, became deputy secretary of the interior. At the Environmental Protection Agency, Linda J. Fisher, former head of government affairs at chemical and agribusiness giant Monsanto, was named deputy administrator and Jeffrey Holmstead, lawyer and lobbyist for industry groups such as the Alliance for Constructive Air Policy that sought looser air pollution standards became assistant administrator overseeing air pollution control. Mark Rey, former timber industry lobbyist, oversees the Forest Service as undersecretary of the Department of Agriculture. James Connaughton, advocate for mining, chemical, and power companies, is chairman of the Council on Environmental Quality. In the courts, S. Jay Plager, a Federalist Society member and former head of Reagan's Task Force on Regulatory Relief, which was aimed at relieving big business of the burden of complying with government regulations, became the leading advocate for the property rights movement as a judge of the U.S. Court of Appeals for the Federal Circuit. President George W. Bush's appointments to the Court of Federal Claims, the primary court for taking cases against the federal government, include Lawrence J. Block, who worked on property rights and tort reform legislation as counsel to the Senate Judiciary Committee, Victor J. Wolski, a former attorney with the Pacific Legal Foundation, and George W. Miller, formerly a member of the Defenders of Property Rights advisory board.[61]

The ultimate network of right-wing lawyers is the Federalist Society. Founded in 1982 as a law school debating club, the Society now has a membership of more than 25,000 lawyers, law students, and law faculty. Its members are devoted to libertarian and conservative principles, and to advancing those principles through the spread of ideology and more direct participation in the legal and political processes; to preserve its tax-exempt status, the Society itself makes no explicit political endorsements.[62]

The leadership and membership of the Federalist Society is a *Who's Who* of the Right. The Board of Visitors includes Robert Bork, Edwin Meese, C. Boyden Gray (counsel to the first President Bush and co-chair of Citizens for a Sound Economy), and Senator Orrin Hatch. The lawyer members are organized into practice groups, to network and coordinate strategy on conservative positions in litigation and legislation. The Environmental Law and Property Rights group, for example, has been chaired by James Burling of the Pacific Legal Foundation and Roger Marzulla. The leadership of the Litigation Group includes former independent counsel Kenneth Starr and Mark Behrens, Victor Schwartz's colleague at Shook, Hardy & Bacon. Leaders of the Administrative Law and Regulation Group include C. Boyden Gray and Judge Loren Smith. Others who have played significant roles include Solicitor General Theodore Olson and a host of conservative judges.

The funders of the Society also are a *Who's Who* of the financial right. Its annual budget of $3 million comes in large part from five- and six-figure grants from the usual foundations: Olin, Scaife, Bradley, Lambe, Koch, and Castle Rock (Coors), among others. Other funds come directly from law firms, drug companies such as Pfizer, and the Product Liability Advisory Council.

Perhaps the Society's greatest significance has been as an employment network by promoting the careers of activist conservative lawyers and, when Republicans are in power, assisting in placing them in government positions. It starts early; listing Federalist Society membership on a resume is a key to prestigious clerkships with some conservative judges, including "feeder judges" for Supreme Court clerkships. As one judge confessed on condition of anonymity, "a clerkship is a useful credential, and if I want to advance my philosophy I'd rather give it to someone who thinks like me."[63] Then, it extends to official positions. Federalist Society leaders claimed that in the Reagan-Meese Justice Department, all of the assistant attorneys general and more than half of the other political appointees were their members. In Michigan, Governor John Engler and five of seven Supreme Court justices are Federalists. A fourth of the candidates for federal judgeships interviewed by the second Bush administration were recommended by the Federalist Society. Most of the lawyers in the White House Counsel's office have been actively involved in the Society. And the Society provides a ready source of lawyers to aid the right's public interest firms, such as the Heritage Foundation and the Pacific Legal Foundation.

Politics by Other Means

The changes in the common law proposed by conservatives are sweeping. That is not surprising given the interests and ideology of those behind the changes. That many changes already have been adopted and more are in prospect is not surprising either, given the broad coalition supporting the changes. The assault on the common law is a coordinated campaign by an army of corporations, foundations, lobbyists, litigation centers, think tanks, politicians, and academics. Law, like war, is politics by other means, and the conservative successes in transforming the common law match their successes in politics.

Conclusion

Conservatives and corporations already have enjoyed many successes in their campaign to diminish the role of government by limiting the rights of personal injury victims, expanding the power of businesses to dictate terms to their employees and customers, and removing land development and environmental degradation from public regulation. The struggle is on-going, and many battles remain to be fought. To the extent the campaign is successful, ordinary people will suffer the consequences: more people will be injured by dangerous products, toxic drugs, and negligent doctors; consumers and workers will find their rights limited by form contracts; and historical landmarks, environmentally sensitive land, and open space will be unprotected.

This campaign might be seen as just part of the normal process of legal and political conflict, tragic but unexceptional. Whether the forum is Congress or the courts, businesses and other interest groups try to shape the law to their liking. What's good for General Motors may not be good for the country, but it is, by definition, good for General Motors, and General Motors is entitled to attempt to change the law to its advantage. (As it literally did in the rewriting of contract law during the drafting of the revised Uniform Commercial Code.) So, too, Pfizer and the American Medical Association can push for tort reform, and the National Association of Home Builders can promote the expansion of land developers' property rights. Big businesses and moneyed interests have more influence in changing the law than consumers do—no consumer group can match the $10 million the U.S. Chamber of Commerce spent on electing judges in a handful of states in a single year—but that does not distinguish the struggles over the common law from any other political issue, such as tax cuts for the rich.

The problem with the conservative campaign, however, is that it is false. Not debatable, or a matter of opinion or political viewpoint, but false.

There are, of course, the small falsehoods, the misleading anecdotes and horror stories. The most famous, described in Chapter 2, is that Stella Liebeck was a sue-happy plaintiff who carelessly spilled coffee on herself and then collected millions of dollars from McDonald's. A lie: the unfortunate

Liebeck was one of hundreds of McDonald's customers who were injured by its indifference to serving coffee it knew was dangerously hot, and her damages were limited despite her week-long hospital stay to treat third-degree burns and undergo painful skin grafts. As the campaign continues, these lies multiply: frivolous lawsuits drive the cost of health care sky high, landowners have their property rights taken away by overzealous regulators, and liberal courts make it impossible for businesses to rely on written contracts.

All of these small lies contribute to a big lie: the common law has been hijacked by aggressive lawyers and liberal judges. The solution is to return to first principles: fundamental principles of law that courts can mechanically apply to decide cases in a way that produces fair results and removes law from politics. The conservative vision offers simplicity, which is first forbidding and then comforting: forbidding in its portrayal of a world of dark forces spinning the law out of control, and comforting in its promise of simple principles of justice and constrained judging leading to a happy and productive future.

Here is a problem simply defined, with a simple solution. But the problem and solution are simply false, and false precisely because they are simple. Conservatives at the end of the nineteenth century tried to construct a similarly pristine legal edifice, with a similar aim of serving the interests of big business, but their effort was completely discredited by generations of scholars and jurists. The Right today is radical, not conservative, in rejecting that history and attempting to resurrect the principles of classical legal thought. Justice Scalia asserts that there are categorical rules of property; Professor Wesley Hohfeld knew better in 1917. The American Tort Reform Association argues for a simple principle of fault as the basis of personal injury law; torts scholar Leon Green showed in 1928 that no simple principle existed. Judge Alex Kozinski claims that we need to restore the "sanctity of contract"; lawyer-economist Robert Hale explained why that was a bankrupt concept in 1943. University of Chicago professor Richard Epstein states there are simple rules that can govern a complex world; Hohfeld, Green, Hale, and other scholars, and Benjamin Cardozo, Roger Traynor, and scores of other judges have known better for generations.

At this point in our history, after decades of critique of classical law and reconstruction of the common law, only a combination of right-wing funding, media manipulation, and political muscle enables claims like these to be made with even the appearance of credibility. The pendulum of legal change has swung from a more liberal era to a more conservative era, but it is not swinging on its own; it is being pushed by large corporations and right-wing ideologues. Accordingly, the primary goal of this book has been to expose the conservative campaign to transform the common law, showing how individual efforts to change particular rules of tort, contract, or property law are part of a broader plan to undermine people's rights.

Where does the law go from here? Contrary to the Right's appeal to simplicity, the essential insight leading to progress in the common law over the past hundred years has been that the world is a messy place.

The world is messy as to facts. The decision of any legal case or the formulation of any legal rule necessarily encompasses a wide range of facts. Law always abstracts to some degree from real life, in order to make rules of law applicable to many like cases rather than to the unique facts of one case. But it needs to recognize that it *is* abstracting and to take account of the most relevant factors in a particular context. An employment contract dispute never involves an abstract employer and employee, explicitly and freely contracting over the terms of the relationship, as the conservative vision would describe it. Instead, it involves a particular employee—Drake Albanza, a prospective fry cook—and a particular employer—Kentucky Fried Chicken, with its standard forms and corporate policies. The context of the making of the contract is important, such as Albanza's level of education, the use of standard forms by KFC, and the misleading terms of an employment application. The substance of the dispute is important, too—whether KFC should be able to use a mandatory arbitration clause to do an end run around the law and the court system, even for claims of race discrimination. And because the case represents many similar disputes, the broader social setting is significant; today, contracts are overwhelmingly made between businesses that dictate standard terms (including mandatory arbitration clauses) and workers and consumers who have little knowledge or choice.

The world is messy as to principles, too. Putting aside the substantial measure of self-interest that motivates the conservative campaign, there is something authentic in its vision of free individuals who desire to pursue their interests with substantial independence from government interference. People do want a broad realm to exercise freedom, economic independence is important, and being productive is a reasonable goal for individuals and society. But this is not the whole story. People are not entirely independent of others, nor do they want to be. We live and work in relations of connectedness in families, communities, the nation, and the global society. People also want the degree of security and protection that only collective action through government can provide. And they recognize communal values of fairness, justice, and equality that are in tension with independence and with a focus on economic acquisitiveness. In deciding employment contract cases, therefore, courts should not assume that employer and employee are steely-eyed bargainers trying to take maximum advantage of each other, and the devil take the hindmost. In many cases, they are trying to create a mutually satisfactory relationship on fair terms that will extend over time, giving each a measure of security and providing mutual benefits. And in a case in which a sophisticated employer uses subterfuge to take advantage of a poorly educated employee who relied on the fairness of the employer, the court properly can apply community standards of reasonableness and fair dealing to refuse to apply surprising and onerous terms.

The messiness of facts and principles conflicts with the conservative vision's nostalgic longing for a simpler time. But the world is what it is, and the law has to deal with its messiness. In science, the Holy Grail is an irreducibly simple principle that explains the natural world, but the reality is that the progress of science embodies the development of increasingly complicated accounts, from Newtonian physics to Einstein's theories of relativity to quantum mechanics. In law, too, progress necessarily entails increasing complexity.

What the law requires, then, is balancing: balancing the need to generalize with the reality of a complex world, and the desire of people to be independent with their desire for a society that is fair and connected. Balancing is complex, so it is impossible to simply prescribe a set of rules that the law should adopt. It is possible, however, to suggest how tort, contract, and property law ought to approach problems, and to describe facts and issues of obvious importance as the law continues to develop.

In tort law, conservatives misstate the complexity of the analysis by focusing largely on the alleged plight of defendants beset by spurious claims. It is unfair, they say, to impose liability on defendants who have done no wrong, or to impose liability out of proportion to the wrong they have done. The social consequences are severe: defendants are hurt immediately, as obstetricians leave practice in high-risk states; the public is hurt more broadly, as essential services such as medical care become unavailable and a tort tax raises the price of products and hurts the economy; and social values are corroded by a decline of personal responsibility in a culture in which everyone seeks to shift his losses to someone else through a lawsuit.

But what about the victims? The complexity of facts in tort law requires us to take account of the need of victims to be compensated for their injuries as well as the interest of defendants in paying less. It also requires us to weigh the interests of potential victims. A key objective of the tort system is promoting safety, and reducing the liability of defendants diminishes an important deterrent to unsafe conduct and so increases the dangers to people as they go about their daily lives. Moreover, fairness to victims is as important as fairness to defendants, and the personal responsibility that should attach to defendants' injury-causing behavior is as important as the personal responsibility of victims for their own behavior.

Tort law also needs to take account of facts beyond the tort system itself. Legislation and administrative regulation promote the objectives of safety and compensation, too. But the larger conservative campaign of which the transformation of the common law is a part aims to reduce government's ability to regulate the safety of products, drugs, the workplace, and health care, and instead to trust the market to make the world safe. The cumulative effect of cutting both tort liability and state regulation would be to substantially increase the dangers to consumers, workers, and patients. If other forms of government protection are decreasing, tort law as a regulator of safety becomes more, not less, important. Likewise, if the social safety net is strung closer to the ground through the privatization of Social Security, the transformation of welfare, and the reduction of federal and state spending for health, education, and poverty programs, compensation through the tort system becomes more necessary, particularly for victims who have fewer other avenues of insurance and income protection, especially homemakers, the elderly, children, and low-income consumers.

Consider how this analysis applies to specific tort reform proposals, analyzing them in light of the complexity of facts and principles that are involved in tort law. One of the most popular proposals among tort reformers caps the damages that a victim can recover, typically damages for noneconomic losses, sometimes punitive damages or all damages; the limit adopted in California a quarter century ago, $250,000, is a frequently suggested maximum for pain and suffering in medical malpractice cases.

From the victim's point of view, although pain and suffering do not come with a dollar figure attached, they are real. As a compensation matter, artificially limiting those losses fails to recognize the significance of the harm to the victim and to provide any means of ameliorating that harm. Capping the recovery also will often reduce not only the victim's noneconomic recovery but his recovery for medical expenses and lost income as well; because the victim pays his attorney a contingent fee, if the damages for noneconomic loss are not large enough to cover the fee and the litigation expenses, part of the fee must come from the victim's recovery for economic loss. From a regulatory point of view, the failure to require full compensation underprices the injury for the defendant. When the wrongdoer does not have to accept all of the costs of the injury, its incentive to safe conduct is reduced. Worse yet, the damage cap has its greatest impact in cases with the most serious injuries. Small injuries, which fall under the cap amount, will continue to be fully compensated, but the most seriously injured victims will not receive full compensation, and the wrongdoers who cause the most harm will get away cheaply.

A cap also means that some victims will never recover because they will never get a lawyer. This burden will fall particularly hard on the elderly, the poor, and women who do not work outside the home. Those are the victims whose economic loss is small, and if the noneconomic loss is capped, it simply may not be worthwhile for a lawyer to litigate a complex case. Once again, the problem is incentives for safety as well as compensation; nursing homes, for example, would have less incentive to care for residents safely because they would be less likely to be sued when their negligence caused injury.

The point here is not just that particular tort reform proposals are flawed, though they are, but that the analysis that produces them and the publicity that attempts to sell them is much too simplistic. It fails to account for all of the facts, for the system in its full context, and for the complex principles that lie behind tort law. In particular, the assault on tort law is biased toward defendants and toward a narrow view of compensation and fairness.

In contract law, the conservative assault focuses on an abstract model of contracting in which independent parties forge agreements that maximize their individual advantage. The essential principle that drives this vision of contract law is that a court must enforce an agreement as it stands, without introducing uncertainty by going beyond the express terms of the agreement or second-guessing its fairness. The market is offered as the remedy for all ills; people who do not like the deals they are offered can go elsewhere or, if they cannot, it is because they are getting the best deal to which their market power entitles them.

The conservative vision ignores the messiness of contracting in the real world, in which an overwhelming proportion of the millions of contracts entered into every day depart from the ideal of the market model. People seldom hammer out the details of their agreements, relying instead on implicit understandings, trade practices, background norms, and the law to fill in the gaps and regulate their transactions. When there is a written contract, it usually does not tell the whole story about the agreement; one of the parties, particularly the less-sophisticated party, will rely on oral representations and promises of a sales representative or a manager as binding the company, for example, even when the representations and promises are not embodied in a written contract and even when they are inconsistent with it. And the most common contracts are those made through standard forms involving standard terms, in which a big business can dictate contract terms to its customers or workers, with the likelihood that the terms will not be presented clearly, understood, or even read.

In these respects, the conservative model of contract is like its model of tort in that it focuses mainly on one side of the equation. With a relatively abstract focus on freedom of contract, it emphasizes the freedom of dominant parties to dictate terms, not to be subject to liability except on those terms, and to be free of court review of the reasonableness or fairness of their deals. For the typical consumer or worker, however, this freedom of contract is simply a means by which the economic power of big business is reinforced with legal authority; their own freedom of contract is theoretical rather than actual, severely constrained by their circumstances and by the dominance of non-negotiable adhesion contracts.

This focus on the freedom to dictate terms also shows that the conservative model ignores the messiness of the principles that underlie contract law. As the critique of classical law made clear, contract law is not essentially about freedom to contract; indeed, freedom of contract is an empty concept. Instead, it is a means by which government empowers people to make enforceable contracts, and simultaneously and necessarily regulates those contracts. Reasonableness, fairness, redress of power imbalances, and a concern for the disadvantaged are all part of contract law, too. In analyzing contract issues and proposals for the transformation of contract law, consideration of all of the facts and all of the relevant policies is required.

Therefore, the conservative attempt to artificially constrain the analysis of contract cases, either, for example, by limiting the factual inquiry to clear expressions such as written documents or by focusing solely on businesses' ability to specify the terms of their own contracts, is misguided. Instead, thinking about contract law needs to be expansive, focusing on the complex factual settings from which the cases arise, and, particularly in cases involving consumers, workers, or small businesses, on the likelihood that the paper deal is not the real deal and that there was no bargaining on an equal footing or actual agreement to the terms of the contract.

Litigated contract cases are relatively infrequent, compared to the ubiquity of contracting. Most contracts proceed without dispute, of course, and even when problems arise, litigation is expensive. Consumers and workers in particular seldom find it worthwhile to sue. Accordingly, courts need to be sensitive to the possibility of establishing rules that will control conduct beyond the particular cases in order to have the desired effect on behavior, as cases will seldom arise. This is why actions for bad faith breach of contract and accompanying punitive damages are important; because ordinary contract remedies are insufficient to deter insurance companies, employers, banks, and others in relations of trust and confidence from taking advantage of their policyholders, employees, and customers, tort remedies are needed. The low incidence of litigation also suggests that legislative intervention in contractual relations is appropriate; more of the improvement of the situation of consumers in the 1960s and 1970s came through statutes such as the Truth in Lending Act than through changes in the law by the courts.

The most important example of the contrast between the restricted, conservative view of contract and the broader approach that is more realistic is the treatment of mandatory, predispute arbitration clauses. In typical cases, an employer, HMO, or credit card company selects an arbitration scheme and includes the term, which is likely to be one of many included in a standard form employment application, patient's handbook, or bill stuffer; until a problem arises, the employee, patient, or customer never sees or reads the clause or understands that it wipes out his or her right to sue.

Under the conservative vision, arbitration clauses in these cases should be enforced as products of freedom of contract working through the market. A prospective employee who signs an employment application or a consumer who continues to use a credit card after receiving a fine-print agreement has exercised a choice to be bound by the terms of the document, or manifested indifference to its terms, which is the same thing. If he does not like the terms, he is always free to take a different job or get a different credit card. The choice to accept arbitration is a rational one, because it provides a means of resolving disputes that is just as fair and much less time-consuming and expensive than litigation. If arbitration were not so effective, at least some savvy consumers would shy away from firms that required it, and the market would force those firms to give up the practice or provide consumers some compensating benefit, such as lower prices.

This happy picture ignores the complexity of the context out of which arbitration clauses arise. Looking beyond the formal act of acceptance, it is clear that the assent to the clause is fictional; even when the clause is presented to the consumer in some way prior to the act of agreement, it is almost never presented in a meaningful way. A consumer who does not bother to read a form knows she is bound by the standard terms it includes, but she expects that if she did read it, she would not be surprised by the terms and would find them to be fair and reasonable. If arbitration were in fact fair and reasonable, consumers would freely choose it after disputes arose, so there would be no need for businesses to foist it on unsuspecting customers. Moreover, the broader context of the transaction includes the terms available in comparable transactions. Credit card companies compete on interest rates and affinity groups, but not on the basis of whether they require the customer to give up the right to sue. This demonstrates the absence of market discipline; contrary to the Right's assumption, the market has not provided an array of choices for consumers, but has limited those choices concerning this important term. The fuller picture, therefore is one of absence of choice and absence of market competition, not freedom of contract on a free market.

Nor is choice the whole story. The fuller account of contract law requires attention to public values as well as the illusory conservative goal of freedom of contract, and the mandatory arbitration clauses are the best example of this as well. Not only are arbitration clauses not the product of private choice, but whether the courts should enforce them and under what circumstances, like any other judicial decision, entails the allocation of public values. Conservatives, following the lead of the Supreme Court, have enthusiastically asserted a broad public policy favoring arbitration of many claims (including civil rights violations) in many circumstances (including employment and consumer cases). But other public policies are at stake, too. One is simple fairness; arbitration schemes that dramatically reduce rights of discovery, examination of witnesses, hearings before impartial judges, and appeal deny the basic principle that everyone is entitled to his day in court. Because arbitration can be secret and does not require the same application of general principles of contract law as occurs in court, and because the consumer only has a limited right of appeal, all of the other values of law are eroded as well.

As with tort law, the broader understanding of contract law shows that the conservative assault on contract law is false because its analysis of contracts is simplistic. It fails to account for all of the facts and for the complex principles that contract law ordinarily brings to bear. The conservative vision, then, becomes simply another means by which big businesses can exert influence, creating systems that disadvantage the less powerful and less sophisticated.

In property law, the conflict between simplicity and messiness is particularly easy to see and resolve. The Right's vision of simplicity has two elements: the ownership of property is an absolute, freeing the owner from government regulation unless the government pays for "taking" the property, and this conception of absolute ownership is enshrined in the Constitution. The effect is to make every regulation of every property interest presumptively a taking, with only minor exceptions that are historically irrefutable. If the government wants to limit the height of a skyscraper atop a historic building or prevent construction on every inch of a beachfront development, it must pay to do so. The logic applies to property interests other than land; government programs that require lawyers to pool small client trust accounts to generate interest for public purposes or assess coal companies for health benefits for miners also are unconstitutional.

Both of these propositions are false. The absolute ownership of property is not simple but simplistic, and as such its absurdity has been understood for almost a hundred years. Private property is important but it is never absolute. The bundle of rights metaphor captures the nature of property; ownership is not one thing but many legal interests, and some elements of the bundle are added or subtracted in individual cases. The law defines property rights, and the definition is always the product of both the desire to give individuals incentives and opportunities to pursue their interests through property and the need to advance the public interest in the use of property in a way that contributes to the common good. The Constitution recognizes that balancing by allowing the government to regulate the use of property without having to compensate the owner. No plausible theory of constitutional history or interpretation supports the idea that any regulation is potentially a taking, and the theories to which conservatives most often claim allegiance, interpretation in light of the intention of the framers of the Constitution or the plain meaning of the constitutional text, lead in exactly the opposite direction; regulation was common and extreme at the time the Constitution was drafted, a reality that was embodied in the wording of the Fifth Amendment, which prohibits the "taking" of property but not its regulation.

Abandoning simplistic ideas of constitutional property makes property law a lot messier, but, as scholars and judges through the twentieth century recognized, there is no alternative. As a result, property, like torts and contracts, becomes a process of balancing. The Supreme Court had it basically right in the *Penn Central* case. There is no set formula for determining when a regulation should be treated as a taking. Instead, the decisions require balancing the individual property owner's interest and the public's interest in each case. Courts need to look expansively at the nature of the interference with the use of property and the public interests involved in the regulation, and the balancing of one against the other.

The need for an expansive factual analysis and balancing of interests does not provide determinate results in many cases, but it does reveal which modes of analysis are valid and which are invalid. The property rights movement has attempted to limit government action by focusing narrowly on the property subject to regulation. This is clever but wrong; if the factual analysis considers the effects on the property owner, it should consider the effects in context. In *Penn Central*, for example, the historic preservation regulation only prohibited the construction of a fifty-five-story office tower atop a historical landmark, but it allowed other valuable economic uses; one segment of Penn Central's air rights was extinguished, but other property interests remained.

Even more broadly, the background of the property rights picture is not absolute ownership free of government regulation, but extensive government control of the use of land and other property from colonial times to the present. From colonial restrictions on which crops could be grown to modern zoning and environmental laws, and from general taxes to fees and assessments on occupations and activities, the ownership and use of property is interpenetrated with government action. Therefore, regulation is not inherently suspect, and the public interest in the regulation deserves deference. Concern for the environment is a strong public value, so protection of forests, beachfront, and wetlands by building restrictions is often reasonable. The people need to be protected from salmonella infections caused by contaminated eggs and from brain-wasting illness triggered by cattle infected with mad cow disease, so destroying some chickens or cattle to test for the problems will rarely be compensable. "Smart growth" to prevent suburban sprawl and the destruction of open space have become important devices of regional planning, and the law needs to respond to that newer public concern as well.

In urging a rejection of the Right's approach to law, we need to recognize that law has its limits. One of those limits is that it is subject to influence by those with wealth and power. But law is also an arena in which small gains can be made and broader questions framed through appeals to principle as well as power. The Right's project of transforming the law has depended on the propagation of a false ideology as much as on the exercise of power, and the first step in confronting that ideology is to prove the ideology false. The array of issues that arise in torts, contracts, and property all present the same basic choices. Will the law use a simplistic analysis that rejects a hundred years of legal development, or will it use a realistic analysis that reflects the complexity of life? Will the law yield control of people's lives to a market dominated by big business, or will it recognize the interests of the public as a counterweight to wealth and power?

Updates

This book describes a struggle over the rights of the American people under the common law. The struggle is ongoing, and the lag between writing and publication guarantees that new developments will not be reflected. With the addition of modest last-minute changes, this book is current as of February 1, 2004. Readers interested in more recent developments should go to the Web site of the broader and continuing project of which this book is a part, accessible through: http://www.beacon.org/feinmanupdates. The Web site contains a directory of organizations involved in these issues, additional sources, reporting of recent developments, and current commentary.

Notes

Introduction

1. Stephen D. Sugarman, "Judges as Tort Law Un-Makers: Recent California Experience with 'New' Torts," *DePaul Law Review* 49 (1999): 455.
2. See Chapter 2.
3. See Chapter 4.
4. See Chapter 6.

1. The Resurrection of Classical Common Law

1. Excellent summaries include William C. Berman, *America's Right Turn: From Nixon to Clinton*, 2d ed. (Baltimore: Johns Hopkins University Press, 1998); George H. Nash, *The Conservative Intellectual Movement in America, Since 1945* (New York: Basic, 1976).
2. Jean Braucher, "The Afterlife of Contract," *Northwestern University Law Review* 90 (1995): 55–56; Thomas Frank, *One Market Under God* (New York: Doubleday, 2000).
3. Richard A. Posner, "Army of the Willing," *New Republic*, May 19, 2003.
4. Kevin Phillips, *Wealth and Democracy* (New York: Broadway Books, 2002), 333.
5. Charles Murray, *Losing Ground: American Social Policy, 1950–1980* (New York: Basic, 1984).
6. Richard A. Epstein, *Forbidden Grounds: The Case Against Employment Discrimination Laws* (Cambridge: Harvard University Press, 1992).
7. Henry Lamb, "Why the government is grabbing our land," Defenders of Property Rights, http://www.yourpropertyrights.org/scandalsheet/030527.asp, 2003.
8. Defenders of Property Rights, *Activities Report* (2000); Nancie G. Marzulla, "Property Rights Movement: How It Began and Where It Is Headed," in *A Wolf in the Garden*, ed. Philip D. Brick and R. McGregor Cawley (Lanham, Md.: Rowman & Littlefield, 1996), 39.
9. *Oki America, Inc. v. Microtech International, Inc.*, 872 F.2d 312, 316 (9th Cir. 1989).
10. Tort Policy Working Group, *Report of the Tort Policy Working Group on the Causes, Extent and Policy Implications of the Current Crisis in Insurance Availability and Affordability* (February 1986): 31–32.
11. Citizens for a Sound Economy, "Lawsuit Abuse," http://www.cse.org/informed/lawsuit.htm.
12. Stephen B. Goddard, *Getting There: The Epic Struggle Between Road and Rail in the American Century* (New York: Basic, 1994).
13. Gregory S. Alexander, *Commodity and Propriety; Competing Visions of Property in American Legal Thought, 1776–1970* (Chicago: University of Chicago Press, 1997); Lawrence M. Friedman, *Contract Law in America* (Madison: University of Wisconsin Press, 1965); Morton J. Horwitz, *The Transformation of American Law, 1870–1960* (New York: Oxford University Press, 1992); William M. Wiecek, *The Lost World of Classical Legal Thought: Law and Ideology in America, 1886–1937* (New York: Oxford University

Press, 2002); Gregory S. Alexander, "The Limits of Freedom of Contract in the Age of Laissez-Faire Constitutionalism," in *The Fall and Rise of Freedom of Contract,* ed. F. H. Buckley (Durham, N.C.: Duke University Press, 1999), 103; Robert W. Gordon, "Legal Thought and Legal Practice in the Age of American Enterprise, 1870–1920," in *Professions and Professional Ideologies in America,* ed. Gerald L. Geison (Chapel Hill: University of North Carolina Press, 1983), 70–139; Thomas C. Grey, "Langdell's Orthodoxy," *University of Pittsburgh Law Review* 45 (1983): 1–53; Duncan Kennedy, "Toward an Historical Understanding of Legal Consciousness: The Case of Classical Legal Thought in America, 1850–1940," *Research in Law and Sociology* 3 (1980): 3–24; Stephen A. Siegel, "Comment: The Revision Thickens," *Law and History Review* 20 (2002): 631.

14. Robert B. Stevens, *Law School: Legal Education in America from the 1850s to the 1980s* (Chapel Hill: University of North Carolina Press, 1983), 52.

15. Bill Moyers, "This Is Your Story—The Progressive Story of America. Pass It On," Commondreams.org, http://www.commondreams.org/views03/0610-11.htm, June 4 2003.

16. Phillips, *Wealth and Democracy,* xvi, 49–51, 201.

17. U.S. (16 Wall.) 36, 127 (1872).

18. Alexander, *Commodity and Propriety, 1776–1970,* 275.

19. Horwitz, *Transformation, 1870–1960,* 12–13, 51–63, 121–127; G. Edward White, *Tort Law in America: An Intellectual History* (New York: Oxford University Press, 1980), chs. 1–2. Cf. Robert L. Rabin, "The Historical Development of the Fault Principle: A Reinterpretation," *Georgia Law Review* 15 (1981): 925.

20. Lawrence M. Friedman, *A History of American Law,* 2d ed. (New York: Simon and Schuster, 1985), 344–345, 355–356.

21. 198 U.S. 45, 57 (1905).

22. Horwitz, *Transformation, 1870–1960;* N. E. H. Hull, Roscoe Pound and Karl Llewellyn: *Searching for an American Jurisprudence* (Chicago: University of Chicago Press, 1997); Duncan Kennedy, *A Critique of Adjudication, fin de siecle* (Cambridge, Mass.: Harvard University Press, 1997); John Henry Schlegel, *American Legal Realism and Empirical Social Science* (Chapel Hill: University of North Carolina Press, 1995); William Twining, *Karl Llewellyn and the Realist Movement,* 2d (Norman: University of Oklahoma Press, 1985); G. Edward White, "From Sociological Jurisprudence to Legal Realism: Jurisprudence and Social Change in Early Twentieth-Century America," *Virginia Law Review* 58 (1972): 999; Robert W. Gordon, "Holmes Lectures," lecture, February 19–20, 1985; Thomas C. Grey, "The New Formalism" (April 2001); Thomas C. Grey, "Modern American Legal Thought," review of *Patterns of American Jurisprudence* by Neil Duxbury (Oxford: Oxford University Press, 1995), *Yale Law Journal* 106 (1996): 493–517; Duncan Kennedy, "From the Will Theory to the Principle of Private Autonomy: Lon Fuller's "Consideration and Form," *Columbia Law Review* 100 (2000): 94–175; Gary Peller, "The Metaphysics of American Law," *California Law Review* 73 (1985): 1219–1240; Joseph W. Singer, "Legal Realism Now," *California Law Review* 76 (1988): 465.

23. Lawrence M. Friedman, *American Law in the Twentieth Century* (New Haven, Conn.: Yale University Press, 2002), 490.

24. Wesley Newcomb Hohfeld, "Fundamental Legal Conceptions as Applied in Judicial Reasoning," *Yale Law Journal* 26 (1917): 710; Alexander, *Commodity and Propriety; Competing Visions of Property in American Legal Thought, 1776–1970,* ch. 11; Barbara Fried, *The*

Progressive Assault on Laissez Faire: Robert Hale and the First Law and Economics Move-ment (Cambridge, Mass.: Harvard University Press, 1998); Horwitz, *Transformation, 1870–1960*, 163–164, 195–198.

25. Arthur L. Corbin, "Offer and Acceptance, and Some of the Resulting Legal Relations," *Yale Law Journal* 26 (1917): 169.

26. Fried, *The Progressive Assault on Laissez Faire;* Horwitz, *Transformation, 1870–1960*, 163–164, 195–198.

27. Robert Hale, "Rate Making and the Revision of the Property Concept," *Columbia Law Review* 22 (1922): 214.

28. Felix S. Cohen, "Transcendental Nonsense and the Functional Approach," *Columbia Law Review* 35 (1935): 809.

2. Injuries, Victims, and the Attack on Tort Law

1. Ralph Nader and Wesley J. Smith, *No Contest: Corporate Lawyers and the Perversion of Justice in America* (Random House, 1998), 256.

2. S. 11, H.R. 5, 108th Cong., 1st sess. (2003).

3. Sara Rosenbaum, "Assessing the Need to Enact Medical Liability Reform," Prepared witness testimony (House Committee on Energy and Commerce, February 27, 2003).

4. Nader and Smith, *No Contest,* 297–298; "After Being Denied an $800 CAT Scan by Doctor, Boy Is Blind and Brain Damaged," Foundation for Taxpayer and Consumer Rights, http://www.consumerwatchdog.org/healthcare/st/st003230.php3.

5. Ronald Bacigal, *The Limits of Litigation: The Dalkon Shield Controversy* (Durham, N.C.: Carolina Academic Press, 1990), 3–9.

6. Thomas H. Koenig and Michael L. Rustad, *In Defense of Tort Law* (New York: New York University Press, 2001), 116–126; *Wooderson v. Ortho Pharmaceutical Co.,* 681 P.2d 1038 (Kan. 1984).

7. Walter Olson, *The Litigation Explosion: What Happened When America Unleashed the Lawsuit* (New York: Dutton, 1991).

8. Citizens for a Sound Economy, "Lawsuit Abuse," http://www.cse.org/informed/key_template.php?issue_it=2.

9. Daniel J. Popeo, "It's Time for Judicial Tort Reform," Advertorial, *New York Times* (September 13, 1999).

10. Health Coalition on Liability and Access, "Safeguarding Patients' Access to Care through Liability Reform," http://www.hcla.org.

11. Theodore B. Olson, "Rule of Law: The Dangerous National Sport of Punitive Damages," *Wall Street Journal* (October 5, 1994).

12. John J. Farley, "Robin Hood Jurisprudence: The Triumph of Equity in American Tort Law," *St. John's Law Review* 65 (1991): 997.

13. Daniel J. Popeo, "The All-American Blame Game," Advertorial (December 14, 1998).

14. Carl T. Bogus, *Why Lawsuits Are Good for America* (New York: New York University Press, 2001): 18–19.

15. Peter W. Huber, *Liability: The Legal Revolution and Its Consequences* (New York: Basic, 1988): 55; Joseph A. Page, "Deforming Tort Reform," *Georgetown Law Journal* 78 (1990): 649, 676–677 n.139.

16. Philip K. Howard, *The Lost Art of Drawing the Line* (New York: Random House, 2001): 3–4; Monty Christiansen, "Playground Safety Around the World," *Parks & Recreation* (April 1, 2001).

17. Koenig and Rustad, *In Defense of Tort Law,* 6; Nader and Smith, *No Contest,* 266; Robert S. Peck, "Tort Reform's Threat to an Independent Judiciary," *Rutgers Law Journal* 33 (2002): 835 n.3.

18. *Pelman v. McDonald's Corp.,* 237 F. Supp. 2d 512 (S.D.N.Y. 2003); David Barboza, "Kraft Plans to Rethink Some Products to Fight Obesity," *New York Times* (January 19, 2004).

19. Tort Policy Working Group, *Report of the Tort Policy Working Group on the Causes, Extent and Policy Implications of the Current Crisis in Insurance Availability and Affordability* (February 1986).

20. Stephen D. Sugarman, *Doing Away with Personal Injury Law* (New York: Quorum Books, 1989), 78–85.

21. *Report of the Tort Policy Working Group,* 1, 25–29, 30–42, 52.

22. *Id.* at 60, 60–75.

23. Sugarman, *Doing Away with Personal Injury Law,* 78–81.

24. *Utah Code Ann.* §78-14-7.5.

25. Adam Liptak, "In 13 States, a Push to Limit Lawyers' Fees," *New York Times* (May 26, 2003).

26. David Hechler, "Tackling Tobacco, and Urging Others to Join In," *National Law Journal* (June 2, 2003).

27. *Connors v. University Associates in Obstetrics & Gynecology, Inc.,* 4 F.3d 123 (2d Cir. 1993).

28. Legal Reform and Consumer Compensation Act of 1996, 104th Cong., S. 1861; Lawsuit Reform Act of 1995, 104th Cong., S. 300; Committee for Economic Development, *Breaking the Litigation Habit: Economic Incentives for Legal Reform* (New York, 2000) 17–22.

29. Bogus, *Why Lawsuits Are Good for America,* 199–200; Koenig and Rustad, *In Defense of Tort Law,* 210–211.

30. Henry Weinstein, "Attack Waged on Fees Anti-Tobacco Attorneys Received," *Los Angeles Times* (March 15, 2001).

31. Bogus, *Why Lawsuits Are Good for America,* 197–199; Koenig and Rustad, *In Defense of Tort Law,* 210–211.

32. *Vernon Tex. Code Ann.* §2254.101 et seq.

33. Juliet Eilperin, "Curbs on Class Action Lawsuits Sought," *Washington Post* (June 12, 2003); Marcia Coyle, "Bill Targets Class Action Lawyer Fees," *National Law Journal* (May 19, 2003).

34. *Report of the Tort Policy Working Group,* 61.

35. Andrew F. Popper, "A One-Term Tort Reform Tale: Victimizing the Vulnerable," *Harvard Journal of Legislation* 35 (1998): 123.

36. Fox Butterfield, "Gun Industry Is Gaining Immunity Against Suits," *New York Times* (September 1, 2002); Dick Polman, "For Gun Industry, Special Standing," *Philadelphia Inquirer* (May 11, 2003); Jim VandeHei, "Gun Firms on Verge of Winning New Shield," *Washington Post* (May 5, 2003).

37. 21 U.S.C. §1604.

38. Ann Marie Murphy, "The Biomaterials Access Assurance Act of 1998 and Supplier Liability: Who You Gonna Sue?" *Delaware Journal of Corporate Law* 25 (2000): 715, 728–734.

39. Seth Borenstain and Sumana Chatterjee, "Energy Bill Would Benefit Industry," *Philadelphia Inquirer* (November 16, 2003): A13. Editorial, "Out of Gas," *News and Observer* (Raleigh, N.C.) (December 16, 2003); Bruce Alpert and Bill Walsh, "On the Hill," *Times-Picayune* (December 7, 2003).

40. *Escola v. Coca Cola Bottling Co. of Fresno*, 150 P.2d 436, 440–441 (Cal. 1944) (Traynor, J., concurring).

41. Dan B. Dobbs, *The Law of Torts* (St. Paul, Minn.: West, 2000), ch. 24.

42. Dobbs, *The Law of Torts*, §353; Stephen D. Sugarman, "Judges as Tort Law Un-Makers: Recent California Experience with 'New' Torts," *DePaul Law Review* 49 (1999): 455, 479.

43. Bogus, *Why Lawsuits Are Good for America*, 33–35.

44. Schwartz, "White House Action on Civil Justice Reform: A Menu for the New Millennium," *Harvard Journal of Law & Public Policy* 24 (2001): 393, 409–411.

45. 391 P.2d 168, 172 (Cal. 1964).

46. Frances E. Zollers, Sandra N. Hurd, and Peter Shears, "Looking Backward, Looking Forward: Reflections on Twenty Years of Product Liability Reform," *Syracuse Law Review* 50 (2000): 1033.

47. *Jackson v. Nestle-Beich, Inc.*, 589 N.E.2d 547 (Ill. 1992); *Soule v. General Motors Corp.*, 882 P.2d 298 n.3 (Cal. 1994).

48. *Mexicali Rose v. Superior Court*, 822 P.2d 1292 (Cal. 1992).

49. John W. Wade, "On the Nature of Strict Tort Liability for Products," *Mississippi Law Journal* 44 (1973): 825.

50. *La. Rev. Stat. Ann.* §§ 9:2800.51 et seq.

51. *Kallio v. Ford Motor Co.*, 407 N.W.2d 92 (Minn. 1987).

52. Bogus, *Why Lawsuits Are Good for America*, 193–196; "Symposium on Generic Products Liability," *Chicago-Kent Law Review* 72 (1996): 3.

53. *N.J.S.A.* §2A:58C-3.

54. *Mich. Stat. Ann.* §27A.2946(4).

55. Bogus, *Why Lawsuits Are Good for America*, ch. 6, 157.

56. *Gryc v. Dayton-Hudson Corp.*, 297 N.W.2d 727 (Minn. 1980); Koenig and Rustad, *In Defense of Tort Law*, 195–199.

57. Marshall S. Shapo, "In Search of the Law of Products Liability: The ALI Restatement Project," *Vanderbilt Law Review* 48 (1995): 633–634.

58. Shapo, "In Search of the Law of Products Liability: The ALI Restatement Project," 645–646; "Symposium: Restatement (Third) of Products Liability," *Kansas Journal of Law and Public Policy* 8 (1998): 1; "Symposium: Restatement (Third) of Torts: Products Liability," *Hofstra Law Review* 26 (1998): 567.

59. *Potter v. Chicago Pneumatic Tool Co.*, 694 A.2d 1319, 1331 n.11 (Conn. 1997); John F. Vargo, "The Emperor's New Clothes: The American Law Institute Adorns a 'New Cloth' for Section 402a Products Liability Design Defects—a Survey of the States Reveals a Different Weave," *University of Memphis Law Review* 26 (1996): 493.

60. Frank J. Vandall, "The American Law Institute Is Dead in the Water," *Hofstra Law Review* 26 (1998): 802.

61. Teresa Moran Schwartz, "Prescription Products and the Proposed Restatement," *Tennessee Law Review* 61 (1994): 1380, 1363.

62. Dobbs, *The Law of Torts*, §384.

63. Cal. Civ. Code §3333.2.

64. Megan Rhyne, "Cap Cuts Virginia's Largest Med-mal Award," *National Law Journal*, April 28, 2003; *N.M. St.* §41-5-6; *Ind. Stat.* §34-18-14-3.

65. 1 N.J.L. 90 (Sup. Ct. 1791), cited in Stephen Daniels and Joanne Martin, "Myth and Reality in Punitive Damages," *Minnesota Law Review* 75 (1990): 7.

66. Dobbs, *The Law of Torts*, §381.

67. Lori Woodward O'Connell, "The Case for Continuing to Award Punitive Damages," *Tort & Insurance Law Journal* 36 (2001): 873.

68. In re Exxon Valdez, 270 F. 3d 1215 (9th Cir. 2001).

69. *Engle v. R.J. Reynolds Tobacco Co.*, 2000 WL 33534572 (Fla. Cir. Ct. 2000); *Liggett Group Inc. v. Engle*, 2003 WL 21180319 (Fla. App. 2003).

70. Michael L. Rustad, "Unraveling Punitive Damages: Current Data and Further Inquiry," *Wisconsin Law Review* 1998 (1998): 24–28.

71. Theodore B. Olson, "Rule of Law: The Dangerous National Sport of Punitive Damages," *Wall Street Journal* October 5, 1994; Stephen Daniels and Joanne Martin, "Punitive Damages, Change, and the Politics of Ideas: Defining Public Policy Problems," *Wisconsin Law Review* 1998 (1998): 71.

72. *Report of the Tort Policy Working Group*, 68–69.

73. Dobbs, *The Law of Torts*, §381, p. 1066.

74. *Common Sense Product Liability Reform Act of 1995*, H.R. 956 (104th Cong., 1995); American Tort Reform Association, "Punitive Damages Reform," http://www.atra.org/show/7343; *HEALTH Act*, H.R. 5 (108th Cong., 2003).

75. *Wis. Stat. Ann.* §895.85(3); *Wischer v. Mitsubishi Heavy Industries America, Inc.*, 673 N.W.2d 303 (Wis. App. 2003); Dee McAree, "$94 Million Crane-Collapse Award Erased," *National Law Journal*, October 13, 2003.

76. American Tort Reform Association, "ATRA Issues—Punitive Damages Reform," http://www.atra.org/show/7343; Zollers, Hurd, and Shears, "Looking Backward, Looking Forward," 1036–1037.

77. 821 F.2d 1438 (10th Cir. 1987).

78. *Colo. Rev. Stat.* §13-21-102; *Conn. Gen. Stat. Ann.* §52-240b; *Ind. Code* §34-51-3-4; *N.D. Cent. Code* §32-03.2-11; Zollers, et al. 2000: 1036–1037

79. 517 U.S. 559 (1996).

80. 532 U.S. 424 (2001).

81. 538 U.S. 408 (2003).

3. A Realistic View of Tort Law

1. Thomas C. Grey, "Accidental Torts," *Vanderbilt Law Review* 54 (2001): 1234.

2. On the nineteenth-century origins of tort law, see Lawrence M. Friedman, *A History of American Law*, 2d ed. (New York: Simon and Schuster, 1985), 299–302, pt. 3, ch. 6; Morton J. Horwitz, *The Transformation of American Law, 1780–1860* (Cambridge, Mass.: Harvard University Press, 1977), 80–101; Morton J. Horwitz, *The Transformation of American Law, 1870–1960* (New York: Oxford University Press, 1992), 13–14, 51–63, 121–127; G. Edward White, *Tort Law in America: An Intellectual History* (New York: Oxford University Press, 1980), chs.1–2; Grey, "Accidental Torts"; Robert L. Rabin, "The Historical Development of the Fault Principle: A Reinterpretation," *Georgia Law Review* 15 (1981): 925.

3. Oliver Wendell Holmes, "The Theory of Torts," *American Law Review* 7 (1873): 662.

4. 3 H.L. 330, 1868.

5. Francis Wharton, "A Suggestion as to Causation," 10–11 (Riverside Press, 1874), cited in Horwitz, *Transformation, 1870–1960*, 54–55.

6. White, *Tort Law in America*, 50.

7. Horwitz, *Transformation, 1870–1960*, 122–123.

8. *Palsgraf v. Long Island R.R.*, 162 N.E. 99 (N.Y. 1928).

9. 162 N.E. at 103.

10. 162 N.E. at 101; *id.* at 103–104 (Andrews, J., dissenting).

11. Leon Green, "Tort Law Public Law in Disguise," *Texas Law Review* 38 (1959–1960): 1, 257.

12. Horwitz, *Transformation, 1870–1960*, 59–60.

13. 150 P.2d 436 (Cal. 1944).

14. 150 P.2d at 440–441 (Traynor, J., concurring).

15. 28 U.S.C. §2875; Dan B. Dobbs, *The Law of Torts* (St. Paul, Minn.: West, 2000), §268.

16. 143 N.E.2d 3, 8–9 (N.Y. 1957)

17. 551 P.2d 334 (Cal. 1976).

18. 551 P.2d at 342.

19. William L. Prosser, "Comparative Negligence," *California Law Review* 41 (1953): 3–4.

20. Lewis F. Powell, Jr., "Contributory Negligence: A Necessary Check on the American Jury," *American Bar Association Journal*, 43 (1957): 1055.

21. *Winterbottom v. Wright*, 10 M. & W. 109 (1842).

22. *Ryan v. Progressive Grocery Stores, Inc.*, 175 N.E. 105 (N.Y. 1931).

23. *Henningsen v. Bloomfield Motors, Inc.* 161 A.2d 69 (N.J. 1960).

24. 377 P.2d 897, 901 (Cal. 1963).

25. *Restatement (Second) of Torts* §402A.

26. Carl T. Bogus, *Why Lawsuits Are Good for America* (New York: New York University Press, 2001), 185.

27. *Cronin v. J.B.E. Olson Corp.*, 501 P.2d 1153, 1162 (Cal. 1972).

28. See *Sindell v. Abbott Labs.*, 607 P.2d 924 (Cal. 1980); *Bichler v. Eli Lilly & Co.*, 436 N.E.2d 182 (N.Y. 1982); *Hymowitz v. Eli Lilly & Co.*, 539 N.E.2d 1069 (N.Y. 1989); *Collins v. Eli Lilly & Co.*, 342 N.W.2d 37 (Wis. 1984).

29. *Zafft v. Eli Lilly & Co.*, 676 S.W.2d 241 (Mo. 1984).

30. 607 P.2d at 936.

31. McConnell, 132 Cong. Rec. S948 (daily ed. February 4, 1986), cited in Marc S. Galanter, "The Day After the Litigation Explosion," *Maryland Law Review* 46 (1986): 3.

32. *Deaths Associated with Playpens*, Consumer Products Safety Commission (July 2001).

33. *Annual Report of ATV Deaths and Injuries*, Consumer Products Safety Commission (May 15, 2002).

34. *Traffic Safety Facts 2001*, National Highway Traffic Safety Administration (December 2002).

35. Michael J. Saks, "Do We Really Know Anything About the Behavior of the Tort Litigation System—and Why Not?" *University of Pennsylvania Law Review* 140 (1992): 1183, 1196.

36. Saks, "Do We Really Know Anything About the Behavior of the Tort Litigation System—and Why Not?" 1184–1185.

37. Marc Galanter, "Real World Torts: An Antidote to Anecdote," *Maryland Law Review* 55 (1996): 1102.

38. Saks, "Do We Really Know Anything About the Behavior of the Tort Litigation System—and Why Not?" 1183–1184; Michael J. Saks, "If There Be a Crisis, How Shall We Know It?" *Maryland Law Review* 46 (1986): 69–70.

39. Paul C. Weiler, Howard H. Hiatt, and Joseph P. Newhouse, *A Measure of Malpractice: Medical Injury, Malpractice Litigation, and Patient Compensation* (Cambridge, Mass.: Harvard University Press, 1993); Harvard Medical Practice Study, *Patients, Doctors, and Lawyers: Medical Injury, Malpractice Litigation, and Patient Compensation in New York* (1990); Saks, "Do We Really Know Anything About the Behavior of the Tort Litigation System—and Why Not?," 1183–1184; Neil Vidmar, "Maps, Gaps, Sociolegal Scholarship, and the Tort Reform Debate," in *Social Science, Social Policy, and the Law,* ed. Patricia Ewick, Robert A. Kagan, and Austin Sarat (New York: Russell Sage, 1999), 187–188.

40. Vidmar, "Maps, Gaps, Sociolegal Scholarship, and the Tort Reform Debate," 185.

41. General Accounting Office, *Medical Malpractice: Medicare/Medicaid Beneficiaries Account for a Relatively Small Percentage of Malpractice Losses,* GAO/HRD-93-126 (August 1993).

42. Galanter, "Real World Torts," 1103; Marc Galanter, "Reading the Landscape of Disputes: What We Know and Don't Know (and Think We Know) About Our Allegedly Contentious and Litigious Society," *UCLA Law Review* 31 (1983): 36–42.

43. Saks, "Do We Really Know Anything About the Behavior of the Tort Litigation System—and Why Not?" 1209.

44. Robert S. Peck, "Tort Reform's Threat to an Independent Judiciary," *Rutgers Law Journal* 33 (2002): 846–847.

45. Marc S. Galanter, "The Day After the Litigation Explosion," *Maryland Law Review* 46 (1986): 23–25.

46. Daniel J. Capra, "An Accident and a Dream: Problems with the Latest Attack on the Civil Justice System," *Pace Law Review* 20 (2000): 339.

47. Congressional Budget Office, "Limiting Tort Liability for Medical Malpractice," Economic and Budget Issue Brief (January 8, 2004): 4.

48. Galanter, "Real World Torts," 1112–1113; Vidmar, "Maps, Gaps, Sociolegal Scholarship, and the Tort Reform Debate," 178.

49. Galanter, "Real World Torts," 1110.

50. Neil Vidmar, "The American Civil Jury for Auslander (Foreigners)," *Duke Journal of Comparative and International Law* 13 (2003): 95, 97–99; Kevin M. Clermont and Theodore Eisenberg, "Trial by Jury or Judge: Transcending Empiricism," *Cornell Law Review* 77 (1977): 1124.

51. Neil Vidmar, *Medical Malpractice and the American Jury* (Ann Arbor: University of Michigan Press, 1995); Galanter, "Real World Torts," 1110–1112, 1120–1124; Michael L. Rustad, "Nationalizing Tort Law: The Republican Attack on Women, Blue Collar Workers and Consumers," *Rutgers Law Review* 48 (1996): 704–713; Vidmar, "Maps, Gaps, Sociolegal Scholarship, and the Tort Reform Debate," 178–1783; Vidmar, "The American Civil Jury for Auslander (Foreigners)," 99–102.

52. Michael L. Rustad, "Unraveling Punitive Damages: Current Data and Further Inquiry," *Wisconsin Law Review* 1998 (1998): 15.

53. Rustad, "Unraveling Punitive Damages," 25.

54. Rustad, "Unraveling Punitive Damages," 32–33.

55. Peter W. Huber, *Liability: The Legal Revolution and Its Consequences* (New York: Basic, 1988), 4.

56. Marc Galanter, "News from Nowhere: The Debased Debate on Civil Justice," *Denver University Law Review* 71 (1993): 83–90.

57. Mark M. Hager, "Civil Compensation and Its Discontents," *Stanford Law Review* 42 (1989): 547.

58. Tillinghast-Towers Perrin, *U.S. Tort Costs: 2003 Update* (2004).

59. Galanter, "News from Nowhere."

60. George J. Church, "Sorry, Your Policy Is Canceled," *Time*, March 24, 1986; Daniel Eisenberg and Maggie Sieger, "The Doctor Is Out," *Time*, June 9, 2003.

61. Leslie Berestein, "An Abandoned Patient," *Time*, June 9, 2003.

62. Eisenberg and Sieger, "The Doctor Is Out."

63. AMA, http://www.ama-assn.org/ama/pub/category/7861.html, 2003.

64. Jane Gordon, "Doctors Upset Over Malpractice. Patients Are, Too," *New York Times*, March 23, 2003.

65. Wendy Ruderman, "Untangling the Knots of Medical Malpractice," *Philadelphia Inquirer*, February 19, 2003; Michael Booth, "Medical Malpractice Measure Fails as Neither Side Wants to Bend," *New Jersey Law Journal*, February 17, 2003.

66. Josh Goldstein, "Malpractice Issue May Not Be About Money, Study Says," *Philadelphia Inquirer*, February 3, 2002; Josh Goldstein, "Medical Lawsuit Payouts Still High," *Philadelphia Inquirer*, September 22, 2002.

67. General Accounting Office, *Medical Malpractice: Multiple Factors Have Contributed to Increased Premium Rates*, GAO-03-702 (June 2003): 15; General Accounting Office, *Medical Malpractice: Implications of Rising Premiums on Access to Health Care*, GAO-03-836 (August 2003): 9.

68. "Study Finds No Link Between Tort Reforms and Insurance Rates," *Liability Week*, July 19, 1999.

69. Mark C. Rahdert, *Covering Accident Costs* (Philadelphia: Temple University Press, 1995), 109–125.

70. Americans for Insurance Reform, "Medical Malpractice Insurance: Stable Losses/ Unstable Rates," http://insurance-reform.org/StableLosses2003.pdf (October 10, 2002).

71. Joseph B. Treaster, "Malpractice Rates Are Rising Sharply," *New York Times*, September 10, 2001.

72. Rachel Zimmerman and Christopher Oster, "Assigning Liability," *Wall Street Journal*, June 24, 2002; Treaster, "Malpractice Rates Are Rising Sharply."

73. Americans for Insurance Reform, "Medical Malpractice Insurance: Stable Losses/ Unstable Rates."

74. General Accounting Office, *Medical Malpractice: Multiple Factors Have Contributed to Increased Premium Rates*, 26–27.

75. Treaster, "Malpractice Rates Are Rising Sharply."

76. Jyoti Thottam, "A Chastened Insurer," *Time*, June 9, 2003: 50.

4. Consumers, Workers, and the Tyranny of Freedom of Contract

1. *Hill v. Gateway 2000, Inc.*, 105 F.3d 1147 (7th Cir. 1997).
2. *Brown v. KFC National Management Co.*, 921 P.2d 146 (Haw. 1996).
3. Restatement (Second) of Contracts §71.
4. *Uniform Commercial Code* §2-316.
5. *C & J Fertilizer, Inc. v. Allied Mutual Insurance Co.*, 227 N.W.2d 169 (Iowa 1975).
6. *Hoffman v. Red Owl Stores, Inc.*, 133 N.W.2d 267 (1965).
7. *Williams v. Walker-Thomas Furniture Co.*, 350 F.2d 445 (D.C. Cir. 1965).
8. *Vokes v. Arthur Murray, Inc.*, 212 So. 2d 906 (Fla. Dist. Ct. App. 1968).
9. *Oki America, Inc. v. Microtech International, Inc.*, 872 F.2d 312, 316 (9th Cir. 1988).
10. Richard A. Epstein, *Simple Rules for a Complex World* (Cambridge, Mass.: Harvard University Press, 1995), 78–79.
11. Epstein, *Simple Rules for a Complex World*, 88.
12. Epstein, *Simple Rules for a Complex World*, 327.
13. Todd D. Rakoff, "Contracts of Adhesion: An Essay in Reconstruction," *Harvard Law Review* 96 (1983): 1174–1284.
14. Edwin Patterson, "The Delivery of a Life-Insurance Policy," *Harvard Law Review* 33 (1919): 198, 222.
15. Charles L. Knapp, "Taking Contracts Private: The Quiet Revolution in Contract Law," *Fordham Law Review* 71 (2002): 761, 789.
16. E. Allan Farnsworth, *Contracts*, 3d ed. (New York: Aspen Law & Business, 1999), §4.26; Joseph M. Perillo, *Calamari and Perillo on Contracts*, 5th ed. (St. Paul, Minn.: Thomson-West, 2003), §§9.41–9.43.
17. *Carnival Cruise Lines, Inc. v. Shute*, 499 U.S. 585 (1991); Jean Braucher, "The Afterlife of Contract," *Northwestern University Law Review* 90 (1995): 49, 61–68.
18. *Carnival Cruise Lines, Inc. v. Shute*, 499 U.S. 585, 590 (opinion of Blackmun, J.); 597 (opinion of Stevens, J., dissenting).
19. 921 P.2d 146 (Haw. 1996).
20. *Caspi v. The Microsoft Network*, 732 A.2d 528, 532 (N.J. Super. App. Div. 1999).
21. *Groff v. America Online*, 1998 WL 307001 (R.I. Super. 1998).
22. UCITA §§112–114, 208.
23. Amelia H. Boss, "Taking UCITA on the Road: What Lessons Have We Learned?" *Roger Williams University Law Review* 7 (2001): 167.
24. *Step-Saver Data Systems, Inc. v. Wyse Technology*, 939 F.2d 91 (3d Cir. 1991).
25. 86 F.3d 1447 (7th Cir. 1996); 105 F.3d 1147 (7th Cir. 1997).
26. "The Gateway Thread: AALS Contracts Listserv," *Touro Law Review* 16 (2000): 1149.
27. *Ting v. AT&T*, 319 F.3d 1126 (9th Cir. 2003), cert. denied, 124 S. Ct. 53 (Mem.) (2003).
28. http://www.comcast.net/comcast.html.
29. UCITA §112(e).
30. Richard E. Speidel, "Revising U.C.C. Article 2: A View from the Trenches," *Hastings Law Journal* 52 (2001): 607, 615.
31. James J. White, "Form Contracts Under Revised Article 2," *Washington University Law Quarterly* 75 (1997): 315.

32. Gail Hillebrand, "The Uniform Commercial Code Drafting Process: Will Articles 2, 2B and 9 Be Fair to Consumers?" *Washington University Law Quarterly* 75 (1997): 69, 76.

33. Speidel, "Revising U.C.C. Article 2: A View from the Trenches," 616.

34. Larry T. Garvin, "The Changed (and Changing?) Uniform Commercial Code," *Florida State University Law Review* 26 (1999): 360n371.

35. 133 N.W.2d 267, 295 (Wisc. 1965).

36. Charles L. Knapp, "Rescuing Reliance: The Perils of Promissory Estoppel," *Hastings Law Journal* 49 (1998): 1191.

37. Daniel A. Farber and John H. Matheson, "Beyond Promissory Estoppel: Contract Law and the 'Invisible Handshake,'" *University of Chicago Law Review* 52 (1985): 903; Juliet P. Kostritsky, "A New Theory of Assent-Based Liability Emerging Under the Guise of Promissory Estoppel: An Explanation and Defense," *Wayne Law Review* 33 (1987): 895.

38. Sidney W. DeLong, "The New Requirement of Enforcement Reliance in Commercial Promissory Estoppel: Section 90 as Catch 22," *Wisconsin Law Review* 1997 (1997): 943.

39. 83 F.3d 431 (10th Cir. 1996).

40. DeLong, "The New Requirement of Enforcement Reliance in Commercial Promissory Estoppel," 1004–1005.

41. 847 F.2d 564, 569 (9th Cir. 1988).

42. Quoted in L. Gordon Crovitz, "Saving Contracts from High Weirdness," *Wall Street Journal,* August 3, 1988, 16, cited in *A Contracts Anthology,* edited by Peter Linzer, 2d (Anderson Publishing Co., 1995).

43. Crovitz, "Saving Contracts from High Weirdness."

44. 7 *Cal. Rptr.* 2d 859 (Ct. App. 1992).

45. 7 *Cal. Rptr.* 2d 859, 861–862.

46. Susan Martin-Davidson, "Yes, Judge Kozinski, There Is a Parol Evidence Rule in California: The Lessons of a Pyrrhic Victory," *Southwestern University Law Review* 23 (1995): 31–32.

47. Kerry L. Macintosh, "Gilmore Spoke Too Soon: Contract Rises from the Ashes of the Bad Faith Tort," *Loyola of Los Angeles Law Review* 27 (1994): 483.

48. *Oki America, Inc. v. Microtech International, Inc.,* 872 F.2d 312, 315 (9th Cir. 1988).

49. Macintosh, "Gilmore Spoke Too Soon," 497–498; Stephen D. Sugarman, "Judges as Tort Law Un-Makers: Recent California Experience with 'New' Torts," *DePaul Law Review* 49 (1999): 455; Robert S. Thompson, "Judicial Retention Elections and Judicial Method: A Retrospective on the California Retention Election of 1986," *Southern California Law Review* 61 (1988): 2007.

50. 765 P.2d 373 (Cal. 1988).

51. *Id.* at 402, 403.

52. *Foley v. Interactive Data Corp.,* 765 P.2d 373, 389 (Cal. 1988).

53. *East River S.S. Co. v. Transamerica Delaval, Inc.,* 476 U.S. 858, 866 (1986).

54. Dan B. Dobbs, *The Law of Torts* (St. Paul, Minn.: West, 2000), §213. As to the tort law, see Chapter 2.

55. 383 P.2d 441 (Cal. 1963).

56. Ralph James Mooney, "The New Conceptualism in Contract Law," *Oregon Law Review* 74 (1995): 1193–1194.

57. *Hulsey v. Elsinore Parachute Center,* 214 *Cal. Rptr.* 194 (Cal. App. 1985).

58. *Saenz v. Whitewater Voyages, Inc.*, 276 *Cal. Rptr.* 672 (Cal. App. 1990).

59. *Randas v. YMCA of Metropolitan Los Angeles*, 21 *Cal. Rptr.* 2d 245 (Cal. App. 1993).

60. *Kubisen v. Chicago Health Clubs*, 388 N.E.2d 44 (Ill. App. 1979).

61. Richard A. Epstein, *Mortal Peril: Our Inalienable Right to Health Care?* (Reading, Mass.: Addison-Wesley, 1997): 412–416.

62. *Grabill v. Adams County Fair and Racing Association*, 666 N.W. 2d 592 (Iowa 2003); *Skotak v. Vic Tanny Int'l, Inc.*, 513 N.W.2d 428 (Mich. App. 1994).

63. *Del. Code Ann. tit. 5*, §952.

64. *Forrest v. Verizon Communications, Inc.*, 805 A.2d 1007 (D.C. 2002).

65. *America Online, Inc. v. Booker*, 781 So.2d 423, 425 (Fla. Ct. App. 2001).

66. Caroline E. Mayer, "Fannie to Set New Policy on Arbitration Clauses," *Washington Post*, February 4, 2004.

67. "Employees Signing Away Right to Sue," *Seattle Post-Intelligencer*, October 15, 2003; Jane Spencer, "Signing Away Your Right to Sue," *Wall Street Journal*, October 1, 2003; Caroline E. Mayer, "There's No Way to Arbitrate This Issue," *Chicago Tribune*, July 30, 2002, 5; Libby Wells, "Mandatory Arbitration Clauses Have Consumers Signing Away the Right to Sue," Bankrate.com, May 22, 2000, http://bankrate.com/brm/news/cc/20000522.asp?prodtype=cc; Stephanie Armour, "Mandatory Arbitration: A Pill Many Are Forced to Swallow," *USA Today*, July 9, 1998; Texans for Public Justice, "Moldy 'Lemon' Homes Denied Day in Court," *Lobby Watch*, http://tpj.org/Lobby_Watch/arbitrationhomes.html.

68. Motor Vehicle Franchise Protection Act, P.L. 107–273 (November 2, 2002).

69. Jack M. Sabatino, "ADR as 'Litigation Lite:' Procedural and Evidentiary Norms Embedded within Alternative Dispute Resolution," *Emory Law Journal* 47 (1998): 1289.

70. American Arbitration Association, "A Due Process Protocol for Mediation and Arbitration of Statutory Disputes Arising out of the Employment Relationship" (1995), and "Consumer Due Process Protocol" (1998), http://www.adr.org.

71. National Consumer Law Center, "Consumer and Media Alert: The Small Print That's Devastating Consumer Rights," http://www.consumerlaw.org/initiatives/debt_collection/content/arbitration_content.html, July 28 2003.

72. *Ball v. SFX Broadcasting, Inc.*, 165 F. Supp. 2d 230 (N.D.N.Y. 2001).

73. Spencer, "Signing Away Your Right to Sue."

74. Richard B. Schmitt, "More Law Firms Seek Arbitration to Settle Their Internal Disputes," *Wall Street Journal* September 26, 1994, B18.

75. Richard M. Alderman, "Pre-Dispute Mandatory Arbitration in Consumer Contracts: A Call for Reform," *Houston Law Review* 38 (2001): 1253–1258; Charles L. Knapp, "Taking Contracts Private: The Quiet Revolution in Contract Law," *Fordham Law Review* 71 (2002): 761.

76. Reynolds Holding, "Private Justice: Millions Are Losing Their Legal Rights," *San Francisco Chronicle*, October 7, 2001.

77. Public Citizen, "Mandatory Arbitration: Opportunities for State-Level Reform," http://www.citizen.org/congress/civjus/arbitration/articles.cfm?ID=9619, 2004.

78. *Id.*[TK]

79. 460 U.S. 1, 24–25 (1983).

80. *Southland Corp. v. Keating*, 465 U.S. 1 (1984).

81. *Shearson/American Express, Inc. v. McMahon*, 482 U.S. 220 (1987).

82. *Gilmer v. Interstate/Johnson Lane Corp.,* 500 U.S. 20 (1991).

83. Alderman, "Pre-Dispute Mandatory Arbitration in Consumer Contracts: A Call for Reform;" Knapp, "Taking Contracts Private."

84. *Council Directive 93/13/EEC of 5 April 1993 on Unfair Terms in Consumer Contracts,* Annex 1 (q), 1993 O.J. (L 095) 29, 34; Jean R. Sternlight, "Is the U.S. Out on a Limb? Comparing the U.S. Approach to Mandatory Consumer and Employment Arbitration to That of the Rest of the World," *University of Miami Law Review* 56 (2002): 831.

85. *Green Tree Financial Corp.-Alabama v. Randolph,* 531 U.S. 79 (2000); Terry Carter, "Arbitration Pendulum," *American Bar Association Journal,* May 2003, 14.

86. *Gilmer v. Interstate/Johnson Lane Corp.,* 500 U.S. 20, 31 (1991).

87. *Doctor's Associates, Inc. v. Casarotto,* 517 U.S. 681 (1996).

88. *Hooters of America, Inc. v. Phillips,* 173 F.3d 933 (4th Cir. 1999).

89. *Ting v. AT&T,* 319 F.3d 1126 (9th Cir. 2003), cert. denied, 124 S. Ct. 53 (Mem.) (2003).

90. Knapp, "Taking Contracts Private," 796.

91. Brief amicus curiae of the Chamber of Commerce of the United States, *Discover Bank v. Superior Court* (Cal. Sup. Ct., August 13, 2003).

92. *George Watts & Son, Inc. v. Tiffany & Co.,* 248 F.3d 577, 580–581 (7th Cir. 2001).

93. *IDS Life Insurance Co. v. Royal Alliance Associates, Inc.,* 266 F.3d 645, 650–651 (7th Cir. 2001).

94. *DiRussa v. Dean Witter Reynolds, Inc.,* 121 F.3d 818 (2d Cir. 1997).

95. Reynolds Holding, "Private Justice" (quoting Justice Terry Trieweiler of the Montana Supreme Court); Richard M. Alderman, "Pre-Dispute Mandatory Arbitration."

5. Freedom of Contract and Fair Contract

1. Henry Maine, *Ancient Law* 163–165 (1864), cited in Friedrich Kessler & Grant Gilmore, *Contracts: Cases and Materials,* 2d ed. (Boston: Little, Brown, 1970), 18.

2. 198 U.S. 45, 57 (1905).

3. 236 U.S. 1 (1915).

4. *Hurley v. Eddingfield,* 59 N.E. 1058 (Ind. 1901).

5. *Moulton v. Kershaw,* 18 N.W. 172 (Wis. 1884).

6. *Thomson v. Libbey,* 26 N.W. 1, 2 (Minn. 1885).

7. David Montgomery, *The Fall of the House of Labor* (Cambridge: Cambridge University Press, 1987), 367–369.

8. Nathan Isaacs, "The Standardizing of Contracts," *Yale Law Journal* 27 (1917): 38–39.

9. George K. Gardner, "An Inquiry Into the Principles of Contracts," *Harvard Law Review* 46 (1932): 20–22, 42.

10. Robert L. Hale, "Bargaining, Duress, and Economic Liberty," *Columbia Law Review* 43 (1943): 603.

11. Anatole France, *The Red Lily,* ch. 7 (1894), cited in *Columbia World of Quotations,* no. 22937 (1996), http://www.bartleby.com/66/37/22937.html.

12. Hale, "Bargaining, Duress, and Economic Liberty."

13. *Heyman Cohen & Sons v. M. Lurie Woolen Co.,* 133 N.E. 370 (N.Y. 1921).

14. Arthur L. Corbin, "Mr. Justice Cardozo and the Law of Contracts," *Harvard Law Review* 52: 408, 409; *Columbia Law Review* 39: 56, 57; *Yale Law Journal* 48: 426, 427 (1939).

15. Arthur L. Corbin, "The Interpretation of Words and the Parol Evidence Rule," *Cornell Law Quarterly* 50 (1965): 161.

16. Arthur L. Corbin, "The Parol Evidence Rule," *Yale Law Journal* 53 (1944): 642–643.

17. *Allegheny College v. National Chautauqua County Bank*, 159 N.E. 173 (N.Y. 1927).

18. *Lusk-Harbison-Jones, Inc. v. Universal Credit Co.*, 145 So. 623 (Miss. 1933).

19. *Uniform Commercial Code* §1-201 (3), (11) (2001).

20. *Nanakuli Paving and Rock Co. v. Shell Oil Co.*, 664 F.2d 772 (9th Cir. 1982).

21. *Id.* at 795, 805 (citations and internal quotations omitted).

22. *Brawthen v. H & R Block, Inc.*, 104 Cal. Rptr. 486 (Ct. App. 1972), 124 *Cal. Rptr.* 845 (Ct. App. 1975).

23. *Williams v. Walker-Thomas Furniture Co.*, 198 A.2d 914 (D.C. App. 1964), 350 F.2d 445 (D.C. Cir. 1965).

24. *Jones v. Star Credit Co.*, 298 N.Y.S. 2d 264 (N.Y. Sup. Ct. 1969).

25. *Ryan v. Weiner*, 610 A.2d 1377 (Del. Ch. 1992).

26. *Green v. Continental Rentals*, 678 A.2d 759 (N.J. Super. Law Div. 1994).

27. *Campbell Soup Co. v. Wentz*, 172 F.2d 80 (3d Cir. 1949).

28. 29 U.S.C.A. §206(d).

29. 42 U.S.C.A. §2000e et seq.

30. 29 U.S.C.A. §630.

31. 29 U.S.C.A. §§701–796.

32. 42 U.S.C.A. §§12101–12213

33. 29 U.S.C.A. §§1001–1461.

34. 29 U.S.C.A. §§2601–2654.

35. *Pugh v. See's Candies, Inc.*, 171 Cal Rptr. 917 (Cal. Ct. App. 1981).

36. *Pugh v. See's Candies, Inc.*, 250 *Cal. Rptr.* 195 (Cal. Ct. App. 1988).

37. *Woolley v. Hoffman-La Roche, Inc.*, 491 A.2d 1257, modified, 499 A.2d 515 (1985).

38. *Reid v. Sears, Roebuck & Co.*, 790 F.2d 453 (6th Cir. 1986).

39. *McDonald v. Mobil Coal Producing, Inc.*, 789 P.2d 866 (Wyo. 1990), modified on rehearing, 820 P.2d 986 (Wyo. 1991).

40. *Fortune v. National Cash Register Co.*, 364 N.E.2d 1251 (Mass. 1977).

41. *Nees v. Hock*, 536 P.2d 512 (Ore. 1975).

42. *Woodson v. AMF Leisureland Centers, Inc.*, 842 F.2d 699 (3d Cir. 1988).

43. 344 P.2d 25 (Cal. Ct. App. 1959).

44. *Wagenseller v. Scottsdale Memorial Hospital*, 710 P.2d 1025 (Ariz. 1985).

45. *Agis v. Howard Johnson Co.*, 355 N.E. 315 (Mass. 1976).

6. Property Rights and the Right's Property

1. Ronald Reagan, "Land Planning," in *Reagan, In His Own Hand,* ed. Kiron K. Skinner, Annelise Anderson, and Martin Anderson (New York: Free Press, 2001), 338.

2. William Blackstone, *Commentaries on the Laws of England* (1765), *40.

3. *Jacobellis v. Ohio,* 378 U.S. 184 (1964)

4. 438 U.S. 104 (1978).

5. *Miller Bros. v. Department of Natural Resources,* 513 N.W.2d 217 (Mich. App. 1994).

6. *Loveladies Harbor, Inc. v. United States,* 28 F.3d 1171 (Fed. Cir. 1994).

7. *Hotel and Motel Association of Oakland v. City of Oakland,* 344 F.3d 959 (9th Cir. 2003).

8. *Maritrans, Inc. v. United States,* 342 F.3d 1344 (Fed. Cir. 2003).

9. *Seariver Maritime Financial Holdings, Inc. v. Mineta,* 309 F.3d 662 (9th Cir. 2002).

10. Dave Hogan, "Oregon Attorney General Gives Broad Opinion on Much-Debated Property Measure," *Portland Oregonian,* February 14, 2001; *League of Oregon Cities v. State,* 56 P. 3d 892 (Ore. 2002).

11. Richard A. Epstein, *Takings: Private Property and the Power of Eminent Domain* (Cambridge, Mass.: Harvard University Press, 1985). For the recent and unrepentant Epstein, see Richard A. Epstein, "The Ebbs and Flows in Takings Law: Reflections on the *Lake Tahoe* Case," *Cato Supreme Court Review* 1 (2002): 5.

12. Richard A. Epstein, *Simple Rules for a Complex World* (Cambridge, Mass.: Harvard University Press, 1995); Roger Parloff, "For the Record: Professor Richard Epstein," *American Lawyer,* September 1997.

13. Parloff, "For the Record: Professor Richard Epstein."

14. Epstein, *Takings,* 85; Richard Epstein, "An Outline of *Takings,*" *University of Miami Law Review* 41 (1986): 3.

15. Richard Epstein, "A Last Word on Eminent Domain," *University of Miami Law Review* 41 (1986): 264–265.

16. Epstein, *Takings,* 95 (emphasis in original).

17. Epstein, *Takings, ch. 9.*

18. Epstein, *Takings,* 322, 323, 303, 299, 327, 328, 281.

19. Thomas C. Grey, "The Malthusian Constitution," *University of Miami Law Review* 41 (1986): 21, 23–24.

20. Robert Bork, *The Tempting of America* (New York: Free Press, 1990): 230.

21. Douglas T. Kendall and Charles P. Lord, "The Takings Project: A Critical Analysis and Assessment of the Progress So Far," *Environmental Affairs* 25 (1998): 509. See also David Helvarg, "Legal Assault on the Environment: 'Property Rights' Movement," *The Nation,* January 30, 1995; Kirk Emerson, "Taking the Land Rights Movement Seriously," in *A Wolf in the Garden,* ed. Philip D. Brick and R. McGregor Cawley (Lanham, Md.: Rowman & Littlefield, 1996), 115; Nancie G. Marzulla, "Property Rights Movement: How It Began and Where It Is Headed," in *A Wolf in the Garden,* 39.

22. Charles A. Fried, *Order and Law: Arguing the Reagan Revolution—a Firsthand Account* (New York: Simon and Schuster, 1991): 183.

23. Georgetown Environmental Law & Policy Institute, Takings Legislation: State-by-State, http://www.law.georgetown.edu/gelpi/takings/stateleg/stateby.htm; Mark W. Cordes, "Leapfrogging the Constitution: The Rise of State Takings Legislation," *Ecology Law Quarterly* 24 (1997): 187; Steven J. Eagle, "The Birth of the Property Rights Movement," 404, *Policy Analysis* (Washington, D.C.: Cato Institute, June 26, 2001): 26.

24. General Accounting Office, *Regulatory Takings: Agency Compliance with Executive Order on Government Actions Affecting Private Property Use* (October 16, 2003).

25. 106th Cong., 2d sess., H.R. 2372, S. 1028. Steven J. Eagle, "The Birth of the Property Rights Movement," 404.

26. Stephanie Osborn, "Takings Dies; Victory for NACo," *County News Online* 32, no. 18 (October 18, 2000), http://www.naco.org/pubs/cnews/00-10-9/takings.htm.

27. *Palazzolo v. Rhode Island,* 533 U.S. 606 (2001).

28. Kendall and Lord, "The Takings Project," 530–538.

29. Osha Gray Davidson, "Dirty Secrets," *Mother Jones,* September 1, 2003.

30. 438 U.S. 104 (1978).
31. *Id.* at 117–118.
32. *Id.* at 123–124.
33. *Id.* at 141, 143, 146 (opinion of Rehnquist, C. J., dissenting).
34. Mark W. Cordes, "Leapfrogging the Constitution: The Rise of State Takings Legislation," *Ecology Law Quarterly* 24 (1997): 187.
35. David Spohr, "Florida's Takings Law: A Bark Worse Than Its Bite," *Virginia Journal of Environmental Law* 16 (1997): 313.
36. Elizabeth Willson, "Property Act Fences Out the Government," *St. Petersburg Times,* July 5, 1995.
37. David Helvarg, "Legal Assault on the Environment."
38. "Oregon Ballot Items Become Money Magnets," *Portland Oregonian,* November 3, 2000; Dave Hogan, "Land-use Wins Buoy Oregonians in Action," *Portland Oregonian,* December 25, 2000; Jeff Barnard, "Environmental Enforcement may be Hindered by Oregon law," *Philadelphia Inquirer,* February 11, 2001; Dave Hogan, "Oregon Attorney General Gives Broad Opinion on Much-debated Property Measure," *Portland Oregonian,* February 14, 2001.
39. *League of Oregon Cities v. State,* 56 P.3d 892 (Ore. 2002).
40. 505 U.S. 1003 (1992).
41. 444 U.S. 51 (1979).
42. *Id.* at 65.
43. 505 U.S. at 1029.
44. *Id.* at 1026, 1029.
45. Richard A. Epstein, "*Lucas v. South Carolina Coastal Council*: A Tangled Web of Expectations," *Stanford Law Review* 45 (1993): 1369, 1369–1372.
46. Glenn P. Sugameli, "Takings Issues in Light of *Lucas v. South Carolina Coastal Council*: A Decision Full of Sound and Fury Signifying Nothing," *Virginia Journal of Environmental Law* 12 (1993): 439.
47. Daniel J. Popeo and Paul D. Kamenar, "In *Lucas's* Wake, Whither the Law of Takings: The Tide Has Finally Turned in Favor of Property Rights," *National Law Journal,* August 3, 1992.
48. *Loveladies Harbor, Inc. v. United States,* 28 F.3d 1171 (Fed. Cir. 1994).
49. 208 F.3d 1374 (Fed. Cir. 2000); 231 F.3d 1354 (Fed. Cir. 2000); 231 F.3d 1365 (Fed. Cir. 2000). On remand, the claims court held that there was no taking of 49 acres that were in navigable waters. 58 Fed. Cl. 657 (2003).
50. *Boise Cascade Corp. v. State ex rel. Oregon State Bd. of Forestry,* 991 P.2d 563 (Ore. App. 1999).
51. 535 U.S. 302 (2002).
52. Mark Twain, *Roughing It* (1872), cited in Patrick A. Parenteau, "Unreasonable Expectations: Why Palazzolo Has No Right to Turn a Silk Purse into a Sow's Ear," *Boston College Environmental Affairs Law Review* 30 (2002): 101, 132–133.
53. 535 U.S. at 331–332.
54. 524 U.S. 156 (1998).
55. 123 S. Ct. 1406 (2003).
56. 55 Fed. Cl. 643 (2003).
57. *Westside Quik Shop, Inc. v. Stewart,* 534 S.E.2d 270 (S.C. 2000).

58. Nancie G. Marzulla, "The High Cost of Highway Robbery," 2000, http://www.yourpropertyrights.org/issues/litigation/robbery.htm.

59. Defenders of Property Rights, "Defenders Warns That SEC's Proposed Rule Will Subject Taxpayer to Multi-Million Takings Judgment," News release, September 22 2000, http://www.yourpropertyrights.org/pressreleases/000922.htm.

60. 312 F.3d 24 (1st Cir. 2002).

61. *Tulare Lake Basin Water Storage Dist. v. United States,* 49 Fed. Cl. 313 (2001); 2003 WL 23111365 (Fed. Cl. 2003).

62. 524 U.S. 498 (1998).

63. 524 U.S. at 541 (Kennedy, J., concurring).

64. Lisa R. Strauss, "The Takings Clause as a Vehicle for Judicial Activism: *Eastern Enterprises v. Apfel* Presents a New Twist to Takings Analysis," *Georgia State University Law Review* 16 (2000): 689.

65. 524 U.S. at 556 (Breyer, J., dissenting).

66. Charles Fried, "Protecting Property—Law and Politics," *Harvard Journal of Law & Public Policy* 13 (1990): 44, 47.

7. Takings and Transcendental Nonsense

1. "Chapter 15: Property Rights and Regulatory Takings," in *Cato Handbook for Congress: Policy Recommendations for the 108th Congress* (Washington, D.C.: Cato Institute, 2003), 145.

2. Felix S. Cohen, "Transcendental Nonsense and the Functional Approach," *Columbia Law Review* 35 (1935): 809.

3. William Howard Taft, "The Right of Private Property," *Michigan Law Journal* 3 (1894): 215.

4. Morton J. Horwitz, *The Transformation of American Law, 1870–1960* (New York: Oxford University Press, 1992), 147.

5. *Munn v. Illinois,* 94 U.S. 136, 140 (1876).

6. Gregory S. Alexander, *Commodity & Propriety: Competing Visions of Property in American Legal Thought, 1776–1970* (Chicago: University of Chicago Press, 1997), ch. 9; Horwitz, *Transformation, 1870–1960,* ch. 5; Molly S. McUsic, "The Ghost of *Lochner*: Modern Takings Doctrine and Its Impact on Economic Legislation," *Boston University Law Review* 76 (1996): 605.

7. Taft, "The Right of Private Property."

8. See Chapter 1.

9. Duncan Kennedy and Frank Michelman, "Are Property and Contract Efficient?" *Hofstra Law Review* 8 (1980): 711.

10. Richard A. Epstein, *Takings: Private Property and the Power of Eminent Domain* (Cambridge, Mass.: Harvard University Press, 1985), 85.

11. Steven J. Eagle, "The Birth of the Property Rights Movement," 404, Policy Analysis (Washington, D.C.: Cato Institute, June 26, 2001): 4.

12. John Locke, *Two Treatises of Government,* 1698, edited by P. Laslett, 3rd ed. (1960), ¶4, 32, cited in Curtis J. Berger and Joan C. Williams, *Property: Land Ownership and Use,* 4 (New York: Aspen Law & Business, 1997): 65–66.

13. Locke, *Two Treatises of Government,* 188, 320, cited in Berger & Williams, *Property,* 90–91.

14. United States Conference of Catholic Bishops, Statement on Takings, October 18, 1995, http://www.usccb.org/sdwp/ejp/takings/take5.htm; United Methodist Church, General Board of Church and Society, Oppose Takings Legislation, March 6, 2000, http://www.umc-gbcs.org/news/viewnews.php?newsId=185, Religious Action Center of Reform Judaism, Issues: Taking Legislation, July 24, 2000, http://www.rac.org//issues/issuetak.html.

15. Thomas Ross, "Taking *Takings* Seriously," *Northwestern University Law Review* 80 (1987): 1591 (reviewing Epstein, *Takings*); Epstein, *Takings*, 17.

16. Alexander, *Commodity and Propriety*; William Michael Treanor, "The Original Understanding of the Takings Clause and the Political Process," *Columbia Law Review* 95 (1995): 782.

17. Stanley N. Katz, "Thomas Jefferson and the Right to Property in Revolutionary America," *Journal of Law and Economics* (1976): 467.

18. John F. Hart, "Land Use Law in the Early Republic and the Original Meaning of the Takings Clause," *Northwestern University Law Review* 94 (2000): 1099; Treanor, "The Original Understanding of the Takings Clause."

19. Morton J. Horwitz, *The Transformation of American Law, 1780–1860*, ch. 3 (Cambridge, Mass.: Harvard University Press, 1977); Treanor, "The Original Understanding of the Takings Clause."

20. Lawrence M. Friedman, *A History of American Law*, part 2, ch. 3 (New York: Simon and Schuster, 1985); William J. Novak, "Common Regulation: Legal Origins of State Power in America," *Hastings Law Journal* 45 (1994): 1061; Treanor, "The Original Understanding of the Takings Clause."

21. *Lansing v. Smith*, 8 Cow. 146, 149 (N.Y. 1828).

22. *Callender v. Marsh*, 1 Pick. 418 (Mass. 1823); *Lansing v. Smith*, 8 Cow. 146 (N.Y. 1828).

23. David A. Dana and Thomas W. Merrill, *Property: Takings* (New York: Foundation Press, 2002): 9–10.

24. *Lucas v. South Carolina Coastal Council*, 505 U.S. 1003, 1028 n.15 (1992).

25. Dana & Merrill, *Property: Takings*, 11–12; Treanor, "The Original Understanding of the Takings Clause."

26. *Mugler v. Kansas*, 123 U.S. 623 (1887).

27. *Powell v. Pennsylvania*, 127 U.S. 678 (1888).

28. *Hadacheck v. Sebastian*, 239 U.S. 394 (1915).

29. 276 U.S. 272 (1928).

30. 276 U.S. at 280.

31. *Id.*

32. 272 U.S. 365 (1926).

33. *Id.* at 395.

8. The Movement to Un-Make the Law

1. John B. Judis and Ruy Teixeira, *The Emerging Democratic Majority* (New York: Scribner, 2002), 151–152.

2. Laura Blumenfeld, "Sowing the Seeds of GOP Domination," *Washington Post*, January 12, 2004, A01.

3. Thomas Frank, *One Market Under God* (New York: Doubleday, 2000).

4. Louis Uchitelle, "Worldbeaters: Puffed up by Prosperity, U.S. Struts Its Stuff," *New York Times,* April 27 1997.

5. William Greider, "Rolling Back the Twentieth Century," *Nation,* May 12, 2003; Robin Toner, "Conservatives Savor Their Role as Insiders in the White House," *New York Times,* March 19, 2001; Bill Keller, "Reagan's Son," *New York Times,* January 26, 2003; Bill Moyers, "This Is Your Story—The Progressive Story of America. Pass It On," Commondreams.org, http://www.commondreams.org/views03/0610-11.htm, June 4, 2003; Richard A. Posner, "Army of the Willing," *New Republic,* May 19, 2003.

6. Greider, "Rolling Back the Twentieth Century"; Toner, "Conservatives Savor Their Role as Insiders in the White House"; Keller, "Reagan's Son"; Robin Toner and Robert Pear, "Bush Proposes Major Changes in Health Plans," *New York Times,* February 24, 2003.

7. Susan B. Glasser and John Mintz, "Capital Plan to Woo Big Business," *Washington Post,* August 1, 1999.

8. Thomas B. Edsall, "In Bush's Policies, Business Wins," *Washington Post,* February 8, 2004.

9. "Tort Reform Interests and Agendas: Proponents of Reform," *Legal Times,* April 17, 1995.

10. John McLaughlin, "Loopholes, and the Bullets That Flew through Them," *Star-Ledger* (Newark, N.J.), April 27, 2003; Dick Polman, "For Gun Industry, A Special Standing," *Philadelphia Inquirer,* May 11, 2003; Jim VandeHei, "Gun Firms on Verge of Winning New Shield," *Washington Post,* May 5, 2003.

11. Ralph Nader and Wesley J. Smith, *No Contest: Corporate Lawyers and the Perversion of Justice in America* (New York: Random House, 1998), 260; Jean Stefancic and Richard Delgado, *No Mercy: How Conservative Think Tanks and Foundations Changed America's Social Agenda* (Philadelphia: Temple University Press, 1996), 102–103; "Tort Reform Interests and Agendas: Proponents of Reform."

12. Carl Deal and Joanne Doroshow, *The CALA Files: The Secret Campaign by Big Tobacco and Other Major Industries to Take Away Your Rights* (Center for Justice & Democracy, 2000), 2; "Tort Reform Interests and Agendas."

13. Deal and Doroshow, *The CALA Files,* 18, 16–17, 20, 15, 27–29; Ken Silverstein, "Smoke and Mirrors: The Tobacco Industry's Influence on the Phony 'Grassroots' Campaign for Liability Limits," *Public Citizen* (March 19, 1996).

14. Terry Carter, "Boosting the Bench," *American Bar Association Journal,* October 2002; Emily Heller and Mark Ballard, "Hard-Fought, Big-Money Judicial Races," *National Law Journal,* November 6, 2000, A1.

15. Alexander Bolton, "K Street Enters Fray Over Bench," *The Hill,* October 8, 2003, http://www.thehill.com/news/100803/kstreet.aspx.

16. Jim Halpin and Paul de Armond, "The Merchant of Fear," http://nwcitizen.com/publicgood/reports/merchant.htm.

17. Ron Arnold, "Overcoming Ideology," in *A Wolf in the Garden,* ed. Philip D. Brick and R. McGregor Cawley (Rowman & Littlefield, 1996).

18. Samantha Sanchez, "How the West Is Won: Astroturf Lobbying and the 'Wise Use' Movement," *The American Prospect,* March–April 1996, 37.

19. Citizens for a Sound Economy, "Lawsuit Abuse," http://www.cse.org/key_template.php?issue_it=2; Media Transparency, "Koch Family Foundations," http://www.mediatransparency.org/funders/koch_family_foundations.htm; Media Transparency, "Citizens for a Sound Economy," http://www.mediatransparency.org/recipients/cse.htm.

20. Citizens for a Sound Economy, "Lawsuit Abuse"; Media Transparency, "Koch Family Foundations"; Media Transparency, "Citizens for a Sound Economy"

21. Sanchez, "How the West Is Won."

22. Egan, "In Energy Plan, Property Rights May Be an Issue," *New York Times*, May 15, 2001.

23. Defenders of Property Rights, *Activities Report* (2000); Nancie G. Marzulla, "Property Rights Movement: How It Began and Where It Is Headed," in *A Wolf in the Garden*, 39.

24. William Perry Pendley, "Responsible Citizenship in a Free Society: It Doesn't Take a Village," http://www.mountainstateslegal.com/articles_speeches.cfm?articleid=7.

25. Media Transparency, "Mountain States Legal Foundation," http://mediatransparency.org/recipients/mountain_states.htm.

26. William Perry Pendley, "Escalation of the War on the West?" http://www .mountainstateslegal.org/summary_judgment.cfm?articleid=35.

27. 515 U.S. 200 (1995).

28. "About ALEC," http://alec.org/.

29. Kenneth J. Chesebro, "Galileo's Retort: Peter Huber's Junk Scholarship," *American University Law Review* 42 (1993): 1715–1716.

30. Lawrence Mone, president, The Manhattan Institute, "How Think Tanks Achieve Public Policy Breakthroughs," address to the Philanthropy Roundtable Forum, May 29, 2002; Chesebro, "Galileo's Retort," 1715–1716.

31. Nader and Smith, *No Contest*, 261.

32. Chesebro, "Galileo's Retort," 1646–1647, 1706.

33. Mark M. Hager, "Civil Compensation and Its Discontents," review of *Liability: The Legal Revolution and Its Consequences*, by Peter W. Huber (New York: Basic Books, 1988), *Stanford Law Review* 42 (1990): 539; Milo Geyelin, "Tort Bar's Scourge," *Wall Street Journal*, October 16 1992.

34. Anthony T. Kronman, *The Lost Lawyer* (Cambridge: Belknap/Harvard, 1993), 226.

35. Nicholas Mercuro and Stephen G. Medena, *Economics and the Law: From Posner to Post-Modernism* (Princeton: Princeton University Press, 1997), 57; Richard A. Posner and Francesco Parisi, "The Economic Foundations of Private Law: An Introduction," in *Economic Foundations of Private Law*, ed. Richard A. Posner and Francesco Parisi (Cheltenham, UK: Edward Elgar Publishing, 2002), ix.

36. Richard A. Posner, *Economic Analysis of Law*, 6th ed. (New York: Aspen Publishers, 2003), 3.

37. Posner, *Economic Analysis of Law*, 25.

38. Anthony T. Kronman, *The Lost Lawyer* (Cambridge, Mass.: Belknap/Harvard, 1993), 226–238; Mercuro and Medena, *Economics and the Law: From Posner to Post-Modernism*, 3, 59.

39. Posner, *Economic Analysis of Law*, 98.

40. Harold Demsetz, "Toward a Theory of Property Rights," *American Economic Review, Papers & Proceedings* 57 (1967): 347.

41. Posner, *Economic Analysis of Law*, 115–118.

42. W. Kip Viscusi, "The Social Costs of Punitive Damages Against Corporations in Environmental and Safety Torts," *Georgetown Law Journal* 87 (1998): 285.

43. Brian H. Bix, "Law as an Autonomous Discipline," in *The Oxford Handbook of Legal Studies*, ed. Peter Cane and Mark Tushnet (Oxford: Oxford University Press, 2003), 982.

44. Media Transparency, "Law and Economics," http://www.mediatransparency.org/law_and_economics.htm.

45. Sally Covington, *Moving a Public Policy Agenda: The Strategic Philosophy of Conservative Foundations* (National Committee for Responsive Philosophy, 1997); Stefancic and Delgado, *No Mercy* (People for the American Way, 1996); *Justice for Sale* (Alliance for Justice, 1993); Karen Paget, "Lessons of Right-Wing Philanthropy," *American Prospect,* September–October 1998; http://www.mediatransparency.org.

46. Covington, *Moving a Public Policy Agenda: The Strategic Philosophy of Conservative Foundations.*

47. Karen Rothmyer, "The Man Behind the Mask," *Salon.com,* April 7, 1998, http://www.salon.com/news/1998/04/07news.html; Karen Rothmyer, "Citizen Scaife," *Columbia Journalism Review* (July/August 1981), 41.

48. Funding data from http://www.mediatransparency.org.

49. "Mountain States Legal Foundation Mission," http://www.mountainstateslegal.com/mission.cfm.

50. Kristina Lanier, "The Home Forum: Whatever Happened to...?," *Christian Science Monitor,* December 31, 1998.

51. "Gale Norton's Association with Anti-Environmental and Wise Use Groups," CLEAR, http://www.clearproject.org/reports_nortonWU.html.

52. Media Transparency, "Mountain States Legal Foundation," http://mediatransparency.org/recipients/mountain_states.htm.

53. Douglas T. Kendall and Charles P. Lord, "The Takings Project: A Critical Analysis and Assessment of the Progress So Far," *Environmental Affairs* 25 (1998): 543n153.

54. Toner, "Conservatives Savor Their Role as Insiders in the White House."

55. Ben Smith, "The Monday Meeting: A Right-Wing Cabal Ready to Convert N.Y.," *New York Observer,* February 9, 2004, 1.

56. Tort Policy Working Group, *Report of the Tort Policy Working Group on the Causes, Extent and Policy Implications of the Current Crisis in Insurance Availability and Affordability* (February 1986).

57. Shook, Hardy & Bacon, "What We Practice: Public Policy Group," http://www.shb.com/display/lawareas/pg_display.asp?pg_id=24.

58. Victor E. Schwartz, "White House Action on Civil Justice Reform: A Menu for the New Millennium," *Harvard Journal of Law & Public Policy* 24 (2001): 393, 409–411.

59. Stefancic and Delgado, *No Mercy,* 102.

60. "Victor E. Schwartz," Shook, Hardy & Bacon, http://www.shb.com/display/pdfs/Schwartz_Vdoc3.pdf.

61. Nader and Smith, *No Contest,* 260; Stefancic and Delgado, *No Mercy,* 102–103; "Tort Reform Interests and Agendas: Proponents of Reform," Osha Gray Davidson, "Dirty Secrets," *Mother Jones,* September 1, 2003.

62. Neil A. Lewis, "A Conservative Legal Group Thrives in Bush's Washington," *New York Times,* April 18, 2001; Jerry M. Landay, "The Conservative Cabal That's Transforming American Law," *Washington Monthly,* March 2000, 19; Rex Bossert, "ABA Watchdog: Conservative Forum Is a Quiet Power," *National Law Journal,* September 8, 1997; "The Federalist Society for Law and Public Policy Studies," http://www.fed-soc.org/, 2003.

63. Bossert, "ABA Watchdog: Conservative Forum Is a Quiet Power"; Lewis, "A Conservative Legal Group Thrives in Bush's Washington."

Acknowledgments

Any book of this kind builds on the scholarship, reporting, and advocacy of many people and organizations. Some of the sources on which I relied are included in the endnotes, but space limitations prevent me from listing all those whose work and ideas contributed to my understanding of this topic. (Some additional resources are listed on the Web site that expands on the topics discussed in this book, accessible through http://www.beacon.org/Feinmanupdates.) I am very grateful to all of them.

This book had its origins at the Annual Meeting of the Association of American Law Schools in January 1998, in a joint session of the Sections on Contracts, Torts and Compensation Systems, and Property Law. I thank those who planned and participated in the session. My thoughts were further developed in preparing a lecture for the fiftieth anniversary of the Camden Campus of Rutgers University, and the invitation from my friend and colleague Roger Dennis and the comments of those who attended encouraged the project.

Research assistants and seminar students over the years contributed in many ways. Matthew Fuchs, Thomas Robinson, Christopher Rosenbleeth, Steven Brill, Emily Ehrhardt, and especially Megan Gorman helped me greatly.

Carl Bogus has enriched my understanding of the subject through our discussions and through his scholarship, especially *Why Lawsuits Are Good for America* (New York University Press, 2001), and his comments on a draft of several chapters were very helpful.

Beacon Press has long published important works on social justice, and I am pleased to participate in its program. Helene Atwan, the director of the Press, provided superb editing.

Rutgers University School of Law-Camden provided financial and administrative support in conducting the research on this book and teaching in the areas it covers. Many colleagues over a span of several decades have made Rutgers an enjoyable and enriching place in which to work; their contributions to this book are immeasurable.

John Wright has been most important to me in bringing this book to fruition. He helped shape this project, never lost faith in it, and found it a fitting home. He has been a wise counselor and a good friend, and I thank him.

Finally, I am least able to express the extent of my appreciation of those to whom I owe the most: My wife, Carole Wood, and our children, Leah and Keith.

Index